History of Political Thought

R.S. Chaurasia

ATLANTIC
PUBLISHERS & DISTRIBUTORS (P) LTD

Published by

ATLANTIC

PUBLISHERS & DISTRIBUTORS (P) LTD

7/22, Ansari Road, Darya Ganj,
New Delhi-110002
Phones : +91-11-40775252, 23273880, 23275880, 23280451
Fax : +91-11-23285873
Web : www.atlanticbooks.com
E-mail : orders@atlanticbooks.com

Branch Office
5, Nallathambi Street, Wallajah Road,
Chennai-600002
Phones : +91-44-64611085, 32413319
E-mail : chennai@atlanticbooks.com

Printed in India at Nice Printing Press, A-33/3A, Site-IV, Industrial Area, Sahibabad, Ghaziabad, U.P.

PREFACE

The study of Political Science is very important in the present epoch of social evolution. The old order seems to be crumbling all over the world and man is faced with a gigantic task of reconstruction. The development of political thought in the historical perspective has a great educative and intellectual value. It trains and develops the faculties of mind to think, to criticise and to construct.

The book is designed to serve as an introduction to the history of political thought. I have placed the ideas of political thinkers in the easiest and lucid language. I have chosen to follow the historical and objective method. An accurate exposition of the views of political philosophers together with fair and reasonable criticism of their views from various standpoints has been carefully elucidated.

There is hardly any suitable book on political thought to meet the needs of M.A. students as well as to meet the requirements of the candidates who prepare themselves for various competitive examinations. This book has been prepared to meet this long felt need.

I shall deem my labour amply rewarded if the merits of the book find due appreciation at the hands of the teachers as well as the students.

I am grateful to Dr. K.R. Gupta, Managing Director and Shri Manish Kumar Gupta, Director, M/s Atlantic Publishers and

Distributors, New Delhi for their sincere efforts to publish the book at a time when it was most needed by students.

Suggestions, if any, for improvement of the book shall be gratefully received.

RADHEY SHYAM CHAURASIA

CONTENTS

Preface *iii*

1. Socialism 1
2. Democratic Socialism 18
3. Communism : Lenin, Stalin, Krushchev and Mao 35
4. Anarchism 69
5. Fascism 80
6. Pluralism 94
7. Harold Laski, G.D.H. Cole and Bertrand Russell 111
8. New Political Traditions in the West 124
9. Gandhi, Sarvodya and Nehru 156
10. Democracy 181

1
Socialism

Difference between Evolutionary and Revolutionary Socialism

Marx is the pivot on which socialistic doctrines revolve. Lenin, Stalin and Mao, and Khruchevian thought developed on the basis of Marx's ideas. These thinkers based their ideas on the basis of Marxian doctrines and call themselves real followers of Marx. On the other hand some thinkers differed with Marx and various schools of socialistic thought came into existence.

Socialism in England. Teachings of Marx failed to influence the workers and thinkers of England. Translation of Communist Manifesto appeared in England in 1850, but its second edition came into existence in 1888 and later on Marx's ideas gained some influence in England after 1917, when Russian revolution succeeded.

Marxism did not succeed in England because Britishers hate revolutionary ideas. According to Ogg and Zink, "Englishmen are conservative even in their revolutions." Popularity of an idea demands the favourable environment and psychological basis and in England none of these elements were present for its favourable development.

So far as surroundings are concerned, in England, workers were given right of vote and were made partners in the prosperity of the nation which was the richest country at that time. With the improvement of the conditions of the workers and grant of political rights to the proletarian class, revolutionary ideas of Marx also failed.

Another reason for the failure of Marxism in England was that instead of capitalism, Fabianism developed in England. With the development of Fabianism, Marxism lost its charm and hold on the workers of England. Thus, revolutionary socialism did not find popularity in England and instead of it, evolutionary socialism or Fabianism developed in England which believed in the maxim that slow and steady wins the race. Basis of Fabianism lies in the teachings of Ricardo and Mill rather than Marx. Ricardo believed that unearned increment created an account of society but it is devoured by the land owners though it belongs to society as a whole. Thus, in England, socialism opposed landowners more than capitalists. Defects of landlordism directed the attention of exponents of socialism to the defects of land-owning class instead of capitalistic class. However, in England, Fabianism proved a rock against the Marxian ideas.

Revisionism in Germany. As in England, so in Germany, neither the circumstances nor the public opinion favoured revolutionary socialism so Revisionism came into existence in Germany. Revisionism also believes that socialism can come gradually by democratic means and revolution for bringing socialism is not necessary. But Revisionism is nearer to Marxism as its basis is opposition of the Marxist ideas, while basis of Fabianism is Ricardo and not Marx.

Syndicalism. In France Syndicalism ideas developed which was nearer to the ideas of Marx than any other form of socialism as it believed in class war and in revolutionary and destructive ideas about which we shall deal later on.

Guild Socialism. G.D.H. Cole and other thinkers did not agree with the Fabianism and developed Guild socialism to remove the defects of Fabianism and Guild Syndicalism. It is a half-way house between Syndicalism and Collectivism and favours a middle path.

State Socialism or Collectivism. Extreme individualism brought into existence state socialism or collectivism. It has been put forward with a view to remedy some of the defects of the capitalist society. According to this view, "The competitive system assures the happiness and comfort of the few at the expense of the suffering of many and that society must be reconstituted in such a manner as to secure general welfare and happiness."

Democratic Socialism. Under Pandit Jawaharlal Nehru and his successors' rule, India steered clear of the two rocks of exploiting capitalism on the one side and the totalitarian communism on the other. Indian National Congress in 1964 decided to follow the path of democratic socialism which according to Kamaraj meant "socialism without loss of freedom".

Survodya or Real Socialism. Mahatma Gandhi believed in Truth and Ahimsa and abhorred absolutism of state. As such, Vinoba Bhave, the true follower of Gandhi developed Sarvodya which believes in the welfare of all. Thus, in India, two schools of socialistic thought have developed. Democratic school of thought believes in nationalization and state omnipotence while Sarvodya believes in the welfare of all and third in वसुधैव कुटुम्बकम *i.e.* in universal outlook.

Political scientist is not an astronomer to forecast which school of thought will succeed in future. But keeping in view the past history of India, it believes in the welfare of all समग्र विश्व का कल्याण हो। Jainism and Buddhism have gone a step further as to seek welfare of all living beings and as such, Sarvodya seems to be the representative of the past ideas of our rishies and sages but keeping in view the modern materialistic trend of India and omnipotence of Government perhaps democratic socialism may go ahead. However, it is clear that India believes in evolutionary socialism than revolutionary socialism but in this modern world, no country can remain aloof from the events of the world and only future will decide which ideology emerges successful in this age of conflicting ideologies and a period of coalition governments.

COLLECTIVISM OR STATE SOCIALISM

Main Propositions of the Collectivist Theory of the State

Collectivist theory discards the Marxian tenets as collectivism is an form of socialism which rose as a reaction against extreme individualism of 19th century. "Collectivism is the imposing word to be set over against individualism. The goal of state socialists can be put in these words". That the competitive system assures the happiness and comfort of the few at the expense of the suffering of many and that the society must be reconstituted in such a manner as to secure the general welfare and happiness.

It is broadly a term for a trend in social development, a programme of economic reform, a theory of general welfare, and a utopian order for mankind, technically a general label for comprehensive schemes of authoritative control such as socialism, communism, syndicalism and Bolshevism; and specifically a name for the trend away from the extreme laissez-faire of the 19th century. Collectivist principles can be found in the words of Eduard Berstein in Germany, Jean Juares in France, Karl Banting in Sweden and Eduard Anseel in Belgium. It wants to employ the state for the promotion of common good, as against the individual good advocated by individualists. Collectivists do not want to abolish the state but desire to retain it. For getting rid of evils of capitalism, private property and competition, they consider state as a positive good, which can be employed to serve the collective good. Collectivists firmly believe that the state action alone can remove exploitation and promote social welfare. According to Coker, "Collectivism is as vague a word as Individualism but there is perhaps no better term to designate the sort of ideas that we consider in the chapter. The Collectivist, as we use the term, rejects, on the one hand, the socialist doctrines of economic determinism, labour created values and class war; he recognises that differences in wealth create divisions of the community into different and often opposing political groups, but discredits the doctrine of a clear-cut distinction of classes and continual antagonism between them."

Objects of Collectivism. As Prof. Ely points out, a Collectivist is "a person who looks to society organized in the state for aid in bringing about a more perfect distribution of economic goods and an elevation of humanity." Collectivism has certain objectives : (1) To abolish private ownership of the means of production, (2) To bring the main industries and services under public control and ownership, (3) To press industry in serving the needs of the community as a whole and not the interests of few, (4) To eliminate the incentive of private profit in favour of the motive of social service and (5) To bring the possession and control of the chief factors of production under the control of democratic authority and not under private capitalists or workers. Means of production which are nationalised are to be under democratic control. Values in society are created by society and therefore the whole society should have them. This is to ensure better production and better distribution of wealth. There should be a national minimum wage for workers, and equal pay for equal work. Collectivists desire to reduce-drastically inequality in income by introducing a highly progressive system of income tax. Hence this type of socialism is called state socialism, and differs from syndicalism and guild socialism.

Methods of Collectivism. The Collectivists believe in evolutionary methods and not in violent or revolutionary changes. Gradualness is the key word of the Collectivists and thus Collectivism differs widely from communism : (1) Democratic methods are to be pursued to bring about change in a peaceful manner. C.E.M. Joad says, "True to the biological conception of society as a social organism, Collectivist socialists have insisted that society is capable only of gradual change, and that each change must be conditioned by the nature of the social structure that preceded it. From this point of view, it is essential to start with what exists and allow the present to decide the direction, as well as the rapidity, of the steps which are taken in the future." (2) The existing state is not to be overthrown but it is to be utilised for making the proposed changes. (3) Those who hold Collectivist views should disseminate their ideas and seek to capture power. They should employ all political, constitutional and educational methods to prepare a ground for an evolutionary change. (4) Collectivists should organize a party of their own, which must have a majority in the legislature. It is then only that they can form a government and introduce the necessary legislation for making Collectivism a reality.

(5) Unlike communists, the Collectivists are for the ballot-box and are against the bullets.

They have a well planned programme and also definite constructive proposals with regard to the future set-up. They stand for universal enforcement of the national minimum wage. It is the business of the state to prevent unemployment. Not only all the factors of production are to be nationalised, these are also to be put under democratic control.

The state socialists aim at bringing about a revolution in the national income. They stand for a highly progressive system of income tax. All the income will go to the National Fund and will be spent in a way which is most conducive to the betterment of society.

Justification of Collectivism. Collectivists justify their plans on many grounds. It is pointed out that nationalisation of industries is absolutely necessary if the interests of the public at large are to be safeguarded adequately. The supporters plead for "the states ownership of land and producer's capital as the means of absorbing for the public, both interest and the various forms of economic rents." There will be no wasteful advertisement or competition.

It is said that under state socialism : (1) All the free gifts of nature will be conserved for the future happiness of men. (2) All collectivist states will be guided by the consideration of service motive. (3) It is pointed out that there will be more unity and the principles of social service, social usefulness, and love of activity will be followed. (4) It is also defended on biological grounds that changes can be only gradual and not violent. (5) The defect of the prevailing political structure can be got rid of only through collectivism. (6) Collectivism assures the welfare of all, while capitalism provides comforts and conveniences only to a few rich persons; it assures comforts to all. (7) The present structure, political, social and economic, brings about starvation in the name of the sanctity of private property and contract but actually these things bring untold sufferings on poor persons. (8) Natural gifts should be owned by state to make the best use of them in the interests of all. (9) Industry should be state-owned so that it can cater to the needs of all. (10) Under capitalism, goods are produced with the profit motive but under state socialism, service motive will replace the profit motive.

Criticism of Collectivism. (1) It is pointed out that the state-ownership, management and control of all the factors of production and distribution will result in an authoritarian and bureaucratic state. There is every likelihood of an increase in corruption, intrigue and personal spite. It may give rise to nepotism, red-tapism and favouritism.

(2) In thinking that state-ownership is the panacea of all the evils, supporters of state socialism are over optimistic. The difficulties of administration will be so many that there is every likelihood of breaking down the machinery. (3) It is feared that state socialism will destroy the chief incentive to individual effort and originality. (4) It is also pointed out that state socialism is inimical to individuals liberty. None can dare to oppose on whose whim depends the livelihood of a person and in state socialism when state will be omnipotent, no one will dare to oppose the state and individual will be forced to work as a dumb driven cattle according to the wishes of the persons who will be fortunate enough to exercise the power of the state. (5) It is pointed out that there may be loss of production under state socialism. (6) It is said that it may make society static. (7) Critics also pointed out that state socialism may be capitalism in another form. The monopoly of the state may not be for the good of all. (8) As all the factors of production and distribution will come under the control of the state, love of wealth will be replaced by the bitter struggle for power. (9) State socialism may bring into existence cliques and bosses who will spend all their resources to capture the machinery of the state and to use it for their own purpose. (10) State socialism may result in cast iron centralisation. (11) Lastly, power corrupts a person and absolute power corrupts absolutely. It is difficult to imagine that the holders of the absolute power of the state will not be corrupt but will utilize this power for the welfare of all.

Evaluation of Collectivism. It is very difficult to draw a definite conclusion, however certain defects and merits can be pointed out : (1) It stands for the welfare of all and not for the welfare of few. (2) It desires to make use of the state for the collective good. (3) It believes in evolution and peaceful means. (4) It also favours decentralization.

Defects. (1) Collectivism is synonymous with statism. The state assumes all power in the name of social welfare. (2) It kills individual initiative and makes man merely a tool and affects adversely so far production is concerned. (3) The individual will lose his liberty and will become merely a tool or slave. (4) It allows totalitarianism through the backdoor. Human nature being what it is, a few clever persons will capture the power of Government to do whatever they like. (5) It will create the evils of bribery, corruption, favouritism and red-tape. (6) Lastly, Marxism ultimately favours utopian ideals but it cannot be said about state socialism.

Revisionist Socialism in Europe

Bernstein is the main exponent of Revisionist philosophy. This philosophy developed in Germany but scholars of many other countries also contributed in its development. Jean Jaures in France, Eduard Ansele in Belgium, Bissolati in Italy, Tugan Baronousky in U.S.S.R., Karl Branting in Sweden contributed in its development.

Revisionists like Marxists regarded socialism mainly a doctrine and programme for the working class. They sought to find the policy that would serve best the interest of working men in improving their physical economic and cultural well-being and strengthing their political position. Bernstein in Germany assailed some of the major tenets of Marxian system, notably the theory of value and its interpretation of history.

In criticizing Marx's theory of value, Bernstein pointed out the confusion arising from an apparent shift of ground in the third volume of Das Kapital. In this volume, market value is represented as equal to the cost of production including average profit, whereas in the earlier volume, exchange value is represented as measured solely by the amount of necessary labour used in production. The earlier view survives in the third volume only in the form of contention that the social value of the total of commodities is equivalent to the total labour time used in their production and that the excess of total product over total wages represents the total social surplus created by labour and wrongfully withheld from it. Bernstein is of opinion that any theory that labour created value is untenable as a basis for disconcerting a just system of distribution. The theory of value gives a norm or the justice or injustice of the partition of the product of labour just as little as does the atomic theory for the beauty or ugliness of a piece of sculpture. We meet indeed today the best placed workers just in these trades with a very high rate of surplus value, the most infamously ground down workers in these with a very low rate. A scientific basis for socialism or communism cannot be supported on the fact only that the wage worker does not receive the full value of the product of his work.

Revisionist theory in general followed Bernstein in rejecting Marxian theory of value in so far as the theory involves the principle that the exchange value of a commodity is measured solely by the efforts of wage earners and that the surplus value absorbed by the capitalists is measurable only by the excess of what the labourers produce over what they receive. But they did not reject the contention that there is a surplus value or that surplus represents generally the excess of what capitalists receive for the sale of commodities over what they contribute to the value of these commodities. And they held to the belief that the effort of capitalists to increase the surplus supplies the propelling force in the natural development of capitalism and creates an exploitation of wage-earners.

In criticising the materialistic conception of history, Bernstein refuted the view of Marx as to predominance of economic factors in the evolution. He held that with the growth of intelligence and insight, individuals and nations acquire increased freedom in shaping their progress.

He also did not agree with the Marxian prophecy of irresistible movement through which capitalism under the laws of its own growth and disintegration would lead to socialism. In refuting that prophecy he argued with an abundance of supporting statistics, that small scale industries are not disappearing, that concentration into large industries through the corporate form of organization tended to diffuse rather than commemorate the ownership of wealth concentrate, that the number of owners of capital was thus increasing rather than diminishing; that the increase in total production was enlarging the per capita wealth and thereby integrating absolutely the extension of markets and improved forms of credit, commercial crises were becoming less frequent and less severe, and the likelihood of a universal and fatal crash were becoming more remote.

Briefly we may say that proletariat is not increasing in number and it is not becoming the homogeneous and united group that the orthodox Marxian visualized. Diversities in interest, sharp contrasts in social and economic status, significant differences in political ideas are found among the various groups that make up the great unprivileged majority to come about through a revolution establishing a dictatorship of the proletariat. The working men must be content slowly to acquire capacity for economic and political supremacy, through whatever training they can obtain in the institution of democracy and in the agencies of industrial self-government.

Jaures rejected the prophecy of Marx. Agreeing with Bernstein, he maintained that since Marx made his prophecy, the prevailing tendency had been for the proletariat to raise rather than increase the ability of the workers to supplant the capitalists; and that economic crises, although demonstrating and confirming that the chaotic tendency of the capitalist system could do little to develop any other system to take its place.

Bernstein and others, however, accepted some of the basic economic and revolutionary theories of Marx. They were of opinion that capitalist society exploits the great majority of working men, constantly allowing them to receive less than they contribute to the production of values; it does tend to undermine itself, by producing more than the underpaid majority can purchase; foment class antagonisms which may result in violent revolution, they contended, although the tendency has been towards an increase in the relative number of owners of capital and towards an elevation of the workers actual wages. Under a system of private ownership for a majority of the workers, there is no chance to reach the position of luxury and care flaunted by the wealthy minority and the improved economic condition of working men generally tends to strengthen, both their desire to achieve their full rights and their ability to work effectively for that achievement whether through revolutionary or through peaceful methods.

Thus, though Revisionists advocated cooperation of wage-earners with sympathetic groups outside, they nevertheless agreed that economic inqualities supply the explanation and justification of socialism. They accepted the class character of socialism in the sense that socialism is a movement denoted to indicating essential rights of workers and to improving their material and social condition, and in the sense that the workers find their natural place in socialist parties. No one said that Bernstein "has questioned the necessity for working classes to gain the control of government". The formation of proletarian socialist party is the indispensable first step towards democracy. James accepted division of society in two antagonistic classes of those who live by ownership of property and those who live by work. The main work of socialism is to break down that supremacy of one class over another. All differences of class must be abolished by transferring the whole body of citizens, the organized community, the ownership of the means of production and of life which today, in the hands of a single class, is a power of exploitation and oppression.

Thus, most Revisionists claimed to be Revolutionist as well as reformers. Bernstein admitted that where political democracy did not exist and the property interests were entrenched in control, revolution may by necessary. James said, "A violent general strike might be the workers, final and desperate course."

In this way, Revisionists like the Fabians want to achieve the socialistic goal through utilizing the agencies of existing state. In the words of Bernstein, "Without a certain amount of democratic institution, and traditions, the socialist doctrine of the present time would not be possible. There would indeed be a worker's movement but no democracy.... Democracy and socialism are not mutually antagonistic, the former is the condition of the latter". Democracy is not only the means but substance of socialism.

For all practical purposes, socialism to the Revisionists meant state restriction upon private capitalism; the restriction might take the form of governmental interference with the property rights of private owners or setting up state-ownership in place of private ownership for a given section of capital. James argued for both reform legislation and nationalization programme adopted by French socialists. In 1902, under his leadership, demands for universal suffrage, proportional representation, initiative, referendum, recall, secularization of the schools, removal of the legal disabilities of women, progressive taxation, social insurance, protection of labour, regulation of industry, international peace were included.

The Revisionists argued for co-operation with other progressive parties which were willing to promote such reforms.

Miller defined socialism as the "necessary and progressive substitution of social property for capitalist property" and insists on (a) state intervention to transfer from the capitalist domain to the national domain the various categories of the means of production and exchange, as fast as they become ripe for social appropriation, (b) the conquest of public power by means of universal suffrage, and (c) the international understanding of the workers.

The Revisionists like Fabians showed the influence of Marx's scientific and synthetic treatment of socialism. A socialist policy must be elaborated according to historic influence. They accepted idea of class war and admitted that a socialist policy cannot ever break the existing social stratification based on economic differences but they differed with Marx on revolutionary means for destroying that stratification. They regarded socialism as part of the whole modern evolution of society — an important phase of a movement, begun in 18th century and advanced continually since then — through which political, social and economic rights had been successively asserted and attained. Sudden upheavals had marched some of the stages but they were no longer essential characteristics of the movement than the slower and quicker advances.

It is evident from all that the Revisionists sought to steer a midway course between mere democratic reformism and an exclusively revolutionary class war socialism. They held on the one hand that political democracy alone would not eliminate class antagonism and on other hand, that a class war alone would not establish socialism. The moral path must be one of negotiation and compromise. The ultimate goal of the Revisionists is that of all socialists, but just because the completed changes which its attainment would involve are so sweeping, complex and remote the only effective plan for socialists today is to work for the partial changes that can be introduced as economic and political conditions permit. If immediate reforms offered or conceded by non-socialist governments, narrow the field of ownership or improve the economic and social conditions of wage-earners, they should be regarded as 'instalments of socialism' and as significant steps towards the disappearance of the capitalist system (Cooker).

FABIANISM

Fabian Socialism

Fabianism made great influence on British thinkers and on Labour Party and also on Jawaharlal Nehru and his successors; therefore brief description is given here.

Introduction. The Fabian Society was founded in 1883 and soon attracted leading British intellectuals such as George Bernard Shaw, H.G. Wells and Sydney Webb and his wife Beatrice who dominated the ideas and policy of Fabian Society. The basic ideas of Fabian Society which have become known popularly as "Fabianism" are given in a book called *Fabian Essays* and published in 1889. The Fabian Society which exists even today, has published many pamphlets and journal and it exercises an intellectual influence and serves as a gathering point for moderate left wing but non-communist intellectuals in Britain.

The name of the Society is adopted from that of the famous Roman General Fabius Cunctator, who defeated Hannibal without actually fighting a battle against him. They believe in transition from capitalism to socialism as a gradual process, look forward to the socialization of industry peacefully through the existing economic and political agencies, and want to arouse the social conscience. In fact, Fabianism was a development on Collectivism or state socialism. But it differed from Marxism in some respects. It rejected Marxists' theory of materialistic interpretation of history. Again it did not believe in the inevitability of social revolution or class struggle. Fabianism was against revolutionary methods.

They believed in evolutionary and constitutional methods and stood for reform and moderation, persuasion and permeation. Similarly they were not against the state.

Origin of Fabian Socialism. It represented a further extension of socialism and liberalism. Like Creen, the Fabians were appalled by the inhumanity of man to man that accompanied an industrial society. Again they wanted to improve the condition of working class through state legislation, but to do it in the manner of General Fabius — through slow, but certain stages.

They believe in delaying tactics of Fabiun who held, "For the right moment you must wait", as Fabius did most patiently when fighting against Hannibal, though many censured his delays, but when the time comes you must strike had, as Fabius did, or your waiting will be in vain or fruitless". Indeed the Fabians propose to improve the conditions of the working class gradually and by stages.

Features of Fabian Movement. The following were its characteristic features :

1. It was essentially a middle-class movement.

2. The champions of movement were persons of high intellectual calibre. Gray remarks in this connection, "The movement was not merely middle class, but highly intellectual-middle class, free from any infusion of those whose wrongs they were lecturing to right. Fabianism was begotten by highbrows in the drawing rooms of London."

3. The movement was launched to spread the doctrine of evolutionary socialism through pamphlets, plays, novels or any other effective medium.

4. The movement aimed at general happiness and welfare of all.

Composition of Fabian Society. As said before, it comprised G.B. Shaw, H.G. Wells, Sydney Beatrice Webb, Graham Wallace, Ramsay MacDonald. Mrs. Annie Besant, Sydney Oliver and Edward R. Pease. Of these, Sydney Webb, Bernard Shaw, Graham Wallace and Oliver were later on famous as the "big four" of the Fabian Society. They made the Society a very powerful intellectual force, armed with a new and practical social gospel. Most of the sponsors of Fabian Society served the Fabianists by head and heart. Edward R. Pease served the Society as secretary for 25 years.

Sources of Fabianism. Fabians studied the works of different reformers such as Mill, Marx, Lassale, Owen Smith, Ricardo, Carins, etc. They were influenced by the Collectivist revision which Mill has made in his early utilitarian philosophy. They were also influenced by Henry George, the American author of *Progress and Poverty*. They adopted marginal utility theory as worked out by later English economists and accepted Ricardo's theory of rent. Karl Marx gave them the theory that common ownership of the means of production is essential for social welfare. But its theories of value, surplus value and class struggle were not acceptable to the Fabians. Again, like Marx they established socialism on economic and historic foundations. But the materials they extracted from economics and history were different from those used by Marx.

Marx believed revolution to be inevitable while Fabians preferred gradual changeover, painless so far as possible. In contrast to Marx, Fabianists did not regard class struggle as the basis of social reality.

Basis and Aims of Fabianism. The Fabians explained the basis and aims of Fabianism in 1887. The Fabian Society had socialists as its members. (1) They aimed at emancipating land and industrial capital from individual and class ownership. Ownership of land and industrial capital was to be vested in the community as a whole. (2) Fabians aimed at the extinction of private property in land and at the prevention of the appropriation of rent by individuals. Fabians considered rent as the price paid for permission to use the earth. (3) The administration of industrial capital as far as possible should be transferred to the community. Such transfers, they considered essential as industrial capital had become a monopoly in the hands of a class of proprietors on whom the majority depended for their livelihood. (4) The idle class living upon the sweat of others can be eliminated when rent and interests are not allowed to go into their pockets but make reward of labour. (5) The Fabian Society desired to conduct wide propaganda of socialist views, which would bring about great social and economic changes, and provide equality of opportunity to all.

Principles of Fabianism. Fabianism was primarily a policy, a question of tactics, rather than body of doctrines. The main aim of Fabianism was to remove the great injustice of the capitalist system. They wanted to spread the theory of evolutionary socialism. They agreed that competitive system assures the happiness and comfort of the few at the expense and suffering of the many and that society must be reconstituted in such a manner as to secure general welfare and happiness. Fabian Society seeks to achieve its ends by general dissemination of knowledge as to the relation between the individual and society in the economic, ethical and political aspects.

The Fabian Programme. Fabians sought to spread socialism through pamphlets, plays, novels and employed many such other effective means. In all, 700 lectures were delivered by the members of Fabian Society in the year 1888-89. Similarly, hundreds of essays were written. In 1912, the Society established the Fabian Research Department with a view to study all experiments on Collectivist production, distribution and exchange made in consequence of the felt need of the society to escape the evils of industrialism and examination of the activities of the various working class societies. A Fabian summer school was established in 1960 to educate socialists.

In this way socialism envisaged a progress of social and economic transformation in terms not of class war but of the gradual and progressive modification of the system by democratic means as a result of pressure from electorate that grow more and more insistent on the claims of social justice and would become convinced that nothing short of the socialisation of the means of production would suffice to ensure their use to achieve the highest practicable level of general well-being. They thought of the advance socialism in terms mainly not of power alone, but of power animated by national convention and inspired by the ethical impulse to achieve social justice (Cole).

Defence of Fabianism. Fabian thought was expressed after studying Owen, Marx, Proudhan, Lassolle, Adam Smith, Ricardo, J.S. Mill and Coairnes. Fabians justified their ideas on historical, industrial, economic, moral and on incentive grounds.

Historical Ground. Sydney Webb elucidates the historical ground of socialism. According to him, 19th century witnessed the almost complete failure of individualism and the continuous record of the progress of socialism. Society is dynamic and not static as proved by Darwin, Compte, and Spencer. As such, Utopian socialists are wrong in asserting that society is static and represents a perfectly balanced equilibrium without the necessity and possibility of future organic changes. Every thinker looks forwards for the general evolution of a new social order. Sydney Webb lays great emphasis on the importance of democracy, as it is acceptable to the majority of people and brings about changes in peaceful and gradual manner without any danger of serious social dislocation. Webb believes that changes that Fabians propose through democracy will be acceptable to people in England who are used to constitutional and peaceful ways. He draws the attention of world to exploitation of men, women and children by industrial capitalists and utter failure of individualism. England, according to Webb, provides a historical basis to socialism by accepting changes which are peaceful, gradual, ethical and democratic.

Industrial Grounds. William Clarke justifies socialism on industrial grounds. According to him, in the beginning, a capitalist worked hard and earned the wages of his superintendence which was very high. But gradually, he handed over the work to others paid by him and gave up the position, he previously occupied. Thus, the capitalist ceased to be useful to the community and continued as receiver of rent and interest. Through joint stock companies, capitalists exercise control over regions they never see or visit and through their hired managers are able to reap the maximum harvest of profits. Managers have to extract as much profit as possible for their capitalist bosses, failing which they will be dismissed. He points out that capitalism is against democracy and hence the two cannot go together. Unless capitalism is restrained, democracy cannot be meaningful. After capitalism is developed, society has no need of the capitalist and he can be gut rid of in the same way in which a slave-owner or feudal baron is eliminated. He pleads for bringing all joint stock companies and combines under public ownership.

Economic Grounds. Bernard Shaw defends it on economic grounds. He criticises rent, which according to him, is "the difference between the fertility of land for which it is paid and the worst lands." Under private property, one who works the best, gets the most and one who works the most, gets the least. In modern times, great fortunes are not built by hard work but by appreciation in the value of land and of the stocks of corporations. The increase in value should be regarded as the contribution of the entire society and not as the contribution of the owners of property. "For all practical purposes, the owners have been able to sit with folded hands, or to devote their lives to golf or fox-hunting, and the rise in value has occurred just the same." Private property has brought about invidious distinction between the class that has much and between the class which has very little. Economic rent should not go into the hands of the individual, but into the hands of community. Shaw speaks of helplessness of workers who breed like rabbits and have no control over their labour. Such poverty exists in society in the midst of plenty. In a play, he proves that slums are created to get the maximum rent to pay interest and generally rich persons become rich only through exploitation.

Moral Aspect. Sydney Oliver deals with the moral side of socialism. According to him, socialism is not the enemy of individualism, but the child of individualism. Socialism is nothing but individualism, which is "rationalised, organized, clothed in its right mind". Private property as it exists now has no moral basis and capitalists do not work for what they get. Capitalism brings about the degradation of human character and misery to the masses of the people.

Incentive to Work. Dr. Mrs. Annie Besant expresses herself very strongly against the lust for wealth in a system in which all people do not have the security of livelihood. The struggle to secure money has become terrific and wealth can get anything. Money stands for all credit and honour, and poverty and misfortune bring disgrace and discredit. Such a social and economic system should be changed and the individual should have the incentive to work. Every where one finds the tyranny of monetary gain. The present social justice should be eliminated and every individual should feel that life is worth living. Mrs. Besant holds out the poverty of the masses of people and want of proper incentive to work before the attention of the world.

"The desire to exalt the joy in creative work, the longing to work, improve, the eagerness to win social approval, the instinct of benevolence; all these will start into full life, and will serve at once as the stimulus to labour and the reward of excellence".

Features of Fabianism. The features of Fabianism may be noted. (1) Fabians are deadly against revolutionary and bloody methods and hence they are against communism and the principles associated with it. They do not believe in the materialistic interpretation of history, dialectical materialism, class war and theory of surplus value. (2) Unlike communists, Fabians would like to employ the state for the good of the community. (3) Fabians regard themselves as social reformers and not socialists in the strict sense of the term. Fabian terms are evolutionary and extremely moderate. (4) The way in which capitalism is criticized is quite different from that of communists. While the communists attack on capitalism is most devastating, the Fabian onslaught is subtle. Guided by a sense of moderation, Fabians spread their ideas through their literature. There is nothing in Fabianism like the mass appeal that Marx or Engels could command. Their appeal is meant not for the masses, but for a small group of people who have influence in public life and who are reasonable. Fabians do not have a party. As such, they believe that in all groups and parties there are people who will be responsive to their views. (5) Fabians do not have dogmas or principles to swear. Their emphasis is on questions of fact. They feel, the questions of fact matter more than questions of principle. (6) The methods of Fabianism are sober and dignified. As they were free from class bias, hatred and fanaticism, they were able to cut much ice in Britain. Though Fabians addressed themselves to a small circle of influential and reasonable people, their influence spread rapidly in Britain. Many people in England were soon won over by Fabianism and the results of 1945 testified to the tremendous popularity of Fabianism in England.

Success of Fabianism. The Fabian principles which were issued in 1887 were augmented from time to time by analysing legislation before parliament and by comprehensive studies of socialism. The Society joined the Labour Party and worked for trade union movement. In 1897, "Industrial democracy" was published in addition to "History of Trade Union" published in 1894.

When in 1883 an independent Labour Party was formed as an organization of working class, it had no clear political programme. Fabians supplied it with a definite philosophy and a clear-cut programme. For a long time, these Fabians and the Labour Party had good relations. In 1918, the Labour Party adopted a programme which was drafted by a staunch Fabianist Sydney Webb. By 1930, the relations between these two became loose, but Labour Party came in power in 1945. After that it again won election and is now in power in United Kingdom of Great Britain and Ireland under the leadership of Harold Wilson.

Evaluation. Fabianism as a separate school of political thought has ceased to exist, as the programme of Fabians came to be identified with that of the Labour Party in Britain.

Fabianism has Certain Merits. (1) Fabian Society having within its ranks eminent men with international reputation exercised great influence in England and the intellectual class in Britain was very much impressed by the evolutionary and sober methods of Fabianism. By their sober and dignified methods, the Fabians were able to push forward socialist ideas. This was no small achievement in view of the fact that socialism was held in deep suspicion by many people. (2) Fabians tried to push their ideas without the least bitterness and fanaticism. While communism spreads violence, Fabianism did not do anything of that kind. With its sweet reasonableness, dignity, sobriety and non-partisan approach, Fabians won over people belonging to different walks of life and impact of Fabianism on parliament was indeed great, (3) Fabians did much to improve the lot of labour. The Labour movement in Britain owed much to the support lent by Fabians.

In spite of the service rendered by Fabians, they have not escaped criticism. In fact, some of the critics have levelled the most scathing criticism against them. Fabians have been criticized for want of honesty and straightforwardness. According to Barker and other critics, Fabians do not speak out plainly and shift their stand according to circumstances. Hence the charge of opportunism has been levelled against them. According to a critic, Fabianism is another name of state socialism.

In spite of all this criticism, it cannot be denied that it exerted a tremendous influence over India as Nehru was the follower of Fabianism. In the words of Prof. Suda, "It is least revolutionary among all kinds of socialism". It can be considered one type of state socialism so far as it supports the state-ownership over land and capital. Perhaps it is permissible to say that it has influenced our democratic socialism most. Ideas of Fabianism gained prominence during the rule of Pt. Jawaharlal Nehru and his daughter Shrimati Indira Gandhi and her son Rajiv Gandhi but later on, coalition Governments began to favour global concepts of privatization, etc.

2

Democratic Socialism

Democratic Socialism and its Impact on UK, USA and India

Democratic socialism originated in England. Now a question can be asked, how is it that democratic socialism rose in England, a capitalist country? The answer is provided by William Ebeustein, "In some ways of course, socialism opposes capitalism, but it is rebellion of the child against the father, not the total war of stranger against stranger. Just as the rebellious child uses arguments he has learned from his own father, socialism employs, in the contrary with its progenitor, a whole arsenal of capitalist values and attitudes especially critical rationalism and pragmatic utilitarianism". England moved with the times and gave rise to forces of democratic socialism. It is necessary to note here that England did not give a chance to the workers to stage a bloody revolution as was done in France in 18th century and Russia in the nineteenth century. England developed parliamentary institutions and brought a compromise between democracy and socialism. Democracy is a government by consent or public criticism; it stands for responsible rule as against autocratic governance. Socialism is the regulation of the use of the means of production for the sake of common good as against narrow good of individuals.

In Britain there was no need for the workers to revolt on a mass scale against the government as the government unlike Russia and China itself took the lead to promote the welfare of workers.

According to Ebenstein, socialist literature in England has no Marx or Lenin who lays down the law for all time. Communists in Russia and China always refer to their high priest, he may be Marx, Engels, Lenin, Stalin, Kruschev or Kosygin or Mao Tse-tung. There is no question about democratic socialism of cultivating the cult of individual; it tolerates or even respects the opinion of others.

Mr. R.H. Tawhney in his book *The Acquisitive Society* strongly criticises functionless property as a charge not only to society, but to legitimate property itself. Capitalism enables individuals to develop property which they regard as a source of power and income and not as an agency of social service. He suggests remedies as given below :

(1) Industry should be subordinated to the larger interests of the community as whole. (2) People who render service should be honourably paid. (3) People should not be ruled by an authority which they do not control.

Socialism in England. The democratic socialism in England aims to the ideas of Robert Owen, Sydney and Beatrice Webb, Tahwney, Laski, G.D.H. Cole, Darwin and others and not to Marx only. In the words of Atlee, ex-Prime Minister of England, "Both fascism and communism in this country are irrelevant. I believe England can afford to the world an example of how society can adapt itself to new conditions and base itself to new principles without breach of continuity and without violence and intolerance." According to Ebenstein, religion, ethical and aesthetic idealism, Fabian empiricism and liberalism are the outstanding elements of British socialism. In England, the change in attitude of capitalists and the presence of a strong middle class worked in favour of democratic socialism as against communism and after a long eclipse, Labour Party again gained power.

Socialism in USA. In the U.S.A., totalitarian communism got the least chance to stage an entry, and socialism has never been able to set its roots. The reason for this is clear. Poverty is never pinching in the U.S.A. On the contrary, workers have amenities of life, which middle class people in many countries will envy. The social equality about which socialists talk too much is guaranteed by the constitution. America is the richest country of the world and they feel that Marxism will undermine the economic foundation of capitalism and attack the very core of American democracy and American way of life. Though the American economic system is regarded as "the last island of sheltered capitalist civilisation", but there has in later years been a steady and increasing extension of state regulation and of state aid by both national and state governments. F.D. Roosevelt's "New Deal" was regarded as "just and inevitable" and state interference and state control are increasing day by day in America, though chances of socialism are still remote there. Now U.S.A. is the leading country of the world which believes in globalization of trade and in privatization.

Socialism Spreads. In France and Italy, socialism gave a setback to communism. Socialism is doing well in Britain, Scandinavia, Holland, Belgium, Australia, New Zealand, Chile, Uruguay, Iseral and in other newly liberated African countries. The most notable attempts to set forth general theoretical principles underlying this moderate and flexible programme for post-war socialists have been made by Otto Baur and Karl Kants in Australia, Ramsay Macdonald, H.N. Brailsford and G.D.H. Cole in Britain and Norman Thomas in U.S.A. They plead for Collectivist system and place studious emphasis upon the gradualness, peacableness, reasonableness, contentiousness and efficiency of a socialist movement towards their goal.

Asian Socialist Conference was held in Rangoon in January, 1953. It was attended by 147 delegates and India, Burma, Indonesia, Malaysia, Siam, Vietnam, Korea and the Philippines and Japan supported it. Clement Atlee, ex-Prime Minister of England was at the head of Socialist International delegation. The Conference declared the principles and objectives of Socialism. "... the socialists state as well as socialist parties have also the right, in fact are duty bound to defend democracy". The second Conference was held in 1956 in K.C. College, Bombay. According to S. Bose, in Asia, socialism has to compete with the forces of conservatism, capitalism, communism and communalism. The countries of Asia are generally more left inclined than Europe, but in Middle Eastern Muslim countries, religion has become the dominating feature.

Socialism in India. India, under Pandit Jawaharlal Nehru's lead, steered clear of the two rocks of exploiting capitalism on one side and totalitarian communism on the other. Pandit Nehru moved with the times. In 1955, the All India Congress Committee in Avadi session accepted the goal of the socialist pattern of society. In 1964, it decided to follow the path of democratic socialism for bringing about a welfare state. Mr. K. Kamaraj, the president of Congress spoke in terms of socialism without loss of freedom. He added, "We hope, we shall be able to establish a society without class conflict and dispel the popular belief that in a socialist state men lose their natural freedom... . The best way of fighting against communism is to inject democratic socialist ideas into the country". India at present is to accept the services of capitalists not as masters but as servants of the state. India turns to British democratic socialism for inspiration. As the Congress itself is wedded to socialist ideas, socialist parties in India cannot do well at the elections particularly due to their division in Praja Socialist and Samuktya Socialist parties, but later on Congress lost its hold and now coalition governments follow rightist policies.

Basic Principles of Democratic Socialism. 1. Socialism wants the state to regulate the activities of the individual so that individual smay not become a stumbling bloc in the path of social welfare.

2. Socialism aims at eliminating exploiting capitalism with its corollaries. Co-operation will do away with antagonism between the employers and the workers.

3. Socialism believes in state intervention to introduce necessary legislation to provide equitable opportunity of life to all.

4. Socialism stands for the principle of equality and works for breaking the chain of material hardships.

5. Democratic socialism stands for the common-ownership of important means of production, which are to be utilized for the common good.

6. Democratic socialism allows freedom of expression and exercise of different rights.

7. Democratic socialism pleads for economic democracy without which political democracy is useless.

8. Socialism stands for equality of opportunities. It is against only privately-owned property, which becomes the means of exploitation. It means collective ownership of the large means of production and is not applicable to goods of consumption.

An Estimate of Democratic Socialism. (1) It believes in dignity of human personality. (2) It stands for liberty and equality. (3) It puts society above the individual. (4) It eliminates the evils of capitalism as the concentration of wealth in the hands of a few and over production, etc. (5) It eliminates private property which can be used for exploitation.

Defects. The following defects may be pointed out :

1. In the name of democratic socialism, excessive power may be put in the hands of the state and socialism may become a stepping stone to totalitarianism. The way in which Government in India is restricting the freedom of the individual abridging fundamental rights has created fear in the minds of people that totalitarianism is subtly effecting its entry through the back-door. The critics of India's socialism point out that the way is being prepared for statism.

2. As the means of production are increasingly being taken over by the state, the incentive to produce is gradually decreased. If the idle are to be treated at par with the intelligent and industrious, there is no need to work hard.

3. Inefficiency increases and volume of production goes down. With the absence of competition, quality in production also deteriorates.

4. As the state undertakes to do what private enterprise generally does, a wide scope is created for redt-ape, bribery and corruption, and for favouratism and nepotism.

5. As individualism is discouraged and individual freedom is curtailed, there is the possibility of degeneration of the individual character.

6. Under socialism, the consumer's sovereignty disappears. The consumer will have to adjust his needs to production and he may be called upon to undergo great hardship and privation.

7. It is also said that the individual loses his liberty as more and more restrictions are imposed on him.

8. Socialism is also criticised as utilitarian and materialistic and it does not care for ethical principles.

9. According to Gandhiji, state is a soulless machine and omnipotence of state will not only harm individuals but that it will always do positive good is doubtful.

10. In socialism, power passes from the masses to bureaucracy and it breeds corruption, bribery and red-tapism and bureaucracy becomes very powerful.

11. In India, democratic socialism has made Government servants omnipotent and masses have become helpless. Peasants and common men lead a miserable life due to disparity of wealth, power and privileges so regional parties and coalition governments have become common feature.

SYNDICALISM

Introduction. "Syndicat" is the French word for trade union, and Syndicalism is the political philosophy of political action by the trade unions mainly in the form of a general strike to overthrow the existing state and to install a socialist regime. The origins of Syndicalism lie in parts in the theories of Karl Marx and in part in the peculiar development of the labour movement in France. According to C.M. Joad, "Syndicalism is the name given both to a body of social organisation and to a plan of action. The plan of action is a particular phase of what Marx called the class struggle, and its object is to bring into being a Syndicalist organisation of society. While, however, the Syndicalist plan of action is direct, vigorous and well-defined, the state of society which it seeks to realise is extremely rebellious."[1]

Barker says, "Syndicalism like Marxism, is a doctorine inimical to the bourgeoisie or capitalist state; but while Marxism erects a whole class, called the proletariat, as the enemy of bourgeoisie state, and proposes to build on that class... Syndicalism creates as the enemy of the bourgeoisie the various and separate syndicates." The important principles were given by Fernand Pelloutier who worked as the general secretary of the National Federation during 1894-1901. Syndicalists based their teachings on revolutionary ideas of thinkers like Proudhan, the Anarchist, so Syndicalims is also called Anarcho syndicalism. Critics regard it as organised Anarchy. As Syndicalism combines revolution with trade unionism, it can be called Revolutionary Trade Unionism.

Origin and Growth of Syndicalism. In second half of 19th century, Syndicalism originated in France, when Government removed hurdles in the way of workers by legislation. Atmosphere of France was favourable particularly after the establishment of Third Republic in 1875, as laws of 1864, 1868 and 1884 conceded to workers the right of forming associations. In 1887, a militant worker's organization was formed in Paris and within six years a National Federation of Brouses was set up, and before long it became the heart of worker's movement in France.

During World War I, the Confederation of Labour gave up their anti-war and anti-government policy and made a compromise with the Government. and socialists in order to promote war effort, but a minority opposed them and in 1922, the party splitted in two organizations and it gave rise to new Syndicalism as the militant group formed General Confederation of United Labour and followed the aims of the Communist International.

New Syndicalism. The principles of New Syndicalism were elucidated by Syndicalist thinkers like Jouhan Perrot and Lerovy. New Syndicalism was to have no truck with communism as the New Syndicalists did not stand for class war and violence. The New Syndicalists desired to supplant the negative, destructive tactics of the older Syndicalism by positive and comprehensive policy and pleaded for state supervision. The rise of New Syndicalism actually spelt the doom of the Syndicalist movement.

Spread of Syndicalism. Syndicalism of France spread in countries like Spain, Britain, U.S.A. and Italy and in England. In Italy it was put down by Mussolini and in Spain by Gen. Franco. In America, socialists established in 1905 their organisation called the Industrial Workers of the World but it followed peaceful methods. During World War I, Syndicalism suffered and now it has lost its popularity and militant role.

Syndicalist Thinkers. Among Syndicalist thinkers, Fernand Pelloutier (1867-1901) and George Sorrel were main thinkers. Pelloutier called upon workers to exert themselves through labour exchanges and better their own condition through corporation. Sorrel was in favour of establishing an industrial self-Government of the working class. He favoured general strike to paralyse government and to put an end to capitalism to capture power.

Features of Syndicalism. Main features of Syndicalism can be given as below :

1. In contrast to Fabianism which aimed at making socialism respectable and peaceful, Syndicalism attempted to make it proletarian and revolutionary.

2. It was a reversion to Marx. Marxian dogma of class struggle occupied an important place in the Syndicalist theory.

3. Syndicalism conceived of state as a bourgeoisie and middle class institution.

4. It was pre-eminently revolutionary.

5. The Syndicalists followed the footsteps of Proudhan rather than of Marx. They derived some elements from Marx's philosophy and some form Proudhan's thought.

6. The Syndicalist movement was in origin a spontaneous movement among the workers. It was an outcome of French labour movement.

Principles of Syndicalism. In brief, principles of Syndicalism may be sumned up as below :

1. A constant struggle is going on between the propertyless wage earning class and propertied employer. This struggle can be stopped only by destroying capitalist class.

2. The state must be destroyed because it is fundamentally an institution of class exploitation, an ally of the capitalists and the enemy of the proletariat.

3. In the new society which will be established after the proletariat revolution, the state would cease to exist and all control of economic as well as of the political life must be vested in the worker's union or syndicates.

4. The method of direct action in the economic sphere will be adopted. Political method advocated by Collectivists, or state socialists will have no place.

Syndicalist Theory of State. Syndicalists advocate direct action. Syndicalism views the trade union as the primary means of achieving the revolution through general strike. The trade unions should first of all intensify class consciousness in workers by participating in the struggle for higher wage, shorter hours and working conditions. They will use the strike, sabotage (injuring machines in the factory) the label (asking consumers not to buy articles produced by the companies mentioned by the trade union organisation) and boycott as a weapon in a spirit of militancy against the system of private property and against the state. The worker will thus be trained for the supreme act of the class struggle, the general strike, which will sound death-knell of the present industrial system and inaugurate the new social order.

The general strike need not necessarily be a strike in all industries; if the workers in electricity, gas and transport go on strike, they can paralyse all production.

Vision of New Society. In the new social order, there will be no necessity for the existence of state. The syndicates or trade unions, functioning harmoniously and without external compulsion will form a general national federation. The federation will not represent the geographical units but the functional interests of the workers. It will carry on the statical and administrative services which are necessary for the smooth operation of the system as a whole. Thus "Syndicalism" pictures the future society as a free and flexible federation of autonomous productive and distributive associations based on collective ownership and carrying on their functions in accordance with the needs of community.

Differences between Socialism and Communism. The Syndicalists accept the dogmas of class war in its most extreme form and adopt it not merely as a philosophy of history but a plan of campaign. Like Marxists, they too advocate the forcible and immediate expropriation of all capitalists and landowners. But whereas the communists aim at seizing power both by political and economic weapons, the Syndicalist srely on direct economic action only. In opposition to proletarian government, they want to eradicate centralised government altogether. In contrast to Socialists the Syndicalists look forward to the welfare and domination of workers and not of community in general. The Syndicalists have taken over from Anarchism, the concept of community without any government and the belief in the moral value of revolt and the strong antipathy to militarism. "Spontaneity in feeling", wrote Ramsay Macdonald, "freedom in action, equality in co-operation within the camp, a sleepless hostility against the enemy carried on sometimes by gureilla tactics, sometimes by grand engagements are along the line of marshalled force that is pageantry of industrial conflict which allures the Syndicalist of the factory and the workshop".

Criticism of the Theory. Syndicalist theory is vague regarding the character of society without the state. It is not clear as to how the interest of consumers will be looked after and how peace and harmony between different categories of workers, can be maintained without political authority. "The view mine for the miners, the railways for the railway men, and dust-carts for the dustmen" such is the common criticism of the implications of Syndicalist doctrine.

Education. Syndicalism as a school of thought did service to the world by making them conscious of their position and glamorising and vitalising them to action. In the words of Bertand Russell, "Whatever may be thought of the practicality of Syndicalism, there is no doubt that the ideas it has put into the world have done a great deal to revive the labour movement and to recall it to a certain thing of fundamental importance which it has been in danger of forgetting. Syndicalists...are more concerned to procure freedom of work than to increase material well-being. They have revived the quest for liberty...they have reminded men that what our society needs is not a little tinkering here and there...but a fundamental reconstruction, a sweeping away of all the sources of operation, a liberation of man's constructive energies, and a wholly new way of conceiving and regulating production and economic relations."

Syndicalism however suffers from serious drawbacks : (1) It is unrealistic and it wants to degrade the state. Abolition of state may create anarchy. (2) It is wedded to violence. (3) It did not give a clear image of Syndicalist society and did not give details of the new social order based on Syndicalism. (4) It cares only for producer workers and not for the consumers or for the society as a whole. (5) It gives a free hand to sabotage and go-slow tactics (6) It is also anti-patriotic. (7) It creates disharmony in the society.

Guild Socialism

Fundamental Principles of Guild Socialism. In fact, Guild socialism was an offshot of Fabian movement. The champions of Guild socialism especially A.G. Pinty, A.R. Oranage. Hobson and Cole were not satisfied with the stand of Fabians on the question of centralization of powers. The Guild socialists shared many of the fears which motivated the French Syndicalists : believing that much government was bad whether it be socialist or not. They proposed a form of socialism beyond the idea of decentralization and divided responsibility.

Meaning of Guild Socialism. According to Coker, "Guild socialism is like the early French Syndicalism in its invasion to all doctrines that make productive activity dependent upon political authority. It would protect the worker not only against exploitation by capitalists but its object is to make work more interesting and the whole economic structure of society more democratic." It aimed at the "abolition of the wages system of national guilds working in conjunction with other democratic functional organisations in the community. Guild socialism followed the golden mean between the extremes of Collectivism and Syndicalism." Guild socialism was inspired in part by the teachings of William Morris, a medievalist poet and artist of 19th century who condemned modern industrialism, because of its ugliness and its destruction of individual craftsmanship. The essence of the Guild socialism was the transfer of ownership of means of production to the state with the management and operation of factories, mines, railroads, etc. to be vested in the guilds of workers. According to Orange, a guild "is a self-governing association of mutually dependent people organized for a responsible discharge of a particular function in society."

History of Guild Socialism. Guild socialism as English school of thought originated in the second decade of the 20th century, though the basic ideas of Guild socialism were given by author Joseph Penty (1875-1935) as early as 1906 in his book *The Restoration of Guild System*. English intellectuals, who at first lent their support to Fabianism gave rise to Guild socialism. This organization could boast of having eminent thinkers like S.G. Hobson, A.J. Penty, A.R. Orage and G.D.H. Cole who expounded the principles of Penty's book. While it was impossible to revive the medieval guild system and implement the utopian ideas of Penty, they tried to modify Penty's ideas to suit modern conditions. Orange powerfully expressed his views through the columns of the weekly *New Age* which he was editing. These articles were in course of time published in a book form. The book National Guilds, "An Enquiry into the Wage System and the Way out" gave a systematic exposition of the view of Hobson and Orange. Guild socialism was intimately connected with Fabianism, as Syndicalism was to communism. Guild socialists honoured ideas from English Fabians and French Syndicalists and so it has been regarded as the "intellectual child of English Fabianism and French Syndicalism". Collectivism or state socialism could not solve the economic ills and so other "ism" was necessary. Those who felt that Collectivism was trying to remove capitalist bureaucracy to make way only for establishing centralised bureaucracy of the state were disappointed. For instance, Penty felt that in the large scale production under Collectivism, the individual worker lost his identify or individualism and it was not possible for him to display the beauty of his individual craftsmanship. Guild socialism would be able to give a place in the sun to the worker.

Factors favourable to Guild Socialism. Certain factors were favourable to the growth of Guild socialism : (1) Carlyle, Morris and John Ruskin criticised the evils of industrial capitalism and praised the advantages of guilds. (2) Similarly G.K. Chesterton and Hilarie Belloc favoured a "distributive state" and strengthened the cause of Guild socialists. (3) In 19th century wage system was criticized which strengthened the cause of Guild socialists. (4) Evils of capitalism brought Guild socialism on forefront.

According to Joad, "In his restoration of guild system," Penty advocates a return to the medieval principle of self-Government in industry whereby the craftsman, who was a member of an autonomous guild, owned the tools with which he worked and determined the nature and extent of production. Penty's arguments are based partly on sentiments, partly on aesthetic grounds and are animated throughout by hostility to modern methods of production and trading and large scale production. The work of Penty represents the utopian phase of Guild socialists' propoganda just as that of William Morris which represents the utopian stage of socialism proper. It profoundly affected the Labour Party also.

Principles and Objects of Guild System. The National Guild system aims at the abolition of wage system and the establishment by workers of self-government in industry, through a democratic system of national guilds, working in conjunction with the other democratic functional organizations in the community. The Guild socialists propose that the state which represents the consumer should own the means of production, but that guilds representing the workers, control the means of production. They believe that state control of industry results in bureaucracy and undemocratic system because it creates a self-interested electorate party controlled by and practically controlling a governing bureaucracy. Therefore, they prefer to set up a federal system in which the state looks after only such makers as public conduct, international relations, and the production of art and higher education — other matters being left to antonomous, cooperating occupational groups. These organisations will determine the wages and prices; they will control all industrial matters and they will have the charge of the national income, paying to the state a certain sum to enable it to perform its duties. There will thus be established two democracies — one economic, second political.

It may be said that Guild socialism represents a reaction against the large scale machine industry of the present day as well as against the state. It looks back to the medieval period, with its small decentralised handicraft industry, which developed the personality of workers and made possible pride in workmanship.

According to C.M. Joad, the general principle on which the statement that wage system should be abolished and workers' self-Government should be established are the following :

1. The principles of functional democracy.

2. The principle that industry should be administered by the common action of workers both of hand and brain who carry on industry.

3. The principle that power and responsibility in society should be related in proportion to the importance of the functions which individuals perform in the service of the community.

According to Joad, the principle of functional democracy is of considerable merit for political theory. He is of opinion that it is not possible for any one person to represent another person; so all so-called representative institutions that have existed in the past are misrepresentative institutions. A man cannot represent another person but he can represent the interest of his profession. Just as a doctor can represent himself as well as his fellow doctors B, C, D, E, etc. if he is elected. It follows that any kind of representation, which really represents must be functional representation, and in real democracy there should be a coordinated network of national representative bodies which each represents wills or purposes that its members have in common.

For political interests such as law, taxation, defence, maintenance of peace and order in the country, etc., there should be election on geographical basis and people's will in all respect of them is best represented on national body not dissimilar to existing parliament. Then for water supply, sanitation and health, etc. there should be regional bodies like existing local authorities for the expression of individual's will in this matter.

Now we come to production and questions relating to status, conditions, hours of weak, wages and many such things can only be settled in accordance with the common will as expressed in workshop and factory, committees elected for the purpose. But the nature and extent of production and the price of articles are questions that also touch the consumer. Consumer bodies are needed to consult with the bodies of producers. The duties of these councils will be to determine, with the factory committee of producers, questions of cost and price.

In this way, "the theory of functional democracy" reacting vigorously from the idea of a centralised and all-embracing state, advocates devolution of powers and functions to a number of different bodies, which will, it is hoped, adequately express all the world interests of man in the complex of modern society.

Following reasons are given for functional democracy to be applied in production first :

1. They follow that "economic power precedes political power". They believed that no democracy was possible in the political field unless there was first democracy in economic sphere. In other words, for success of political democracy, economic democracy was necessary.

If industries are organized democratically, the democratic organisation of society will necessarily follow.

2. Guild socialists plead that modern industry is in such a chaotic condition that until it is re-established on an ordinary basis, there can be no health in any other department of social life. These principles, later on, according to Joad, may be extended to local and national Government and proposes so to extend it after it has been applied in industry.

3. If applied to industry, the principle takes the following form. The chief public service and industries are to be owned by the state. But though nationalization is desirable, it must not be assumed that industrial problems will be solved by the mere transference of industry to public ownership.

Essentials of Guild Socialist Philosophy. Guild has been defined as "a self-governing association of mutually independent people organised for the responsible discharge of a particular function in society". Guild socialists stand for the functional democracy on the basis of guilds having antomony in their work.

Though a lot of antonomy is given to guilds but provision was also made for taking appeal to the national guilds. According to G.D.H. Cole, a National Industrial Guild Congress was to be set up. That was to represent all the national guilds. It was to act as a representative of the producers in their negotiations with the representatives of the consumers. Every guild was to be so organised so as to coordinate its productive activity with that of other guilds on a national scale. To safeguard the consumer's interests, Guild socialists advocated the joint consultation of the producer's guilds and consumer's councils. It was in these meetings that the questions of cost and prices and other questions concerning both were to be discussed and settled. Existing trade unions may be transformed into guilds under a Guild Socialist Society. Guild socialists advocated the use of constitutional and peaceful methods for the establishment of a Guild Socialist Society and pleaded for "encroaching control", *i.e.,* snatching of control bit by bit from the hands of the capitalists as well as later on from the control by the Government.

Position and Functions of the State in Guild Society. The main object of Guild socialists was to help the workers to stand on their own feet. According to Hobson, the state was to continue as the representative of the community as a whole. The authority of the state was to be lessened but not to be eliminated altogether. The state was to own all the plants and tools and was to lease them out to the various guilds. It was to act as a court of final appeal in cases of disputes between the guilds. It was to set up civil and criminal courts and enforce the laws of the country. It was also to regulate the international relations, both in political and economic field.

G.D.H. Cole did not give the state the same authority which was given by Hobson. According to him, Government is to manage the whole of production and the state to look after the interest of consumers by regulating prices and distribution of income. In case of conflict between the guilds and the state, the institution known as supreme council of Functional Equity was to have the final word. In this way, sovereignty of the state was to be taken away from it.

According to Joad, the National Guilds League, however, adopts a hostile attitude towards the state and follows Marx's teachings in regarding it as an executive committee for administering the affairs of the whole capitalist class. The hostility to the state regarded as a repository of sovereignty continues after the transformation of society into a guild socialist community has been achieved. There is a tendency to relegate the state to the role of an association of consumers represented on a number of bodies elected on a national basis for the purpose of negotiating with the big producing guilds.

Some Guild socialists take the view that under a Guild socialists regime, the state should be allotted certain functions which no other association can do. They wanted to make the state the supreme authority but assign it less functions as stated by Hobson.

Methods of Guild Socialism. They want to modify the trade unions by incorporating two functions of the Guild :

1. They must be made all-inclusive of workers in the industry.
2. They must take certain measures of controlling the working of industry.

According to Joad, Guild socialists advocate larger and fewer trade unions and endeavours to remodel trade union structure along the lines of vertical as opposed to horizontal organisation. A horizontal organisation would embrace all the workers in a particular industry from top to bottom.

They also desire to follow the policy of encroaching control, *i.e.*, workers should wrest bit by bit from the hands of the possessing class the economic power which they now exercise, by a steady transference of functions and rights from their nominees to representatives of the working class. Its object is to transfer to the workers as many as possible of the functions of control by having power to elect overseer and foreman and of collective contract and of distribution.

Evaluation of Guild Socialism. Though the Guild socialism has lost its former glamour but it has exercised some influence on political thought in Britain and U.S.A. The idea of joint management of industries by the representatives of employers and employees had a strong appeal to many. After World War I, Guild socialists raised the question of housing in England and enthusiastically undertook the job of constructing buildings and different guilds were integrated into the National Building League. But the laudable construction plan to solve the shortage of housing came to grief owing to various causes, and in 1925 the National Guilds League had to be abolished. This marked an end to the Guild socialists, movement in England. Then its members had to go over to other forms of socialism. Formerly Guild socialists brought the evils of absolute sovereignty of the state on forefront and strengthened pluralist thought with all merits. Guild socialism suffered from very serious drawbacks which almost sounded its death-knell. Following demerits are notable :

1. Guild socialism cannot stand the test of reason and in the practical field it is bound to fall. The co-existence of two parliaments representing territorial interests and functional or economic interests is hardly possible. While Guild socialists point out that a joint committee of two parliaments will solve disputes between them, in actual practice there will be nothing but deadlock.

2. In championing the cause of complete autonomy of guilds, Guild socialists give rise to two states: political and economic. The co-existence of two states makes a ridiculous picture.

3. In Guild socialism, production may go down as incentive to hard work will be lacking and this will cut the very roots of production.

4. The approach of Guild socialists is doctrinaire as, according to Cole, state sovereignty will have to make way for guilds' sovereignty.

5. Guild socialists will take retregrade steps like reviving the medieval guilds. It is difficult to deem it a practical suggestion that the revival of the medieval guilds with their glaring defects will be able to solve modern questions.

6. This principle lacks charm to capture fancy of the masses.

7. Autonomy in each industry will also promote strifes. Due to functional representation of manufacturers, teachers and steel workers, etc., interests of the people and their common welfare may suffer.

8. The extreme insistence of Guild socialists, observes Mac Iver, "on functional representation becomes on attack upon the state itself".

About Guild socialism, it has been said, "But although Guild socialism represents an attempt at adjustment between two equally legitimate points of view, its impulse and force are derived from what it has taken over from syndicalism", Betrand Russell.

It has been remarked that Guild socialism is the intellectual child of English Fabianism and French Syndicalism and according to Rockow, "Liberal Collectivism under Fabian inspiration is mainly a theory of evolution, while communism is a theory of revolution. Guild socialism attempts to combine both."

Difference between Syndicalism and Guild Socialism

Guild socialism stands for worker's control and self government in industry. It is opposed to collectivism in as much as it does not want that the industries should be conducted, when they have been socialised, under bureaucratic system based on appointment from above. It is equally opposed to Syndicalism, because it does not dispense with the state and because it puts in the forefront of its programme the idea of the service of the consumer. Guild socialists want to abolish the passive capitalist class by denying all rights to rent and interest.

Syndicalists regarded the trade union organization as the foundation of a new society and instrument by which such a society is to be brought into being. Syndicalism laid emphasis on the trade and industrial union movements. It laid emphasis on producers rather than consumers as the controlling factor in industry. Syndicalists believed in revolutionary change. They believed in general strikes, sabotage and other kinds of direct action as means of social transformation. They emphasised the importance of political parliamentary action for bringing about the empancipation of working class. Their method was that of direct economic action.

State socialism or collectivism believes in the state control of means of production to be managed by the state and to be distributed through the state. They desire to make state all powerful. Fabianism also desires to employ state to control the industry and to nationalize large scale industries and to manage equitable distribution. The idea of snatching the control from capitalists and to organize equitable distribution was taken over by the Guild socialists from the state socialists but they differ as Collectivists desire its control by the state or bureaucracy but Guild socialists desire the control of industry by workers themselves though both oppose direct action and other unfair means of Syndicalists.

On the other hand, Guild socialists wanted to realise socialism on the basis of guilds. They believe in the evolutionary transformation of society like Fabians. They have no place for general strike in Guild socialism. The object of Guild socialism was abolition of wage system and the establishment by the workers of self-government in industry through a democratic system of National Guilds working in conjunction with other democratic organizations in the society. Its exponents believed in the three basic principles of functional representation, working participation in management, and proportional responsibility.

It is true that Guild socialism is a half-way house or middle path between Syndicalism and Collectivism as it combines the features of both. Agreeing with collectivists or Fabians it desires to take control of industry from capitalists by peaceful methods gradually but collectivists desire state control and desire to make state omnipotent but on the other hand, Guild socialists want antonomy for the guilds which neither Collectivists nor Fabianists can agree. Like Syndicalists they believe in trade unionism and desire to control the sovereignty of the state which is the essential feature of Collectivism. Thus though Guild Socialists have elements of both but their inclination is more towards syndicalism or they believe in management by workers' antonomy and equal powers of the guilds and all alone in curtailing the sovereignty of the state to which state socialists cannot agree.

Regarding choice if we take the aims and methods both of these "isms", *i.e.,* Syndicalism and Guild socialism into consideration we will find that guild socialism is definitely better and suitable for India but seeing the practical side of these three "isms" perhaps Fabianism is the best among them, but Democratic socialism is most popular which aims to create welfare state to provide food, livelihood, house, health and education for all and tries to improve the lot of the down-trodden people and of women and children. Pt. Jawaharlal Nehru, his daughter Smt. Indira Gandhi, Acharya Narendra Dev and his followers such as Chandra Sekhar, ex-Prime Minister, Subhash Chandra Bose, Ram Manohar Lohia and Jayaprakash Narain, etc., and their followers believed in Democratic socialism but now coalition governments having pragmatic outlook have become a common feature of Indian politics.

NOTE

1. Joad, *Introduction to Modern Political Theory,* pp. 62-63.

3

Communism : Lenin, Stalin, Krushchev and Mao

LENIN

Life Sketch of Lenin and Salient Features of Leninism and Teachings of Lenin

The real name of Lenin was Vladimir Ilyitch Ulinou. Lenin was merely his pen name. He was born in 1870 and he was the second child of his father Iliya Ulinou who had six children. Lenin was inbibed with the revolutionary tradition, when he was 17. His elder brother Alexander was executed for complicity in a plot to assassinate Alexander III, the Czar. While at the University of Kazen, Lenin was converted to Marxism and eventually expelled for revolutionary activities. In 1892, he came to Petersburg, where he organised a league for the emancipation of the working class by combining a number of small Marxist groups which had developed in Petersburg. He was arrested for revolutionary activities and exiled to Siberia in 1878. In the meanwhile a significant development took place and a Socialist Workers Democratic Party was formed.

On his release Lenin got himself associated with the revolutionary movement which had its affiliation with the Social Democratic Party. He became one of the editors of the weekly *Iskore* (*Sparhs*). It was in this paper that Vladimir signed his article as Lenin. He was soon brought face to face with other controversies with the various sections of the working class movement. Economists were more faithful to Marx when they maintained that the class consciousness must come spontaneously. As against this, Lenin believed in the conscious activity directed to stimulate class consciousness among the working class. In fact, Lenin gave an important place to party in the Marxian Socialist Movement. It was the party that represented the vanguard of the working class movement, to stimulate class movement, to stimulate class consciousness, to determine the tactics of Social revolution, to establish and consolidate directorship. In its struggle for power, remarked Lenin, the proletariat has no weapon but organisation.

In "What is to be done" Lenin held his views about the party organisation and contested the views of the economists. More important was the controversy centering round the organisation and tactics of revolutionary movement which confronted Lenin in 1903. Mensheviks favoured the formation of a political party of the proletariat which would include both active revolutionaries and sympathisers. In its organisation, the party should adopt democratic principles. Lenin was opposed to it and favoured strongly centralized and hierarchical principles. It was this controversy that made the Russian revolutionaries fall apart as Mensheviks and Bolsheviks and really, Mensheviks who were more faithful to Marx. Lenin was the leader of the Bolsheviks. In fact, Lenin's conception of party, as carefully picked body of the intellectual and moral elite "makes Marxism different from what had been conceived to be by Marx and Engels"; that this conception of a disciplined and centralized party in the revolutionary movement is Blanquinon rather than Marxism. While the Bolsheviks thought that time had come to strike, the Menshiviks thought that conditions were not mature for a revolution. They were in favour of a bourgeois revolution and formation of a democratic government with a capitalist economy. A bloody revolution could take place in Russia only after a certain period. In 1917 Lenin wrote *State* and *Revolution*. The Government was overthrown by the Bolsheviks who were led by Lenin and Trotsky. The success of Bolshevik revolution in November. 1917 paved the way for the supremacy of Lenin and his ideas. He had to face tough opposition and civil war up to 1921 but later on he emerged as the greatest leader of Russians. He died in 1924.

Lenin's Views. Lenin was the architect of the Bolshevik revolution. Nikolai Bukharin and Leon Trotsky were Russian theorists who shared his views about Soviet policy. According to Maxey, "Lenin, now the beatified saint of Bolshevism was not only a revolutionary leader of great sagacity and practical ability, but was also a writer and thinker of exceptional penetration and power. He claimed to be nothing more than a faithful disciple and authentic interpreter of Marx and Engels, but he was also a thorough student of Hegel, and his writings reveal a mind quite aware of the deeper philosophical implication of Marxist creed."[1] As a leader he was practical minded. While following Marxism, he continued to see that what could not be realised was not followed. His approach was never doctrinaire but all time empirical. As a hard willed leader, he knew the pitfalls of Marxism and so he was overc areful in dealing with his adversaries (champions of the Czarist regime). To suit the conditions in Russia, he modified Marxism and revealed himself as a master strategist :

1. Lenin was a born leader and organizer. Communists were to conduct their activities through their labour organizations like Trade Unions and Co-operatives openly and legally. Besides this, selected and highly efficient professional revolutionaries were to secretly infiltrate all political, social, economic, educational and religious organisations. They were to form cells everywhere. Even the bureaucracy, the police and the army were not to be spared. Under Lenin, the communists knew their destination; the goal was clearly marked out and the way to reach the goal was well known. The real work was to be conducted by fanatical secret agents of the Communist Party, working underground and infiltrating everywhere.

2. Lenin used the party as a strong party to see through his communist programme. Marx had only laid stress on class consciousness; but credit of employing the party in favour of proletariat should go to Lenin.

3. Lenin put emphasis on discipline and felt that if a party member accepted the party programme, he should obey the instructions of the party.

4. Lenin was in favour of a world communist revolution, as its enemies, world capitalism and imperialism had to be got rid of. But as an experienced revolutionary leader, he thought about the possibility of "Socialism in a single country". This idea was pursued by his successor Stalin, who was as practical as Lenin but was decidedly inferior in intellectual calibre. Lenin believed that export of capital and the cultivation of huge capitalist monoplies led to imperialism and scramble for markets. Capitalists, according to him, had high stakes not only in their own countries but all over the world. In a war, the product of capitalism and imperialism, the workers had no state.

5. As such, Lenin withdrew his country from the World War I and emerged victorious in civil war and by applying socialism in one country, made Russia first-rate power.

6. Lenin was in favour of institutions run by elected representatives, but was dead against bourgeoisie parliaments, which he characterized as talking shops.

7. Lenin accepted the idea of Marx of withering away of the state.

Lenin's Contribution. 1. Lenin's greatest contribution lies in giving practical demonstration of Marxian ideas. Lenin conditioned Marxian ideology to suit the Russian context. The ideas of Marx were clearly spelt out in the form of the Bolshevik organisation. "The dictatorship is a matter of revolutionary tactics", and while Marx was no stranger to agitation, he really had little so say about the details of revolution and almost nothing about what would follow it.[2]

2. Lenin followed Marxism wherever possible and modified it, wherever necessary. Between the dictatorship of the party, as a realist, he preferred the latter. Under him, Russia became not a dictatorship of the proletariat but a dictatorship of the Communist Party. Lenin felt that there could be dictatorship of the proletariat without the rise of the Communist Party. Trade union consciousness among workers is not enough; it was necessary to have a strong consciousness. According to Maxey, "Theory and practice should be absolutely integrated with reference to ultimate goal." Violence should be used when practical gains would result, likewise moderation. Compromise and retreat should be governed by the same rule. To attempt to leap at once at communism, was a madness.[3]

3. Lenin was a dynamic and practical minded leader and so he announced concessions to private property through his new economic policy.

4. Lenin actually showed by the Bolshevik revolution that contrary to Marxism, which expected revolution in a highly industrialized country, it was possible to have revolution in Russia, the stronghold of feudalism and not of high industrialism.

5. As a realist again, Lenin revised Marx by giving a national interpretation to Marxism, which had been primarily international. He invented the theory of possibility of socialism in one's own country.

Lenin's Contribution. According to William Ebenstein, "Lenin's most important contribution to the theory of Marxism is his concept of the professional revolution." Sabine states, "Lenin's Marxism presents the anomaly of being at once the most dogmatic assertion of orthodox adherence to the principles of the master and at the same time the freest rendering of it on points where circumstances required its modification." According to Wayper, "Yet, even if his is a bastard Marxism, no one will minimise the significance of what he bequeathed to Russia and to the world".

LENIN

Democratic Centralism

Theoft interpreted and misinterperted with a ring of controversies, the term "Leninism" should not be taken as a doctrine in essence. "It is nothing but Lenin", says Prof. Priezle Griffin. There was no "ism" in Lenin, as there is in Marx of course.

Marx gave us theory which we may call "historical materialism" or "economic determinism" or "materialistic interpretation of history". This theory was supplanted by plan of action which was again both evolutionary and revolutionary. But what we call Leninism is only the political actions for which he supplemented some thoughts borrowed from Marx, whose great admirer he was. Lenin's genius was primarily practical and political.

Does it mean that we are to sidetrack Leninism as merely an application of Marxism to the conditions in Russia? Certainly not, for to maintain that means to believe that Lenin was searching for a ground for the plantation of Marxism. The ground in Russia was not fertile enough to him put to Marxism in practice there, thus he modified it to an extent that it might be easily planted there. It was not a modification in the strict sense of the term "modification". It was complete deviation.

Marx's ablest contribution is the analysis of historical developments, pointing to the inevitability of the socialist revolution. But the purpose to which Lenin dedicated himself was practical, despite the fact that he was also active as a theorist. Therefore, he adopted the teachings and theories of Karl Marx to the demands of the situation which arose out of peculiar circumstances of Czarist Russia. According to Bukharin as quoted by Alexander Grey from "Lenin as a Marxist", that time Lenin was a translator "a genius theoretician". But it is more correct to say that he was more a practical party man than a theoretician.

Leninism lies in the fact that it does base its practical activity on the needs of development of the material life of society and never divorces itself from the real life of society.

One of the most enduring contributions of Lenin to practical politics was his theory of party organisation which he called the party of a newtype. A political party that intends to carry out a revolution successfully must be thoroughly disciplined, alert and ably led just like an army.

Lenin's concept of revolutionary party was determined to a great extent by the situation obtaining in Russia during the revolutionary period. The Czar ruled without the consent or co-operation of the people and the political party the Lenin led, had to work underground. It had to be conspiratorial, ever watchful of the activities of the enemy which was the secret police that would destroy it. Lenin's theory of the organization and role of the political party was made under these conditions. The basic principle of party organization was democratic centralism.

Democratic centralism means, onthe one hand, that the party is democratic. Every office-bearer is elected by the membership. The full congress of the party is the ultimate and supreme authority. The party is self-governing. And each organ of the party, whether the lowest cell or the highest central executive, conducts its deliberations and arrives at the discussions on a democratic basis. Each member of all communist bodies has the right of speech and expression. Decisions are by majority. In this way, party is democratic. But the party is highly centralized and in the normal course of functioning, the decisions of higher organs are binding on the lower organs. In other words, while the members are emowered to elect the leadership, they have to follow leadership after it is elected. Any disagreement of a lower with higher body must be kept in abeyance until the next congress, but until that time the lower organ must obey the higher one. This solved the problem of leadership, which is vital in political action, by legitimising and yet fully empowering the highest levels of the party organisation.

Similarly, there is freedom of expression and full discussion before the issue is undecided. But after full discussion, when once the decision has been taken, it is fully binding on all participants. They have to obey it fully and unquestionably. This type of democratic centralism is the contribution of Lenin. In addition to it, Lenin also made contribution to Marxian theory. Perhaps the most significant is the theory of imperialism as the last stage of capitalism. During the later part of 19th century, capitalist governments entered into a phase of rapid international expansion. Practically the whole world was divided up among the major powers of Europe, Britain, France, Holland, Belgium, Germany and Portugal, etc. Thus, a new phenomenon of imperialist rivalry appeared in the world politics. The various great powers were manoeuvring against one another forming blocks and counter-blocks aiming to win new colonies or to retain old ones, to gain or to retain mastery of the balance of power in the world. The world scene was dominated by the conflict among the imperialist giants. Similarly, the national capitalist enterprises were being transformed into international monopolies. There were often economic wars between these monopolists leading to mergers which gave rise to economic empires no less vast and powerful than political empires.

As the imperial power of the capitalist nations increased, the class struggle inside their boundaries declined, even the working class in the imperialist countries became involved with pride in worldwide colonial possessions. It thought of itself as part of the ruling nation rather than as the oppressed proletariat whose main enemy would be the bourgeois at home. It was opposite to the views of Marx who had pointed out that with the growth of and spread of capitalism, the class struggle will grow in intensity. Marxists had to seek some solution or some way of rekindling class struggle or take advantage of the new imperialist phase of capitalistic development in order to reach their goal of a socialist revolution.

The main explanation put forth by Lenin was that imperialism or capitalism could offer some (bribe) to a part of the working class out of the ill-gotten gains that it extracted through the exploitation of colonial countries. The workers who received material benefits out of the loot of imperialism and constituted labour aristocrats were leaders of the working class movement. They misled and frustrated it by adopting theories of gradualism and mechanical (inevitability) socialism; such ideas prevented the workers from developing class struggle.

Lenin introduced a ground change in the nature and method of political action by the proletariats. He came to the conclusion that the leadership of even the poletariat party should be in the hands of the educated class, not of workers themselves. Workers did not look beyond their immediate economic and material interests, while revolutionary action required a broad vision which could come only from a knowledge of historical revolution. What imperialism had done was to deprive the workers of the revolutionary middle-class leadership.

However, the way out of this difficult situation was provided by imperialism itself. Rivalry between various classes led to various crises and wars, in which working class and poor peasantry had to suffer. War between imperialist countries provided an opportunity to revolutionary leaders to rekindle the class struggle of the proletariat. Thus Lenin described First World War of 1914 between the time-old robbers (England and France) and one new robber (Germany) and hailed it as a heavenly sent opportunity for revolution. He gave a call to all socialist parties to declare war upon their own governments and to start civil wars for overthrow of the bourgeois. But nobody cared for Lenin's appeal and war went on mercilessly. But in Russia, Lenin's appeal was put into practice and the revolution succeeded.

In leading revolution of 1917, Lenin assigned leading role to the peasantry. In Marxian theory, the peasantry has no role to play in the socialist revolution. But Lenin realised that no revolution could succeed in Russia unless it was supported by the peasantry and working class. Perhaps the most important slogan of the revolution was "Land for the peasants"; at least it was next in importance to one that promised *i.e.*, an end to war and thus peace to the suffering Russian people. Actually the Russian revolution was a bourgeois democratic and a proletarian revolution combined, two revolutions squeezed into one.

This had been considered hardly possible by orthodox Marxism although Marx had acknowledged personally that it was not necessary for a country such as Russia to go through full-fledged capitalism before entering into socialism.

According to orthodox Marxism and the even Russian Bolsheviks, revolution may break out in industrially developed countries. According to Marxist philosophy of breaking revolution in many countries, they hoped for a revolution in Western Europe. But Western Europe disappointed their hopes and Russia had to sail a lonely furrow in the midst of a hostile capitalist world. Success of revolution in Russia was Lenin's achievement who steered the ship of the state successfully among the storms and whirlwinds.

Leninism is Marxism of the Era of Imperialism and Proletarian Revolution (Stalin)

Lenin as a matter of fact "added" no "new principles" to Marxism nor did he abolish any of the "old" principles of Marxism. But Lenin merely did not carry out the teachings of Marx and Engels. He developed further the teachings of Marx and Engels in conformity with new conditions of development, with the new phases of capitalism, imperialism. In developing further the teachings of Marx in the new conditions of the class struggle, Lenin contributed some-thing new to the general treasury of Marxism as compared with that which was created by Marx and Engels with what should be created in the pre-imperialist period of capitalism. At the same time Lenin's new contribution to the treasury of Marxism is based on the principles laid down by Marx and Engels. It is in this sense that we speak of Leninism as Marxism of the era of imperialism and proletarian revolution.

Lenin's Development of Marxist's Concept

Lenin dealt first with the question of monopoly capitalism and of imperialism as the new phase of capitalism.

Marx and Engels, who analysed the foundation of capitalism in *Das Kapital* lived in the period of pre-monopoly capitalism, *i.e.* in the period of the smooth evolution of capitalism and its "peaceful" expansion over the world. With the beginning of 20th century, old phase of capitalism came to close when Marx and Engels were no more. Marx and Engels could only guess at the new conditions for the development of capitalism that arose as a result of the imperialist monopoly phase of development when the smooth evolution of capitalism was succeeded by spasmodic, cataclysmic development of capitalism, when the unevenness of development and the contradictions of capitalism became particularly pronounced, and when the struggle for markets and fields of capital exports in the circumstances of the extreme unevenness of development, made periodical imperialist wars for periodic revisions of the world and of spheres of influence inevitable.

Lenin on the basis of the fundamental principles of capitalism made a substantiated Marxist analysis of imperialism as the last phase of capitalism, and expressed its ulcers and the conditions of its inevitable doom. That analysis formed the basis of Lenin's thesis that under conditions of imperialism, the victory of socialism is possible in individual capitalist countries separately.

Secondly, he dealt with the question of dictatorship of the proletariat. The fundamental ideas of the dictatorship of the proletariat as the political rule of the proletariat and as a method of overthrowing the power of capitalists by class, the use of force was advanced by Marx and Engels.

Lenin's new contributions in this field were :

(1) He discovered the Soviet system as the best state form of the dictatorship of the proletariat utilizing for this experience of the Paris Commune and Russian, revolution.

(2) He elucidated the formula of the dictatorship of the proletariat from the angle of the problem of the allies of the proletariat, defining the dictatorship of proletariat as a special form of class alliance between the proletariat, as the leader and the exploited mass of non-proletarian class (the peasantry, etc.) as the led.

(3) He laid particular emphasis on the fact that the dictatorship of the proletariat is the highest type of democracy, which expresses the interest of the majority (the exploited) in contrast to capitalist democracy, which expresses the interest of the minority (the exploiter).

Thirdly, the questions of the forms and methods successfully building socialism in the period of the dictatorship of the proletariat, *i.e.*, in the period of transition from capitalism to socialism, in a country surrounded by capitalist states.

Marx and Engels regarded the period of the dictatorship of the proletariat as a prolonged one, full of revolutionary clashes and civil wars, in the course of which the proletariat being in power, would take the economic, political, cultural and organisational measures necessary for creating a new socialist society, a society without classes and without a state. Lenin agreed with that view and based his contributions on these principles.

Lenin's New Contributions

(1) He proved that a complete socialist society can be built in the land of the dictatorship of the proletariat surrounded by imperialist states; provided the country is not strangled by the military intervention of the surrounding capitalist states.

(2) He traced the concrete lines of economic policy (the New Economic Policy) by which proletariat having possession of the economic positions (industry, land transport, bank, etc.) link up socialised industry with agriculture (the link between industry and peasant economy) and thus lead the whole national economy towards socialism.

(3) He traced the concrete ways of gradually guiding and drawing the main war of the peasantry into the channel of socialist construction through the co-operatives which in the hands of the proletarian dictatorship are a most powerful instrument of or the transformation of small peasant economy and for the reduction of the main mass of the peasantry in the spirit of socialism.

Fourthly, Lenin developed and expanded the outlines provided by Marx and Engels for the hegemony of the proletariat into a harmonious system of leadership of the working masses in town and country by the proletariat not only in overthrowing Czarism and capitalism but also in the building of socialism, under the dictatorship of the proletariat. This hegemony of the proletariat principle was applied in Russia and the revolution succeeded.

Fifthly, regarding colonial and national questions, Lenin's ideas can be summarised as below :

(1) He unified those ideas in one harmonious system of views on national and colonial revolutions in the era of imperialism.

(2) He linked the national and colonial question with the question of overthrowing imperialism.

(3) He declared the national and colonial question to be a component part of the general question of international proletariat revolution.

Lastly, Lenin's contribution regarding the part of the proletariat may be summarised below :

(1) The party is the highest form of class orgnisation of the proletariat as compared with other forms of proletarian organisations (trade unions, co-operatives, state organisation). It is the party's function to generalise and direct the work.

(2) The dictatorship of the proletariat can be implemented only through the party, as the guiding force of dictatorship.

(3) The dictatorship of the proletariat can be complete only if it is led by one party, the communist party, which does not and must not share the leadership with other parties.

(4) Unless there is iron discipline in the party, the tasks of the dictatorship of the proletariat in regard to suppressing the exploiters and transforming those societies into socialist society cannot be accomplished.

In short, Lenin gave a concrete form to Marx's teachings and developed them further in conformity with the new conditions of the struggle of the proletariat in the period of imperialism. As such, Leninism can be said Marxism of the era of imperialism and proletarian revolutions. It is difficult to separate it from Marxism and most difficult to counterpoise it against Marxism.

Sometimes a question is posed that would it be correct to say that Lenin believed in creating revolution whereas Marx was more inclined to wait for the culmination of the development of the economic forces?

For answering this question, we have to keep in mind that, it would be correct to say that every popular evolution is a creative revolution for it breaks up the old and creates a new one.

Even the glorious revolution of England of 1688 created a change and power from king passed in the hands of the parliament. Similarly French revolution gradually snatched the power from the king and nobility and gave it to middle class. Thus except some toy-like risings which take place in backward countries and transfer power from one tribe to another tribe, real revolutions bring a change in social values. And only a revolution which brings a change in social rules can only be termed as a real social revolution. Marx and Lenin upheld precisely such a revolution. Perhaps it goes without saying that such a revolution cannot arise under all conditions, that it can take place only under definite favourable conditions of an economic and political nature.

Lenin's Views on Dialectical Materialism

Lenin's Marxism was by profession utterly dogmatic and orthodox. The bitterest and most constant condemnation that he hurled on the opponents were charges of adulterating Marx's meaning. Engels had also referred to in 1893. Lenin always described theory as a guide to action. It is not a body of static doctrines but rather suggestive ideas to be used in assessing concrete situations and to be modified in application.

The official definition of Lenin's philosophy laid down by Stalin in his "Foundations of Leninism (1924) is that Leninism is Marxism in the epoch of imperialism and of the proletarian revolution". "Lenin realised that no revolution could succeed without at least acquiescence of the peasants and on his readiness to postpone his own preferred policy of nationalizing the land, he got success. Thus, Lenin's Marxism was always flexible enough in practice to permit him to take a line that Russian Marxistscommonly regarded as not Marxian at all" (Sabine).

Regarding party organisation, Marx and Engels after 1850, severed their connections with the underground, a course which Russian revolution could not initiate under Czar and so Lenin changed his tactics about party organisation; so he introduced democratic centralism. Thus his theories in spite of their constant reaffirmation of Marxian generalizations always had reference to a specific course of action in a definite situation. Lenin's Marxism was, therefore, at once intensely dogmatic and highly pragmatic, a combination that can be as puzzling to historians as it often was to his Marxian associates. Lenin published in 1902 a pamphelet entitled "What is to be done?". He differed fundamentally with Marx on two grounds : (1) Advanced stage of capitalism was necessary for bringing about a communist uprising and (2) the organization of the party; yet he held that Russian communist programme was in entire conformity with the Marxian principles.

Lenin on Dialectical Materialism. Dialectical materialism is the essence of Marx-Leninist doctrine. "My dialectic method" says Marx, "is not only different from the Hegelian, but directly opposite." To Hegel, the process of thinking, which under the name of "the idea" he even transforms into an independent subject, is the demiurge (creator) of the real world, and the real world is the only external phenomena form of "the idea". "With me" on the contrary, the ideal is nothing else than the material world reflected by the human mind and translated into forms of thought.

Dialectic comes from the Greek word "dialgo" which means to discourse, to debate. In ancient times, dialectic was the art of arriving at truth by disclosing the contradictions in the argument of an opponent and overcoming these contradictions. There were philosophers in ancient times who believed that disclosure of contradictions in thought and the clash of the opposite opinions was the best method of thought of arriving at truth. This dialectic method of thought later extended to the phenomena of nature and thus it is the direct opposite of metaphysics.

Lenin's book *Materialism and Emperio* criticism published in 1909 dealt with general philosophical problems, the nature of dialectic, its relation to nature and sociology, the validity of materialism, idealism and scientific positions as philosophical systems. In this book Lenin adopted from Engels the dogma that every philosophy must be either idealist or materialist, any third form being merely confusing or a pretence. Idealism is clericalism since non-spatial and non-temporal beings were inventions of the clergy to deceive the masses, a bad product of a bad social order. But idealism is not nonsense. Scientific position on the other hand is merely "a pseudo-erudite pretence to transcend idealism and materialism" and is in reality covert clericalism "conciliatory quackery", a bourgeoie philistine, cowardly tolerance. Lenin like Engels regarded it as refuted by the fact that statements can be empirically verified. Throughout he represented positivism as merely a modified form of Bolshevian idealism and therefore equivalent to denial that there is any such thing as objective truth or any reality other than conditions of consciousness. Its only purpose is to offer a confused or hypothetical defence of religious faith. Materialism was reduced in Lenin's exposition to the not very profound proposition that objective reality exists independently of ever knowing it which he stated as meaning indifferently that perceptions give us correct impressions of things that we directly know of objects themselves and that objects casually on our senses. Hence our ideas "reflect" objects or give us pictures or "images" of them. His account of dialecticism is in almost the same terms used by Engels. Truth is atonce relative and absolute that is partly incorrect and an "approximation" to absolute objective truth. Every ideology is historically conditioned but it is an unconditional truth that there is an objective truth corresponding to every scientific theory. This he said has the merit of being indefinite enough to prevent science from becoming dogmatic but definite enough to exclude any form of faith or agnosticism. Throughout Lenin's argument there ran a curious sympathy for clericalism and a moral abhorrence for scientific positivism. He hated clericalism or idealism as he called it, but he did not fear it because he knew the answer. As he wrote in his notebook, clericalism is indeed a sterile flower, yet one growing on the living tree of a prolific truth powerful, omnipotent objective and absolute human knowledge. On the other hand, the indifference of scientists like much to metphysics disputes and the empirical and non-authoritarian temper of his philosophy, produced in Lenin's mind a sense of profound moral repulsion. It was so foreign to his way of thinking that he could not believe it honestly.

In one important respect Lenin's treatment of dialectical materialism is different from Marx and engels. Marx following Hegel had regarded the dialectic as a method specially suited to the social studies because these have to do with a subject matter in which development or growth is an important factor. Sciences that deal with inanimate nature like physics and chemistry, Marx assumed, these sufficiently well served by a materialism of the non-dialectical type. In short, dialectical materialism, as Lenin conceived it, became a universal method applicable in every field of science, and the only safeguard in any matter. In effect, this turned it into a higher form of knowledge, a species of theology that can act as arbiter of all questions of all sciences. Thus dialectical materialism can set the mathematician right about euclidean and non-Euclidean geometry and can instruct the physicist about the "correct" relations between matter and electricity.

The relation of dialectical materialism to the social studies as Lenin conceives them is, of course, much closer than its relationship to the natural sciences, though not different in kind; philosophy and social studies, Lenin asserted, are inevitably partisan. Professors of economics, he said, are nothing but scientific salesmen of the capitalist class and professors of philosophy are scientific salesmen of theology. The most that a scientific theory of society can discover is general out-line of the objective logic of economic and historical evolution, and this is provided by dialectical materialism. In philosophy, economics and politics, impartiality or scientific detachment therefore is merely a pretence adopted to cover a defence of vested interests. Within the framework of dialectical materialism, there are time systems of social sciences, the one produced in the interest of middle class, the other produced in the interest of the proletariat. The superiority of the proletariat consists in the fact that in dialectic, the proletarian is to be the "rising" class which is in the forefront of social progress. The middle class on the contrary is engaged in a hopeless struggle to hold back the inevitable transition from capitalism to communism. In 1932, Stalin's account of "Dialectical and Historical Materialism" followed closely the models set by Engels and Lenin but emphasized the relations between dialectic and policy.

The dialectical method therefore holds that the process of development from the lower to the higher takes place not as a harmonious unfolding of phenomena, but as a disclosure of the contradictions inherent in things and phenomena as a "struggle" of opposite tendencies which operates on the basis of these contradictions.

Hence, in order not to musterr in policy, one most pursue an uncompromising proletarian class policy, not a reformist policy of harmony of the interests of the proletriat and the bourgeoisie, not a compromiser's policy of "the growing" of capitalism into socialim.

Further, according to Lenin, this world is knowable and our knowledge of the laws of the development of nature is authentic knowledge, having the validity of objective truth. It follows that social life and the development of society are also knowable and that the data of science regarding laws of development of society are authentic data having the validity of objective truths.

Hence, the science of the history of society, despite all complexity of the phenomena of life, can become as precise as science, let us say biography, and is capable of making use of the laws of the development of the society for practical purposes.

Hence, the party of the proletariat should be guided in the practical activity not by casual motions but by the laws of development of the society by practical conclusions from these laws. Hence, socialism is converted from a dream of a better future for harmony into a science.

According to Sidney "Lenin gave a new orientation to the Marxist analysis of imperialist capitalism". According to Lenin. "Imperialism is the last stage of capitalism". This was the view of Lenin which he exhaustively dealt with the characteristics of capitalism that it must reach its highest stage which he calls as the highest stage and from which must come its downfall. Imperialism, according to Lenin, is the monopoly stage of capitalism. Capitalism becomes imperialism at a definite and a very high stage of its development, when some of its fundamental characteristics begin to change or transform into their opposites, when the features of the epoch of transition from capitalism to a higher social and economic system have taken shape and reveal themselves all along the line. From economic point of view, it is the replacement of capitalist free competition by capitalist monopoly. Free competition is the fundamental characteristic of capitalism but monopoly is the opposite of free competition. The transformation of free competition into monopoly is characterized by the creation or origin of large scale industry which results in forcing out small industry, replacement of large scale industry by still larger scale industry, concentration of production and capital to the point where out of it has grown and is growing monopoly development of cartels, syndicates and trusts, and merging with them the capital of a dozen or so banks which manipulate thousands of millions. One peculiar feature of this development is that monopoly which grows out of free competition does not abolish or eliminate free competition, but exists over and above it and alongside of it and thereby gives rise to numerous, very acute, intense, antagonisms, frictions and conflicts.

The briefest definition of imperialism is that imperialism is the monopoly stage of capitalism. It means two things :

(a) Finance capital is the banks' capital of a few very big monopolist banks. These monopolist banks are merged with the capital of the monopolist combines of industrialists.

(b) The division of the world is the transition from a colonial policy which has extended without any type of hindrance to territories unoccupied by any capitalist power to a colonial policy of monopolistic possession of the territory of the world which has been completely divided up.

Broadly stating the imperialism contains following features :

(a) The concentration of production and capital developed to such a high stage that it created monopollies. These monopolies created by the high stage of concentration of production and capital play a decisive role in the economic life.

(b) Imperialism is characterized by the merger of bank capital with industrial capital. Banks' capital merged with industrial capital, becomes finance capital or is known financial capital. This financial capital creates financial oligarchy.

(c) Under imperialism or imperialistic monopoly, the export of capital as distinguished from the export of commodities, acquires exceptional importance. Putting it differently we may say that export of capital becomes exceptionally important.

(d) Imperialism is also characterized by the formation of international monopolist capitalist combines. These international monopolist capitalist combines share the world among themselves.

(e) The territorial division of the whole world among the highest capitalist power is completed.

Summing up the above points, Lenin says, "Imperialism is capitalism in that stage of development in which the domination of monopolies and finance capital has established itself, in which the export of capital has acquired pronounced importance in which the division of the world among the internationalist trusts has begun, in which the division of all territories of the globe among the biggest capitalist powers has been completed".

Lenin made a special point in connection with the drive of imperialist countries. To speak in general terms, the drive of each and every imperialist country for expansion had been considered, regarded, or treated as only aimed at colonial countries. The special point that Lenin made in this connection was that, according to Sabine, the drive of each and every imperialist country was not essentially or necessarily aimed at colonial countries. The imperialist drive for expansion, according to Lenin, was general in nature. In this connection, the drive of German finance capital in the Nazi period is worth mentioning. The imperialist stage of capitalism, Lenin concludes, brings with it, greater economic crises, wars, the on a world scale, on the one hand, and labour class revolts and revolutions of the oppressed, suppressed and exploited people of colonial and semi-colonial areas against their exploitation by imperialists, on the other hand. One of the characteristic features of imperialism is the concentration of capital in the hands of small groups. It follows that these groups have more and more power over the state machine. With increase in power over state machine, of these small groups, the policy of the various countries becomes very closely associated with the interest of these groups. This characteristic feature of capitalism makes it possible for the finance capital group in every country to fight against their foreign rivals by quotas, tariffs and by war.

The above-mentioned conflict between the rival groups is inevitable. Though it is true that the monopoly groups in different countries make so many agreements in order to divide the world market among themselves, but such arrangements are not lasting. According to Baile Burns, "Economic agreements are only, so to speak, armistices in a continuous trade users between the finance capital group of different countries."

The concentration of capital and wealth in the hands of finance capital groups in each and every country resulted in large scale wars or war between great powers. There is a constant competitive struggle between rival imperialist groups resulting in general worsening of conditions. Every imperialist group wants to win or keep markets. With this aim in view, wages are forced down to reduce cost of the commodity produced. Economic crises are characteristic of decaying or dying capitalism. In imperialism, economic crises become more prolonged and deeper.

Prolonged and deeper, economic crisis, cutting down, all this result in an acute form of class struggle, which is also the characteristic feature of imperialism. In imperialism, it is not only the class struggle which becomes acute, but the struggle of the colonial people against imperialism also becomes very acute.

He further states that in imperialist stage of capitalism, the monoplist groups, according to Lenin, in the imperialist regions or in the imperialist countries are in a position to make profit over and above the average, by exploiting backward people. According to Emrile Burns, "This is partly because of the low standard of living of these people whose methods of production are primitive partly because of the terrible conditions forced on them by completely callous rulers and capitalists; and partly because of the fact that the products of machine industry can be exchanged with handicraft products at a very specially high rate of exchange".

According to Lenin, monopoly is the foundation upon which, the whole structure of imperialism stands. Economic monopoly like any other monopoly, inevitably produces a tendency to stagnation and decay.

"Imperialism" as Lenin says "is an immense accumulation of money capital in a few countries". This immense accumulation of money capital in the hands of a few countries leads to an extra-ordinary growth of a class of rentiers. These persons do not take part in any sort of enterprise and their only profession is idleness. The isolation of rentiers from production is increased by one of the most essential bases of imperialism, *i.e.*, export of capital. As Lenin says, it more completely isolates the rentiers from production and sets the seal of parasitism on the whole country that lives by exploiting the labour of several overseas countries and colonies. That is why the term "rentier state or usurer state" is commonly used in the economic literature that deals with imperialism. The rentier state, according to Lenin, is a state of parastic decaying capitalism. This parasitic and decaying capitalism is bound to effect the true fundamental trends in the working class movement.

Hobson has described the connections between imperialism and the interests of financiers. He says, "While directors of this definite parasitic policy are capitalists, the same motives appeal to special class of workers". Giving example, Hobson further says, many towns and most important trades are dependent upon government employment of contracts; the imperialism of the metal and shipbuilding centres is attributable in no small degree to this fact. These points are notable.

1. "Economic parasitism".

2. Formation of armies composed of subject people. About economic parasitism, Hobson says, "There is first the habit of economic parasitism, by which the ruling state has used its provinces, colonies and dependencies in order to enrich its ruling class and to better its lower classes into acquiescence." High monopolist profits are necessary for such bribery. Regarding the second point, Hobson says, one of the strongest symptoms of the blindness of imperialism is the reckless indifference with which imperial nations are embarking on this perilous independence. This is essence of imperialism and imperialistic parasitism. Joseph Schumpeter contests Lenin's thesis regarding the origin of imperialism. A capitalist world, according to Jospeh Schumpeter, can offer no fertile land or soil to impulses. He holds that people of capitalist world are very likely to be of an essentially un-warlike disposition. Through the capitalistic world or the world of capitalism in general and among the elements formed by capitalism in modern social life, in particular, has arisen fundamental or basic opposition to war expansion of armaments, which are characteristic features of imperialism. Modern pacifism is also a phenomenon of modern capitalism. Industrial workers of capitalist world do not take any initiative for forcible policy of expansion. Types of workers created by capitalism are ignorantly anti-imperialist. Despite manifest resistance on the part of powerful elements, the capitalist age or the capitalist area has seen the development of methods of prventing war or the peaceful settlement of disputes among states as U.S.A. and as such it can be said that industry is by nature anti-mperialist.

According to Prof. Staley, the relationship between the movement of capital and poverty seems to be the direct opposite of what Lenin declared it to be.

According to Wayper, "His theory of imperialism, in fact, in so far as it is a defence of Marxism, is both dishonest and untrue; in so far as it is true that it is not defence but an effective renunciation of teachings of the master".

Lenin's ideas failed in practice. Russia which never reached the climax of its imperialist policy got a revolution but England had reached the climax but remained anti-revolutionary.

Critical Appreciation of Leninism

According to Sydney Hook, "Lenin was both architect as well as product of a great revolutionary phase in world history. He is what the revolution of 1917 made him appear to be, and had there been no revolution in Russia in 1917, then the name of Marx and Marxism would have hardly been known outside Russia and probably he (Lenin) too would have been cast into oblivion".

Marx Lerner is of opinion that "There is probably nothing in the history of political thought that equals in dramatic power of Lenin's achievement in linking his own life with the analysis and enactment of revolution. He was one of those rare persons in whom life derives no paralysing wedges and in whom therefore there is no gap between the idea and the fact".

As a theorist, Lenin is quite famous and best known for his analysis of revolutionary tactics and for his study of imperialism. "Foundation of Leninism" according to Stalin is the era of results and of imperialism. Mary James Nobler, to a very great extent, is of the same opinion. Expressing her views regarding Leninism, she says, "If Marxism is a scientific dogma what Lenin did was that he supplanted Marxism in various important ways." This is why Leninism is defined as "the Marxism of the era of imperialism and the proletarian revolution".

About revolution Lenin was of the aim that compromise with bourgeoisie liberals was quite inadmissible and a violent change was necessary. Lenin was of the opinion that socialism could not be introduced without a revolution.

As against Marx, Lenin attached more importance to the influence of ideas in the creation of revolutionary ideology, than to influence of economic factors.

In the words of Sabine, "Leninism presents an anomaly of being at once dogmatic assertion of orthodox adherence to the principles of

Marxism and at the same time free at rendering of it on points where circumstances require its modification".

It is evident from the study of Lenin and Marx that the meanings which Lenin attached to tenets of Marx were to a very great extent different what Marx himself gave them. Prof. Sabine adds, "Indeed if piety towards the master permitted, Leninism might have claimed to have stood the Hegelian dialect on its feet. The simple truth is that the Marxian dogmas which Lenin piously held were simply abandoned when they came into conflict with his profounder belief in organisation and his will as a revolutionist. Lenin's formulas remained the formulas of Marx, the meaning of Leninism departed very widely from the meaning of Marxism".[4]

We may conclude our discussion on Leninism with the following remarks of Joad :

"While Marx's approach to life is a big philosophical, Leninism has no such fragrance; it is a scientific truth, not a dogma, purely a materialist approach to life and its actualities".

Stalin's Theory of Communism

Joseph Stalin was born in the year 1879 in the Province of Georgia. He was the son of a peasant shoemaker. He joined the Marxian movement at an early age and ever since was a revolutionary. When the communist uprising was successful, he was made a commissar for nationalities. When Lenin died in 1924, he managed to dispose of Trotsky by conspiring with other top leaders. Later on he disposed of other leaders and emerged as a successful man who shaped the destiny of Russia from 1924, till his death in 1953 at the ripe age of 74 years. He consolidated Russia, made it a world power, gave it a constitution and was backbone of Russia's tremendous progress and prosperity.

Stalin differed with Trotsky regarding the international character of the working class movement. He here appears to be a realist. His main object was to first of all consolidate the communist revolution in Russia and then to see its international character. Trotsky on the other hand was in favour of simultaneous communist uprisings. Afterwards Stalin himself supported communist revolutions in East Europe and China. All the communist parties of the world looked towards Moscow.

So far as Lenin is concerned, Stalin points out, "Lenin had indeed revived the revolutionary content of Marxism suffocated by the opportunists of the Second International. Imperialism has made the revolution a practical necessity. Could the Russian communists, in such a situation, confine themselves to a narrow national framework of a Russian revolution? Of course not, they were forced to smash social patriotism and social pacifism finally to overthrow capitalism in their own country, and hammer out a new weapon, the theory and tactics of proletarian revolution."

Regarding wages Stalin writes, "This sort of socialism in which every one received the same wages, the same quality of meat, the same quality of bread and received the same products in the same quantity — such a socialism is unknown in Marxism. It only says until the final annihilation of the classes instead of labour being a means to existence, has become the final necessity of life, voluntary labour for society, every one will be paid in accordance with the work done. Equalisation in the sphere of consumption or in personal life is reactionary, petty bourgeois nonsense, worthy of some primitive set of ascetics but not of a socialist country." He believed in communist age in which everybody will work according to his ability and will get according to his needs, a golden age but such a condition is not possible in socialist age.

Joseph Stalin supported the theory of socialism in one country. He regarded Russia as a force in her own right while Leon Trotsky regarded Russia as a springboard for world revolution. In the words of Wayper, "To the old Bolsheviks who agreed with Trotsky, Western Europe was the real centre of the world, and Russia a back-ground community on the edge of outer darkness which never the less can help Europe and which must in its turn await the saving strength of Europe." To Stalin Russia was the centre of the world. It was her destiny to become the centre of the new civilization superior to that of capitalist Europe.[5]

Trotsky was of opinion that the theory of socialism in one country is against the views of Lenin. Lenin holds that the relationship between socialism in one country and world economy is economic in nature. Joseph Stalin's theory of socialism in one country "makes the relationship political". As per Prof. Sabine, Joseph Stalin's theory of socialism in one country amounted to assuming that a socialist economy in Russia could insulate itself and could pursue political tactics alternatively of co-operation or intervention as circumstances dictated, while it waited for capitalism to collapse. Such a policy would be practically indistinguishable from Russian nationalism or imperialism, and would have no logical relation to Marxism.[6]

Later on, as said before, he began to possess a firm faith in the theory of moral revolution. According to Wayper, "His belief in the possibility of a peaceful transition to socialism through socialist encirclement was also a belief in force. The differences were differences of degree not of kind."

Change introduced into Marxism by Stalin

Lenin was leader of the revolution of Russia, but he died in 1924. From around 1924 to 1953, Stalin was the supreme leader of Soviet region and of the international communist movement. The communists in Russia had believed that their revolution was only a prelude to the revolutions that would break out in other countries. Marxism taught that the task of the communists starts when that of capitalists ends. In fact, only when the capitalists have exhausted their potentialities for progress, the communists would have the chance of coming to power and setting right the economic and social imbalances which the capitalists system had created. Marx believed that the capitalists system would die of its own contradictions because capital is owned by a group of men, each of whom acts in self-interest; but hopes of revolution in other countries were belied on the sharprocks of reality and Stalin had to face the task of building socialism in a single country and that too dominated by the peasantry.

According to Karl Marx, communism is a movement of industrial proletariat. But Stalin stated that the task of communist regime in Russia was to create proletariat which were a small minority of the population. The Soviet regime under the leadership of Stalin was different from that anticipated by Karl Marx, to Stalin had to conciliate the peasant masses in order so win their support when it was needed. In the first phase of the Russian revolution, land was distributed to the peasants and New Economic Policy allowed considerably free trade to a great extent. But these policies were soon followed by collectivisation of agriculture which was fought bitterly by prosperous peasants.

To develop industry, the standard of living of the people had to be kept low in order to direct the bulk of production to industrial development. But certain people whose co-operation was necessary were kept well paid. They included important government and party officials, scientists, engineers and military officers. The obedience and loyalty of the population could be ensured by creating a vast secret police, by holding spectacular trials of alleged spies in order to check the activities of the capitalist countries. But the people were mobilised for economic development and basic facilities of free education, free medicine and cheap medicine were provided.

In short, Lenin adopted the Marxist doctorine for the purpose of creating a communist party in Russia, and leading the revolution to success. But Stalin had to wield the power which Lenin had won. On the one hand, Stalin had to preserve and strengthen the Soviet government in the world of hostile capitalist powers; on the other hand, his task was of making the peasants accept a communist regime. He had to work with an iron hand. He isolated the Russian people from the outside world and spent a great deal of resources on building the armed forces but he succeeded in strengthening the communist regime at the cost of much suffering and sacrifices and, as has recently come to be alleged, distorting communist theory and practice.

Evolution of Marxian thought in Soviet Russia

Stalin made Russia a world power but he did not believe in the withering away of the state. In place of bringing state towards an end, he made the state omnipotent and according to some persons gave socialism or rather to say state socialism to Russia instead of communism. Marxism became the handmaiden of Soviet regime which could not really follow or practise the precepts of Marxism because of its cultural and economic state of development. It became Marxism, Leninism and Stalinism.

Apart from the improvement of communist revolution in Russia, the failure of proletariat in the capitalist countries to rise in revolution or at least to remain sympathetic to the Soviet Union, is another feature of the Marxism view of history. The failure of the revolution in the West and its success in the east, created unusual conditions for the application of Marxist philosophy by the Soviet leaders. Marxism had to serve a dual purpose. Firstly, to be an organic part of the Soviet Russian regime, which used Marxism pragmatically, in order to justify whatever measures it had to adopt. As Marcuse put it, "Soviet Marxism appears as the attempt to reconcile the inherited body of Marxism theory with a historical situation which seemed to initiate the central conception of this theory itself, namely the Marxism conception of the transition from capitalism to socialism." Thus, adds Marcuse, "Soviet Marxism has assumed the character of behavioural science". Most of the theoretical pronouncements have a pragmatic instrumental intent. They strive to explain, justify, promote and direct certain actions and attitudes which are actual date for these pronouncements. Secondly, however Marxism, had to be kept pure for the day when it would be used for actual attainment of socialism. Soviet leaders had to find everything within the four corners of Marxism, even if it had to be extended into Marxism-Leninism-Stalinism. Russia proclaimed Marxism communist utopia, which would establish a true humanist society which can be free from enslavement to material needs. The Soviet leadership was unable to act according to Marxian theory and it might have suited their immediate purposes to discard Marxism altogether but this they could not do, because they would not have any other theoretical or philosophical locus standi, so they developed a direct set of theories on pure classical Marxism and offer a popular practical Marxism. Humanistic outlook of Marxism was discarded and practically applicable part of Marxism was utilized. the Party was made ultimate judge of all matters, the ultimate source of all authority, political or moral, and would not permit the acceptance of any beliefs whereby it itself could be judge. The situation has quite aptly been compared with that of the Roman Catholic Church, whose Pope proclaims infallibility on matters of faith and morals.

Transition from socialism to communism is a most important one in Soviet Union but it raises many delicate issues. Since the deprivation imposed upon Soviet Union is justified as a necessary sacrifice to achieve utopia, the repeated references to the transition to communism are meant as an earnest desire of the Soviet leadershipvs, sincerity on that score.

In the Soviet Union moral values are externalised. These are decided by the society in theory but by the Communist Party in practice. The question whether the Soviet experience verifies Marxism remains unanswered. But Marxism has inspired the Soviet Union to become a highly industralised country and to keep clear of capitalist ideology. These are its most important achievements. The truth of falsity of Marxism cannot be established, but its effectiveness as faith cannot be denied.

As we have seen, Marxism's interpretation varied from time to time, so the 22nd Congress of Communist Party was held in 1961 under the leadership of Kruschev and following draft was adopted :

> "The draft programme of the Party raises and resolves a new important question of communist theory and practice, the development of the dictatorship of the working class into a state of the whole people, the character and purpose of the state and its future under communism. The state of the whole people is a new stage in the development of the socialist state on all important phases on the road from socialist statehood to communist public self-government."[7]

Lenin said that "The bourgeoisie state is a dictatorship of the exploiting minorities over the overwhelming majority of society, whereas the proletarian state expresses the interest of the vast majority of the society." Thus, he aimed for the establishment of communism after achieving the victory of socialism. As such, it was declared that "It (state) being retained because the tasks which society can so use only with the aid of the state are not as yet consummated, these purposes and functions of the socialist state are defined conclusively in the draft of our party. The state will remain long after the victory of the first phase of communism, the process of its withering away will be very long one; it will cover an entire historical epoch and will not end until society is completely ripe for self-government; it is only after a developed communist society has been built in the USSR and provided socialism wins and consolidates in the international area, that there will no longer be any need for the state, and it will wither away".[8] In foreign relations, the general principle of co-existence of states with varied social systems was accepted. The USSR needs arms as the threat of war may come from imperialist camps.

Thus, in the light of actual experience Russian communists had to modify their views and sometime go against what they upheld most fanatically. Lenin himself had to make concessions to private property through his New Economic Policy (1921-28) when production figures went alarmingly low. Besides this, the Russians agreed to pay according to actual results of work and finally they had to give up the principle "from each according to his capacity to each according to his merit." The withering away of the state is not in sight and history did not afford any example where lust for power had been given up by the dictators themselves. However, after the exit, of Kruschev from power, Mr. Brejenov and Kosygin have been elected as office-bearers but due to dispute with China, nothing new has taken place. For dispute with China and its ideology, we will discuss later on.

Communism in China and Basic Concepts of Maoism

China is the most populated country of the world, having population of more than 130 million. Its civilization is very old, but later on, it embraced Buddhism and Manchu dynasty ruled over it. After the over-throw of the Manchu dynasty, China became a republic in 1911 with Dr. Sun Yatsen as its first President. Dr. Sun, who has been regarded as the father of modern China strongly upheld the three principles of Nationalism, Democracy and People's livelihood (or socialism). But the republic did not succeed in China and Litao-Chau and his follower Mau-tse Tung became communists. Dr. Sun Yatsen himself became communist sympathiser. Republican, government of Kuomintang and the corrupt leadership of Chiang Kaishek failed to check the rising tide of communism and in 1949, Communists succeeded in expelling Chiang to Formosa. Chiang could be easily expelled from Formosa too but for the continued military and other assistance that he had been receiving from the USA.

Mao and his comrades have learnt much from Russia and they

succeeded in dealing with feudal, capitalist and imperialist elements in the communists for their liquidation. Mao did not go so far as Stalin in dealing with the enemies. Russia introduced collective farms, but China allowed peasant proprietorship to continue provided the land was tilled by the peasant himself. Mao distinguished the rural proletariat from the urban and laid particular stress on the former. Mao followed Marxism-Leninism and adopted a ruthless attitude towards the capitalists. Theoretically Mao-tse Tung speaks in terms of New Democracy or People's democracy in which the people have freedom. The workers, the peasants, the petty and national bourgeoisie form the people. Mao combines "democracy for the people and dictatorship over the reactionaries". Whatever may be the theory, Mao's China has become authoritarian and socialist. People have no rights and no intellectual freedom. Though Mao's principle "Let hundred flowers bloom" intellectual freedom, it did not last long for the power-drunk communist leaders found their position untenable and naturally the original tight control over all aspects of life had to be retained. But not China is also following policy of Globalisation of Economic aspects and they have liberalised tight control over economic activities and have allowed foreign investments.

The views of the Communist leaders of China are not in tune with the leaders of Russia. The ideological gap between Russia and China became very wide. The Chinese are against new Kruschevian attitude of collaboration with capitalist powers, particularly after the Cuban crisis in 1962 and Russian help to India against China increased their differences.

Ideological Differences between Russia and China

With the emergence of Communist China, a power came on forefront to challenge the Russian leadership of the communist world. Stalin, the senior-most Communist leader died in 1953 and his place was taken oner by Kruschev in Russia, but according to seniority and experience, Mao is the senior-most leader of the communist world. Soon differences developed between China and Russia.

Differences about Stalin. Differences came on forefront in 1956 when Kruschev condemned Stalin and Stalinism in the 20th Congress of Communist Party of USSR. Chinese were of opinion that through Stalin committed some mistakes but he was a defender of Marxism and Leninism.

He contributed a lot to communist ideology and international communist movement. He also crushed the internal and external enemies of communism and defended the USSR. against fascist powers. He emerged successful in the Second World War and sailed the ship of the state successfully against the whirlpools created by the capitalist and fascist powers.

Differences about the Means of Revolution. The second difference is more serious and ideological. Lenin and Stalin both believed that revolutions cannot take place without armed unheaval, but Kruschev and his successors, Kosygin and Breznov believed that now world situation had changed and there was possibility that working class may capture power by peaceful methods without armed revolution. Russian leaders say that in the present situation, labourers and workers can capture power in capitalistic countries by and through constitutional and parliamentary means. Mao is of opinion that there is no country of the world where workers may capture power by peaceful means and workers will have to adopt violent methods. Mao also accused Russian leaders that they have abandoned the Marxist and Leninist methods and have adopted revisionism and are in collusion with U.S.A.

Differences about Imperialism. Lastly there is difference in their attitude towards capitalistic countries. Russian leaders are of opinion that now capitalistic countries such as U.S.A. do not desire more and Russian workers can have friendship with them to save the world from the scourge of war. Communist countries should compete with capitalist countries in peaceful progress, economic development, cultural aspects and in administration, and communist countries can score over capitalistic countries in those respects. But Chinese believe that there has been no change in the nature of imperialism and can only be wiped out through violance and it war. To beat down the capitalist powers, communists should increase their armed power and should also encourage and support workers and peasants' revolutions all over the world. Mao is in favour of indirect wars against U.S.A., and is behind the other countries. Vietnam war is the burning example of this strategy.

Conclusion. It is beyond the power of any political scientist to arrive at a definite conclusion but it seems that the conflict is not only ideological. In this conflict, natural jealousy and individual ambitions have also played a notable part. Peaceful co-existence, peaceful competition and peaceful co-operation, ideologically are against the basic teachings of Marx and Lenin, but regarding world peace Kruschevian policy seems to be correct. But for this abandonment of Marxism and Leninism by Russia, open declaration is necessary. Russian leaders not possess courage to publicly abandon the Marxism Leninism to support their policy and here lies the greatest weakness of Russian ideology. On the other hand, Mao is strictly adhering to Marxism and Leninism and did not agree that with the advent of nuclear weapons, policy of violent revolutions and war cannot succeed. He is even willing to plunge the world into war for the sake of ideology. He forgets that, in war, God is always in favour of large battalions. In war, not the ideology but armed might decides the issue and in this respect China is thousand miles behind in comparison to U.S.A. and U.S.S.R. Mao's bogey of war and ideology that power comes through the barrel of gun may plunge the whole mankind into war. If such a dream materialises then not only China but the whole world may have to pay the price and even existence of whole humanity may be at stake. Only the future may tell what will happen but it can not be denied that China has now become a menace to whole world.

It was expected that after the fall of Kruschev, differences may subside but the differences between Russia and China have increased and are increasing day by day. Later on, U.S.S.R. became divided in 16 states and lost its former influence and glory but China increased her power by adopting changes in its policy. Now Russia has become a state devoid of communism and China preaches communism but follows pragmatic policies to suit its requirements.

Criticism of Communism. Marxism has gone far off from Marx's basic teachings. Now it may be called Marxism, Leninism and Stalinism and Krushevianism in Russia, and Marxism, Leninism. Stalinism and Maoism in China. Secondly, though Marx supported armed revolution and proletarian dictatorship but he believed basically in democratic ideology. He desired the majority government of workers and supported freedom of expression and press but now in communist countries there is party dictatorship and no freedom of press. Communist rule is not the rule of people by the people though it is possible that it may be rule for the benefit of the people.

Secondly, the present communist regimes are most authoritarian in which all things and every aspect of life is governed by the state and man's spirit cannot work freely.

Thirdly, openly or secretly communists support armed conflict and armed revolution and with the increase of communist power it is feared that in armed conflict of communist and capitalistic world, existence of humanity itself may be at stake, as Carew Hunt has said that communism is now the greatest destructive force of the world. Lastly, goal of communism that everybody will work according to his ability and will get according to his needs is a far off goal and unrealistic dream. Power corrupts a man and absolute power corrupts absolutely. Perhaps no communist country rulers can abandon the power of their own accord for the sake of communist utopia.

Lastly, in the words of Laski, in a general sense doubtless, the error of communism lies in its refusal to face the fact that this is a complex world. Its panacea is unreal simply because the world is too intricate for panaceas as to have universal guidance.

EFFECTS OF THE RUSSIAN AND CHINESE REVOLUTIONS

The Bolshevik revolution in Russia and Chinese communists, revolutions had far reaching effects. In less than 80 years after the death of Marx, about one-third of world population became red. Stalin took full advantage of Russia's position as one of the leading victors of World War II. The democracies in the second World War context made concessions to Russia. This enabled Russia to develop her imperialism and spread communism in Europe and Asia. Consequently, communist governments came in power in Romania, Bulgaria, Hungary and Poland and East Germany and in Czechoslovakia, etc. With the emergence of China as a communist power, communism spread over North Vietnam, North Korea, etc. Outer Mangolia became a Russian satellite and Latavia, Lithunia and Estonia were annexed by it. China annexed Tibet.

International. International organisations were formed for spreading socialism or communism. The First International was formed in 1864 under the leadership of Marx. The Second (Socialist) International was established in 1889. World War II gave a death blow as all socialist parties forgetting their international alliances supported their national governments. The Third (Communist) International was formed at Moscow in 1919 under the leadership of Lenin. It was dissolved in 1947.

The Cominform. An International Communist Information Bureau was formed on October 6, 1947 at Belgrade.

Communism and Socialism. It is necessary to know the difference between socialism as found in Britain and India and communism as seen in Russia and China.

1. While socialism wants to bring about common ownership of all means of production, communism stands also for their common enjoyment. In other words, communism unlike socialism is applicable to consumption goods also.

2. Socialism is evolutionary; it believes in constitutionalism and peaceful methods to construct society. Communism as shown by Russia and China believes in class war and supports violent methods to liquidate capitalism and imperialism.

3. Socialism tolerates all classes but communism opposes some classes from tooth to nail.

4. Socialism wants to use the state as aninstrument to realise human welfare. On the other hand, communism wants to seize the state in favour of so-called dictatorship of the proletariat; the state is to destroy the capitalist and bourgeoisie. The state is to last only in transitional period at the end of which the state will begin to wither away.

Drawbacks of Communism. Communism as preached by Marx, Engels, Lenin, Stalin, Kruschev and Mao Tse-Tung has been criticised on various grounds.

1. According to Milowan Diljas, the ex vice president of Yugoslavia, communist leadership exercises absolute power under the cloak of "public ownership".

2. Communists give no quarter to their opponents and support use of violence for revolution. Jawaharlal Nehru says, "Communism has definitely allied itself to the approach of violence. Its language is of violence, its thought is violent and it does not indulge normally in physical violence. It is throughout violent and it does not seek to change by persuasion or by peaceful and democratic methods, but by coercion and indeed, by destruction and extermination."

3. Communists believe that end justifies the means and leaders do not hesitate to make alliance with the fascists and use dictatorial powers of the same if it suits their purpose.

4. Communistic utopia of each according to ability, to each according to needs seems unrealisable in this realistic world.

5. The principle of withering away of the state has been falsified. The communist state, on the other hand, grows from strength to strength.

6. Communist power has developed another type of imperialism against which communists profess to fight.

7. Communism in actual practice has led to authoritarian rule of one party.

8. Lastly there is a vast difference in communist theory and practice. Communist states are not going to wither away nor they have been able to eliminate difference.

The Effects of Russian and Chinese Revolutions. The Bolshevik revolution in Russia and Communist revolution in China had the following far reaching important effects :

1. Capitalism all over the world got a rude setback, from which it may not recover.

2. Two powerful big countries, Russia and China adopted communism and each of them has its own communist satellites.

About one-third population in the world has been forced to accept communism.

3. Violence, bitterness and hatred have spread all over the world, owing to the communist strategy and tactics.

4. Totalitarianism and authoritarianism have spread all over the world in one shape or the other.

5. Communist empire like British and French empires has grown rapidly.

6. The world has been divided into communist and capitalist camps. The presence of these diametrically opposite camps is felt all over the world.

7. In democratic countries, radical socialist parties have accepted communism as their goal.

8. Traditional social and spiritual values are in danger due to new communistic values.

Communism under the influence of Russian Bolshevism has become almost exclusively a philosophy of method theory, that is to say, of the manner in which transition from capitalism to socialism is to be effected. Sometimes it is used to denote a theory of society, such as that of Christians and Buddhists in which all property is held in common, at other times it is used synonymously with socialism. It is also the name given to a system under which food, clothing, medical care and all other necessaries are freely administered according to want. But we have to search for its proper meaning through communist manifesto.

Communism in this sense of the word is essentially a theory of method. It seeks to lay down the principles upon which the transition from capitalism to socialism is to be accomplished, and its two essential doctorines are class war and forcible transference of power to proletariat.

Marx believed that capitalism would come to an end as the result of contradictions inherent in the very nature of capitalism. Of these contradictions, the most important are first that capitalism is compelled in order that it may extract the surplus value on which it lives to create and to concentrate class consciousness of proletariat in such a way as to make it organize for victory over the capitalism that it creates, and secondly due to overproduction, it had to seek markets abroad. It combines in turn and eliminates the small capitalist in order to gain monoply. As production increases, the competition for overseas markets grows fiercer; there is rush to exploit and appropriate under developed territories and capitalism, passing through the states of imperialism and world war reaches its climax.

Communists in order to prove the prophecy of Marx advance the following reasons. The origin of the world wars was economic. The force of production outstripped the existing social organization, with the result that goods were produced at such a rate that society could not control the use of them. Hence arose in a world property-less workers and idle rich together with competition for fresh markets, which under the guise of imperialism, produce war.

Lenin, for example, defines imperialism as capitalism in that stage of development in which monopoly and financial capital has attained a prepondering influence, the international trusts have begun the partition of the world and the biggest capitalist countries have completed the division of the entire territorial globe among themselves. At this stage, the concentration of capitalism leads to its overthrow. The proletariat created by capitalism is the force which destroys that what it has created. Growing over in numbers and in the insistence of its demands, it refused ultimately to be satisfied with anything less than the expropriation of the exploiters, the social ownership of property which had hitherto been held privately and transference of power militant workers.

In history, class wars have frequently occurred. Thus the bourgeoisie created by feudalism caused the overthrow of feudalism by means of the expansion of industry and the spread of commerce. But though history affords parallels to the uprisings of the proletariats, the latter is in one respect unique. All previous revolutions have resulted in the suppression of a class by a class in the usurpation of power of a minority by a minority. But the victory of working class carries with it emancipation of humanity. Though the revolution itself is carried out on a class basis, the state of society that follows the revolution will be based on abolition of classes. Thus the communists maintain that the battle they are fighting though outwardly based on behalf of a dispossessed class, is really the battle of the whole mankind, and it is the conviction embraced with the intensity born of a disinterested ideal, which generates the self-sacrifice and self-devotion underlying a superficially somewhat arid and doctrinaire programme.

Though the ultimate aim of communism is the emancipation of humanity and abolition of all classes but it cannot be realized immediately. It can be achieved by stages. A transitional revolutionary stage is based on domination of the state by the working class and lastly communistic stage in which the state is abolished and classless society is established.

1. Revolutionary Stage. The communists believe that workers' victory is of no use if capitalists remain in possession of the means of production because they can exert influence over the parliament. If parliament may pass resolutions against the capitalists, they will evade its enforcement and in the last resort they may fight in defence of their privileges. For example, they point out that the capture of power by Labour Party has made no impression upon the dominance of the capitalists in Great Britain.

It is argued accordingly that constitutional means must be abandoned, the machinery of the existing state superseded. Modern communists have never hesitated to emphasize the severity and bitterness of the struggle which will accompany the overthrow of the capitalist class. All-round violence will be necessary on the part of the workers, not only to dispossess the capitalists, but to crush the counter-revolutions, designed to restore them. As Engels says, "The party which has triumphed in the revolution is necessarily compelled to maintain the rule by means of fear with which its arms inspire the reactionaries". It is pointed out that the bourgeoisie have all the advantages of superior education, discipline and military talent. They have fighting material at their disposal and money for their equipment. It is not to be expected, therefore, that even if dispossessed by a sudden revolutionary coup, they will refrain from using these advantages.

Lenin says, "In any and very serious revolution, a long, obstinate, desperate resistance of the exploiters for who many years enjoyed great advantages over the exploited, never will the exploiters submit to the decision of the exploited class without making use of their advantage in the last desperate battle or in a series of battles." Thus, the transition from capitalism to communism forms a whole historical epoch.

During this epoch what Lenin calls a quasi-state of the workers will be created in place of the existing bourgeoisie state. This will of necessity be a class organization but it will function as the representative of the revolutionary working class. In order to break down the resistance of the bourgeoisie, says Marx, "the workers invest the state with a revolutionary form". This communist regime is intended to destroy eventually every group that insists on remaining a class. The proletarian class rule is an intermediate transition stage of society between capitalist class rule and classless commonwealth of the future.

The Post-Revolutionary Stage. According to communistic conception, class rule is only transitional rule. And when classes disappear, coercive social rule will disappear. The communists hold that under socialism, the state "withers away". "State power" "stays "Bukharin, which is the embodiment of class rule vanishes in proportion to the vanishing of classes." The proletarian only needs the state temporarily.

The communists acknowledge that the temporary period of proletarian state's omnipotence, intervening between capitalist dictatorship and the free communism of the future, may be a long "historic epoch". Anarchism is in that doctrine something to be achieved and with great difficulty. In this way, it is a way of achieving the ideal organization of classless and stateless society. In a classless and stateless society there will be real freedom as in capitalist system it is idle to talk about the freedom and democracy. So long as the masses of men are propertyless, it is idle to talk about individual freedom as a propertyless individual has no alternative but to sell his labour to the highest bidder; he can exercise no effective control with regard to the kind of life he wishes to lead. Thus communism believes in the utopia of classless and stateless society in which everybody will work according to ability and will get according to his needs which has not been realised.

Now USSR has been disintegrated into 16 states and has lost its former influence, power and glory. Moreover, now Russia, the greatest state of USSR and its former states have given up communist ideology so communism has got a set-back. Now China is following pragmatic policies to suit its needs and help its development. Germany has become a united nation devoid of communism. Similarly Eastern European countries such as Poland, Romania, Hungary and czechoslovokia, Bulgaria, etc., have also given away communism. Thus, communism has lost its former popularity, power, influence and glory.

NOTES

1. C.C. Maxey, *Political Philosophies* (1959), p. 667.
2. W. Lancaster, *Masters of Political Thought,* Vol. III, 1959.
3. Maxey, *Political Philosophies,* 1959, p. 672.
4. Sabine, *History of Political Theory*, 1.6. 39 (1957).
5. Wayper, *Political Thought*, p. 234.
6. Sabine, *History of Political Theory*, p. 700.
7. Kruschev, On Programme of C.P. of the Sovit Union, delivered in October 1961.
8. Lenin, *Collected Works*, 4th edition, Vol. 29, p. 358.

4

Anarchism

Anarchism was previously popular. Now it has lost its importance but still a few thinkers defend it, so a brief description has been provided.

Anarchist philosophy regards that state is an evil and it should be abolished altogether. Hence it is diametrically opposite to idealist philosophy and Fascism. The essential features of Anarchism are the abolition of all constituted authority and the complete emancipation of the individual from every form of control — political, social or religious. Oscar Jazi defines it as "an attempt to establish justice (that is equality and reciprocity), in all human relations by the complete elimination of the state (or by the greatest possible minimization of its activity) and its replacement by an entirely free and spontaneous co-operation among individuals, groups, regions and nations." Prof. E.M. Burns thinks that Anarchism is against government by force.

According to Kroptkin, "It is a principle or a theory of life and conduct under which society is conducted without government, harmony in such a society being obtained not by submission to law or by free obedience to any authority, but by agreements concluded between various groups, territorial and professional, freely constituted, for the sake of production and consumption as also for the infinite variety of needs and aspirations of a civilized being". F.W. Cooker says, "Anarchism is the doctrine that political authority in any of its forms is unnecessary and undesirable. In recent Anarchism there is theoretical opposition to the institution of private property and also there is hostility to organized religious authority".[1]

Origin and Growth of Anarchism

The principles of Anarchism are expounded by thinkers like pierre Proudhon, Henry Thoreau, Leo Tolstoy, Mikhail Bukanin, Prince Kroptkin and Emrico-Malatesta (1863-1932), an Italian. The gist of thought of these philosophers is that human beings can live well without a government.

According to Prof. E.M. Burns, modern Anarchism falls into two groups : (1) Economic individualists like Godwin and (2) Collectivists and revolutionaries like Bukanin. Godwin and Proudhon mixed Anarchism with individualism while Bukanin and Kroptkin combined Anarchism with Collectivism.

William Godwin. The first modern Anarchist to think strongly against the authority of the state was William Godwin. He expressed his ideas in his book, *An Enquiry concerning Political Justice and its influence an General Welfare and Happiness*. According to him, state prevents the individual from acting in a just and reasonable way by upholding injustice and inequality with the help of its authority. In the atmosphere provided by state, there is no scope for the individual's free expression. When man is born, he is neither virtuous nor vicious. It is the environment that makes him good or hed. Evils arise in society owing to government and property, which should be abolished. Government is an evil as it is based on violence and property is an evil as it creates vanity and depravity among the propertied people and servility and immorality among the poor.

Proudhon. "Governments are the scourge of God". The state is against reason, justice and understanding. Instead of having the state, individuals and voluntary groups should engage themselves in productive enterprises. Regarding property he said, "Property is theft" and advocated equal property rights for all. He spoke of giving everyone three acres of land and a cow. In short, Proudhon was against authority, privileges and the form of private property which leads to exploitation. He wanted a society seeking the highest perfection "in the union of order and Anarchy."[2]

Henry Thoreau (1817-62). Another Anarchist was the American Henry Thoreau. He also spoke against the existence of the state. He did not approve of the authority of the state and was against the payment of taxes. He himself did not pay taxes, others paid for him. According to him, government exercises authority wrongly and unjustly and good persons have to suffer. Men need not cultivate respect for law. He was in favour of offering active and passive resistance to the government of USA.

Count Tolstoy (1828-1910). Tolstoy who belonged to an aristocratic Russian family also condemned the state and supported the cause of Anarchism. He disliked a culture based on violence and exploitation. The state according to him rose and existed as an evil institution. He believes that private property and state are against the teachings of Jesus Christ as the former violates the principle of charity and brotherhood, and the latter is based on force. Tolstoy's doctrine has been called Christian Anarchism. He stated that the state deprives a man to do good to humankind. He made it clear that the presence of the authority of the state prevents people from doing work which was good and desirable. The state compelled man to do what he does not like and prevent him from doing what he liked. Moreover people were forced to pay taxes to support authority, which stood for evil.

Mikhail Bukanin (1814-76). Another Anarchist who upheld anti-authoritarian philosophy was Count Mikhail Bukanin of Russia. He came in contact with Proudhon, Marx and Engels who influenced him much. He visited countries like Germany, England, France, U.S.A. and Japan. He criticised the Russian Government strongly as communist and Anarchist. Born as a member of the Russian aristocracy, Bukanin dedicated his life to the cause of revolutionary Anarchism, spent twelve years in prison and was twice sentenced to death. For a time he was associated with Marx, but Marx repudiated him when he realised the significance of Bukanin's belief that the state could be abolished overnight. According to him, state is an evil, which degrades and demoralises people. Whatever may be the form of government, it is an evil. He said, religion and private property are the instruments with which the rich exploit the poor.

Prince Peter Kroptkin (1842-1921). Kroptkin, a Russian, was another great Anarchist. In 1872 he went to Switzerland and became a member of the International Working Men's Association at Geneva, which he had to leave as his views were very radical. For participating in the Nihilist movement, he was arrested in 1874, but he escaped from prison in 1876. He visited foreign countries like England, France and Switzerland. In London he wrote a book *Modern Science and Anarchism*. According to him, there was a time when people worked thorough natural institutions which gave liberty to the people. But when state emerged, it imposed its authority on people, who lost their authority. People obeyed laws not because laws were good, but because authority forced them to do so. The state is not only useless but is a positive hindrance to liberty. The state as an evil should be eliminated and other associations should be entrusted with the work. There is too much injustice in society and hunger drives people to work like slaves.[3]

Other Anarchists are Jossiah Warren (1799-1874), Stephen Pearl Andrews (1812-86), Benjiman R. Tucker and Lysander Spooner (1808-87).

The views of Anarchists may be given as below :

1. Anarchism regards state as an unmixed evil, against which people should fight and get it abolished. State authority is unnecessary

and undesirable; injustice and inequality are blessed by state authority. Law, the instrument of state, is an evil and people obey it, as they are compelled to do so.

2. Anarchists oppose capitalism as in this system, a few persons enjoy and other persons starve due to unemployment.

3. The church obliges poor persons to reconcile their lot with a system which brings them sorrow and degradation by teaching them that blessed are they that mourn.

4. Anarchism opposes the continuation of a state whose authority is based on compulsion, fear, egoism and exclusion. The state should be abolished to make room for voluntary associations based on fraternity, freedom, union, love and co-operation. Anarchists desiredecentralization and a classless and stateless society.

Methods of Anarchists. Anarchists like Tolstoy desire to employ peaceful methods and intend to establish a peaceful society through love and persuasion. Other Anarchists along with nationalists and communists are in favour of constitutional methods, if possible, and violent methods, if necessary. Nihilism is an extreme form of Anarchism based on violence. Though communists and Anarchists want state to wither away but there is a vast difference about transitory period. Main difference between Syndicalists and Anarchists is that the Anarchists speak for all and Syndicalists speak for workers' associations only.

Evaluation. Anarchists are unsatisfied with the present state of affairs in which there is unemployment, misery and suffering. People have to work in which they have no interest for the sake of bread and butter. It is a fact that in several countries, in which the form of government is democracy, people suffer from degradation, misery and unemployment and real liberty is only enjoyed by rich. Though there is some truth in what Anarchists say but they advocate methods which are violent and mischievous and mark out aims which can be never realised.

1. Aristotle says, "The state came into being for life and it continues for the sake of good life". Anarchists desire to get rid of the state without which human beings cannot live. It is difficult to imagine that associations function without some kind of authority and if authority exists, state becomes necessary.

2. It cannot be said that states do not perform welfare activities as modern states are welfare states which perform many welfare activities.

3. It seems that in paradise which Anarchists seek to create, there will be no authority, exploitation, misery and compulsion. In a

stateless, classless and churchless society, all will be happy. It is too good to be true. Unless human beings become angels or saints, such a dream can never be realised in this materialistic world.

4. Anarchists use destructive methods and desire a society based on love and co-operation. In this, Anarchists suggest a remedy worse than disease.

Lenin held the view that after the dictatorship of proletariat has served the purpose, the machinery of the state will be destroyed. The quasi-state "based on the power of workers will wither away" and give place to a free organization of society which will be stateless and classless in which everybody will work according to his ability and will get according to his needs. It is the free organization of classless and stateless society which Anarchism advocates. To quote Kroptkin, "Anarchism is a principle or theory of life and conduct under which society is conceived without government. Harmony in such a society is being obtained not by submission to law or by obedience to any authority but by free agreements concluded between the various groups, territorial and professional, freely constituted for the sake of production and consumption, so also for the satisfaction of the infinite variety of needs and aspirations of a civilized being."

With regard to the question how such a society is to be brought about, Anarchism has little to say. Kroptkin claims that Anarchist conception of society far from being a practicable Utopia, is derived from analysis of the tendencies existing and growing in community today. He supports this by pointing out to the enormous simplification in the provision of the necessaries of life which the growth of machinery has rendered possible, and the great increase in voluntary associations formed for other than political purpose. But although the facts to which he refers are undoubted, it is questionable whether they do tend together in the direction he supposes. It is doubtful whether the natural course of evolution, without a revolution, would develop on Anarchist lines. However, it can be said that tendency is towards localization rather than centralization which communism preaches.

Anarchists claim that only in Anarchist society, an individual can fully develop himself. Thus, full development of individuality would be rendered possible by the entire absence of external restraints : the individual would in fact for the first time be really "free" from every kind of authority. Three sources, of authority from which Anarchism would free an individual are important :

(a) It would free an individual from the yoke of a state which is based on coercion and violence.

(b) It would free man as producer from the yoke of a capitalist.

(c) It would free man as an individual from the authority of religious morality derived from hypothetical, metaphysical entities, etc.

Arguments of the Anarchists. Basic concept of Anarchism is that the state is against human nature as it curbs the individual freedom and consequently full development of individual's personality.

1. They argue that state does not lay emphasis on equality. Ultimately state power is controlled by a particular class. It may be bureaucracy or capitalist class or oligarchy but a particular class captures the power of the state and utilizes the state machinery for its own benefit. According to a scholar, rule itself means coercion and authority while Anarchism means love and unity.

2. Anarchists agree that state protects capitalism and consequently encourages exploitation of the poor class.

3. Thirdly, they agree that the state does not render any valuable or useful service. It fails to give security and bread or butter to poor persons. Not only this, they argue that no state has been able to uproot the crimes. Crimes are not committed due to habits but the state creates circumstances that force a man to commit crime.

4. Anarchists also argue that the state is symbol of autocracy. In monarchy, one person, in aristocracy a few persons and in democracy majority or bureaucracy exploit the other persons.

5. State is against the human nature. Government means compulsion, exclusion and separation while Anarchism is freedom, union and love. Government is based on egoism and fear and Anarchism on fraternity.

6. Lastly Anarchists say that there is no justification of state historically. In primitive age, three was no state, people used to live formerly in voluntary groups or tribes and activities were conducted on the basis of traditions and customs.

As such, Anarchists agree that government is not necessary at all. They further present following main arguments to support their point of view :

1. Distrust of Existing State. The state as it exists today, they argue, is used by the few as an instrument to protect their unjust monopolies of those things which rightly belong to all. For this very reason, therefore, the state cannot be used to accomplish the monopolies it protects. It means that until the state is replaced by some organization, present evils cannot be removed.

2. The Fallacy of Representative Government. No elected government can know the will of the people on each and every question as it arises and must therefore, if it is not to be an open tyranny, be carried on by means of representatives. As such, representative government makes a show of election after a few years. But no man can represent another man much less a group of other men. Elected man cannot possess the knowledge of all questions and subjects, but what he is supposed to do, is to direct the experts of the departments. Representative government are therefore government by men who know just enough about everything badly and not enough about one thing to do anything well. It generates the professional politician, the professional lawyer, the professional priest, general dealers in human relationships whose business it is to perpetuate the human weaknesses on which they are nourished. Thus, politicians will draw boundaries without any proper knowledge of ethnology or geography and lawyers decide questions of will, purpose and motive without the slightest knowledge of psychology. Anarchism, therefore, evinces itself rather than surprisingly as a plea for directions by experts rather than for government by amateurs.

Secondly, the common will expres itselfdifferently with regard to each one of the questions that the state has to settle. Either the representative had to work in dark which is not to the advantage of those to whom he represents or he will have to call a meeting of his constituents every time a question arises for settlement, and get them after discussion to formulate an expression of their will. But in this event, his office will be unnecessary.

Thus, representative government is unnecessary and it does not represent. The only method is that a delegate should be elected to express the feelings of a meeting or constituency and he should finish his job as soon as his question is over and for other questions in the similar way other representatives should be elected to express general feelings.

3. Effect of Power. Power corrupts even the noblest of the mankind. The exercise of power over other men corrupts the best intentioned natures. It makes them selfish, arrogant and oppressive, seekers after their own ends and neglectful of the interests of those who place them in power. The politician, for example, is wicked not because of his nature but because he is a politician. No man and no-body of men should, therefore, be entrusted with governmental authority over their fellows.

According to Kroptkin, "This or that despicable minister might have been an excellent man, if power had not been given to him." But the love of power which government fosters can only be nourished on the exercise of power and the exercise of power necessarily requires persons over whom it may be exercised. Therefore governments from the very nature use force, to separate men who are naturally friends into hostile and different nationalities, force to separate brothers who are naturally brothers into different hostile classes. Thus, the evils of internal strife and external war arise on account of governments based on force. According to Mr: Lowes Dickeinsons, wars arise "because we divide ourselves into nations and we endure the oppression of armaments, because we isolate ourselves as individuals and we invoke the protection of laws."

4. How the State is Superfluous. Anarchists believe that state is superfluous and they try to prove it by concrete examples. For example, "Is the state necessary for defences against outside aggression?" the answer is that it is not. Standing armies, says Kroptkin, are always beaten by invaders who have historically been repulsed only by spontaneous uprisings unorganized by the state. The record of the state in guaranteeing security to the individual is no better. Far from protecting the citizen from ill-disposed persons, it creates them. It drives man to crime through the misery caused by its ill adjusted economic system and then punishes them for its own handiwork by throwing them into prison thereby confirming their criminality for the future by making it impossible for them to earn a living by honest means.

In art, in science and in business, most progress is achieved through voluntary organization, clubs, academies and societies. The bodies which regulate these activities such as Royal Societies and the British Association rely upon free co-operation.

The Organization of Anarchist Society. According to Anarchists, after the abolition of state, all activities will be carried on by voluntary associations formed ad hoc for carrying out special purpose. Each trade and business should be carried by a society voluntarily formed by those who choose to engage in it, which will elect and remove its own officials, determine its own policy and co-operate by free arrangements with other similar bodies. A complex interweaving of associations will manage the whole show. Anarchy as Mr. Lowes Dickenson says, is not the absence of order : it is absence of force.

These associations, groups, federations will be of all sorts, of sizes and degrees and they will be formed for all sorts of different purposes. Harmony will be achieved in society by the equilibrium of these forces and influences. Voluntary societies will exist for the fulfilment of every purpose that men have in common; some will be organized on vocational and some on territorial basis and they will carry on all the work.

Regarding adjustments, Anarchists say that with the advancement of education, abolition of disparity in wealth and monopoly, occasions for conflict and disharmony will be few. Instead of rivalries and competitions there will be friendliness and co-operation among the fellow beings. Material grouping will eliminate the quarrels.

In this respect we may briefly discuss the views of following main Anarchist thinkers :

1. Bukanin
2. Kroptkin
3. Leo Tolstoy

Bukanin, the son of a diplomat and a student at the universities of St. Petersburg and Moscow is regarded as the founder of modern Anarchism.

According to Bukanin, "Human history consists in the progressive negation of man's original necessity, the evolution of his humanity." Political authority, private property and religion are natural institutions for the lower stage of man's development for they are associated in one way or another with physical desires and fears; private property cultivates man's interest in material goods; the state supports private property through the physical compulsions; religion sustains, both state and property. These institutions, the characteristic expression of man's primitive nature under the natural laws of human evolution are destined to disappear.

Bukanin strongly opposes every form of political authority. Despotism, he holds, lies not in the form of state but in its essence and the most democratic devices are of no avail, whatever, in modifying the essential character of the state.

The state is morally debasing for it acts by compulsion, rather than by enlightenment and persuasion. Political authority demoralizes those who participate in its exercise. It breeds attitude of superiority quite out of relation to any actual distinction in merit and they desire prerogatives, class differentiation and sacrifice, welfare for the sake of office. The goal of Anarchism is to be attained both through evolution and revolution. Anarchism by evolution can be achieved by removing the ignorance of the natural laws of social evolution and by demolishing the institutions which interfere with evolutions. Revolution means removal of all authorities by violence and to discard authority in any form or shape.

In place of state, Bukanin would establish a free society from which all classes and relations of authority have disappeared and which every one without distinction of race, colour, nationality or belief is permitted to labour and enjoy the fruits of labour on equal terms. The basis of this society will be contract and voluntary association instead of law and compulsive allegiance. The new society will operate on some basic economic principles. Society will itself own the lands and all materials and instruments of production; it will permit them to be taken into possession by these persons acting individually or in freely formed associations who are willing to use them productively without any compulsion. The abolition of state will mean the end of political boundaries and co-operation will be not only on national lines but on international lines and it will open am era of golden-age.

2. Kroptkin. Kroptkin's analysis of Anarchism is more varied. He sponsors two phases of evolution. Firstly, he holds that in both individual and social life natural evolution takes place not only through a process of steady development but also, at times, through accelerated, abrupt, apparently distinctive transformations. The second principle is of predominant part played by the co-operative as distinguished from competitive attributes of animals and men. The law of organic evolution is primarily a law of natural aid and not of conflict. He argued that law of natural aid manifests itself in social life, in a principle of equality, justice and social solidarity, which is nothing but the golden rule "Do to others as you would have it done to you in like case."

The state, says Kroptkin, is without any natural or historical justification. It is opposed to man's naturally co-operative instincts. Men lived together for ages without any politically enforced rules. The state is of recent origin, having displaced the free and peaceful life. State enacted laws appeared only when society became divided by economic conditions into mutually hostile classes.

Kroptkin argues that history reveals both the state's incompetence for the achievement of any high purpose and its positive contributions to human suffering injustice. The state has not protected peasants and workers. Kroptkin has no faith in representative governments. Representative governments have served its purpose and are unsuitable for socialist society.

Regarding future society, Kroptkin says that men will continue to live together, but they will no longer be held by governmental authority. Free associations will prevail throughout society. People will form groups and group associations on voluntary basis. Disputes will be settled by voluntarily established courts of arbitration. As the social order will be based upon principles of freedom and justice, the incitement to anti-social acts would disappear. When such acts do occur, moral influence and sympathetic intervention will normally suffice to end them. Lastly expulsion which will be exercised rarely will work as a corrective.

Economically that order will be of complete communism. He opposes the preposition that producer goods should belong to the state and consumer goods to private ownership. He is of opinion that the individual should be free to join any group and to enjoy what his group produces by doing one thousand hours' work in a year.

He placed emphasis upon man's social responsibility, his feelings of human brotherhood and his disposition to engage in between that satisfies both an impulse to create and desire to see commodities produced sufficient to meet the needs of the fellow-men. He regarded these natural human attributes as adequate guarantee of peace, order and fair dealing in a society, that got rid of the unnatural institutions of private property and political coercion.

Leo Tolstoy. He was a pacific Anarchist relying on the teachings of Christ so he is called Christian Anarchist. He is one of the greatest literary giants of the world. His writings influenced Mahatma Gandhi very much.

Both the state and private property are in Tolstoy's theory incompatible with true Christianity. The state is based on force and executes its will through armed men, policemen and soldiers trained to kill; thus it transgresses Christ's command not to resist evil by force.

About future, he believed that future "... will only be what man and circumstances make it". "Awaken the conscience of the people; live according to the principles of love and equality, practise passive resistance; refuse obedience to the already un-Christian commands of a government refuse to pay tax or to serve as juries." He believed in goodness of human nature and desired to utilize it for the service of mankind.

In Indian literature also, supposition of Satyayoga सतयुग or सत्ययुग resembles the Anarchist thought. Mahatma Gandhi also imagined society based on truth and non-violence but whether such a dream is realisable in this materialistic world is too difficult to answer as in modern situation it is Utopian, *i.e.*, unrealizable.

NOTES

1. J.S. Roachu and others, *Introduction to Political Science*, p. 98.
2. Pere Joseph Proudan, (1808-65) *India in Conflict* (1960), p. 37.
3. E.M. Burns, *Ideas in Conflict*, p. 38.

5

Fascism

The Origin and History of Fascism. The term Eascism is derived from the Latin werd Fasces which means bundle. In ancient Rome, a bundle of rods with an axe was the sign of authority which included the power of life and death. Fascism emerged in the 20th century as a reaction against liberalism and democracy.

Mussolini has disclosed that Fascism was an ideology compounded of the teachings of Machiavelli's doctrine of opportunism, Hegel's political absolutism, Sorrel's doctrine of violence, and William James's pragmatism. Fascism did not have a dogmatic ideology and adopted its doctrine as the exigencies of the moment required.[1]

According to Otto Dictrich, "Fascism is essentially a reaction to Western individualism to what is considered corrupt, hypocritical and decadent bourgeois democracy".[2] Fascism was spawned in the economic and military strife which grew out of the apparent peace of 19th century culminating in the World War. Italy, bitter over her treatment at the Versailles' treasure hunt and rent with internal discord, had forgotten the ideals of Mazzini and Garibaldi and surrendered to a Fascist dictatorship that was rapidly anti democratic.[3] The original forerunners of Italian Fascist political theory were a group of intellectuals who had adopted with varied modifications the philosophy of Hegel. The prominent Fascist philosophers were Giouanni Gentile (1875-1944), a disciple of Hegel and Guisseppe Prezzolini, a great admirer of Benito Mussolini.

Fascism is the totalitarian organization of government. and society by a single party dictatorship intensely nationalist, racist, militarist and imperialist. To trace all the sources of the political philosophy, now known as Fascism is not easy. It is compounded of many ingredients which have been blended together with great ingenuity. We may perceive among others borrowings from Machiavelli, Hobbes, Fichte, Hegel, Treitschke, Nietzsche, Marx Sorrel, Mosca, Schopenhauer, Bergson, James and Preto. Mr. R.P. Dutta, in his book *Fascism and Analysis* has defined Fascism in following words :

"Fascism is in fact, no peculiar, independent doctrine and system arising in opposition to existing capitalist society. Fascism, on the contrary, is the most complete, and consistent working out, in certain conditions of extreme decay, of the most typical tendencies and policies of modern capitalism ... it is a movement of mixed elements, dominantly petty bourgeois but also slum proletariat and demoralised working class, financed and directed by fiance capital, by big industrialists, landlords and financiers to defeat the working class organization."[4]

Its Development. The period of history between the end of the First World War and end of the Second World War was dominated to a large extent by the Fascist powers. The first avidly Fascist regime was that which was established after a coup detat by Benito Mussolini in Italy in 1924. Later on, a militarized regime grew up in Japan that had many features common with fascism. But the most powerful Fascist regime to gain power was that under the dictatorship of Adolf Hitler. He led his Nazi Party to power in 1933 and initiated war which caused destruction and ruin such as had never been seen before. Some minor Fascist powers such as notorious General Franco's Falangist regime survives in Spain even today. The dictatorship of Salazar in Portugal and the present government in South Africa and in some other countries are also Fascistic. Thus, although main centres of Fascist powers have been destroyed, the movement is by no means extinct.

The popular image of Fascist government is that of militant and aggressive nationalism. It is one of the puzzles of history that how this movement succeeded in seizing power in countries where the level of education and culture was high. Their victory was an episode in the constant battle between progress and reaction.

French revolution divided politically active individuals into progressives, *i.e.*, who believed that it is in the power of human reason to change social and political institutions more in helping with moves and welfare of mankind and reactionaries who did not agree with this progressive outlook.

Industrial society brought into existence the new class of capitalists, financiers and industrial workers, who were filled with new ideas and came in conflict with the constructive class of agricultural persons consisting of landlords, artisans and peasantry. The way of life, beliefs and customs, social relations of the agricultural classes were different from those of the new industrial classes. Agriculturists were tradition minded, deeply religious, conventional and involved with the ideas of loyalty to their superiors as well as conscious of their family ties and race. As several political writers have pointed out, agriculturist society is based on status, something similar to but not always identical with the caste system in India. In a society based on status, man enjoys privileges of his ancestors.

Industrial society is based on contract, where on the social scale a man is born, is of no concern. The question that governs his relations is what he can do, and how much he possesses. In capitalist system, man's wealth counts while in agriculturist society status counts. Thus growth of industry upsets the old social system, but in France, where the revolution was successful in destroying the power and privileges of feudal class, the issue was not fully settled.

In Germany, Japan and Italy, feudal aristocracy survived and what we know Fascism or Nazism is essentially an attempt of reactionary leaders who are inclined with the mentality of feudalism to control and run an industrial society with the help of conservative agriculturist class and urban middle class which support them due to economic crisis caused by industrial growth.

The conservative sections of the society oppose rational activities in the name of law and order. In other words, forces of feudalism at the end of First World War were like wounded tigers and Fascists who believed in the principles of feudal agricultural societies such as of fixed status, anti-individualism, loyalty to the superiors, war and violence, fought the lost battle and captured power in Germany, Japan, Italy and in other minor countries where industry had developed but the forces of progress were weak. This was superimposition of feudal principles on societies that were largely industrial and rule could be imposed only by war and violence.

The totalitarianism of the Fascists stemmed from their opposition to the values and virtues of industrialism and their loyalty to feudal virtues in which individualism plays no part, but the principle of unquestioning obedience to the superior is accepted. They collected material to justify their actions on philosophical basis from various sources and adopted hypocritic name of socialism but they failed to develop systematic theory because of its anti-intellectualism.

Marxists and socialists, who base their political philosophy on the growth of fully developed industrial society are the chief enemies of Fascists. Similarly democratic societies oppose their authoritarian outlook. In World War II, democratic powers led by UK, USA and France and socialist powers led by USSR gained a decisive victory over the Fascist power of Italy, Germany and Japan and shattered the remnants of conservative class.

It is difficult to answer whether the forces of reaction are still a menace, but it can be said that on a worldwide scale, industrialism and progress are now firmly established and difficult to be uprooted.

Now we may discuss something about the sources and principles of Fascism.

Sources of Fascism. We have already discussed the sources of Fascism but some sources may be further added :

1. The political doctrine of Fascism (it was an address delivered by Perugia in 1925).

2. Gentile's philosophical basis of Fascism published in 1928.

3. The doctrine of Fascism (it was an article contributed by Mussolini in 1932).

4. History of Fascism written by Volpa.

5. Philosophy of Fascism written by Palmieri.

Mussolini was greatly influenced by American, French and German scholars in shaping his views. The pragmatism and anti-intellectualism of the American philosopher, William James, French philosopher Sorrel, the theory of "will power" of German philosopher Nietzsche and the anti democratic views of V. Pareto, an Italian sociologist profoundly influenced the outlook of Mussolini, and Carlyle of England also influenced him. From these sources, Mussolini derived his anti-intellectual, anti-liberal and anti democratic views.

The Principles of Fascism. In the first section of the doctrine of Fascism, Mussolini writes :

> "The world seen through Fascism is not the material world which appears on the surface, in which man is an individual separated from all others and standing by himself and in which he is governed by a natural law that makes him instinctively to live a life of selfish and momentary pleasure. The man of Fascism is an individual whom nation is fatherland, which is a moral law, binding together individual and generation, into a tradition and mission, suppressing the instinct for a life enclosed within the brief round of pleasure in order to restore within duty a higher life in which the individual through the denial of himself, through the sacrifice of his own private interests, through death itself, realises that completely spiritual existence in which his value as a man lies."

To Mussolini, Fascism was a reaction against the flabby doctrines of 19th century. It desires an active man, one engaged in activity with all his energies, it desires a man conscious of all difficulties, that face him. Fascists held life to be serious, austere and religious. They disclaimed the comfortable life and Mussolini desired "Action not talk." "There is no need for dogma; discipline suffices." In 1924 he wrote, "We Fascists have had the courage to discard all traditional political theories and we are aristocrats and democrats, revolutionaries and reactionaries, proletarians and anti proletarian, pacifists and anti-pacifists. It is sufficient to have a single fixed point, the nation. The rest is obvious."

Fascism has recognized the following principles :

1. Nation is born out of the state.

2. War is necessary for the development of human personality.

3. Faith, obedience and war — these are the three weapons of Fascism.

4. Unopposed government is necessary for common good of the society.

5. The system which is beneficial in the economic sphere should be adopted for the whole nation.

6. Private property is very helpful for production.

7. Fascism opposes capitalism.

8. It also opposes democratic feelings and parliaments which are nothing more than talking shops.

9. Fascism believes in imperialism, *i.e.*, Italy must expand or perish.

10. Fascism is opposed to socialism which teaches class conflict.

The Fascist Conception of the State. The leading Fascists conceived of state as the "conscience and universal will of man in his historical existence .... Liberalism denied the state in the interests of particular individual. Fascism reaffirms the state as the true reality of the individual .... Therefore, for the Fascists everything is in the state, and nothing human or spiritual exists, much less has value, outside the state. In this sense, Fascism is totalitarian and the Fascist state, the synthesis and unity of all values, interferes, develops and gives strength to the whole life of the people." Fascists conceived of the state as a spiritual entity and stressed the importance of elevation to it.

Mussolini observes in his book *Political and Social Doctrine of Fascism* :

"For us, Fascists, the state is not merely a guardian, preoccupied solely with the duty assuring the personal safety of the citizens, nor it is an organization with purely material aim .... Nor it is a purely political creation, divorced from all contact with the complex material reality which makes up the life of the individual and the life of the people as a whole. The state as conceived of and as created by Fascism is a spiritual and moral fact in itself, science its origin and development as manifestation of the spirit. The state is the guarantor of security, both internal and external and it is also the custodian and transmitter of the spirit of the people, as it has grown up through the centuries in language, in customs and in faith. And the state is not only living reality of the present, it is also linked with the past and above all with future."

The Fascists believe in an organic state with a varied symmetry of classes organized in syndicates and corporation of syndicates directed by hierarchies.

Fascism and Liberty. The fascists did not believe in individual liberty. They declared that there is no liberty but the liberty which is inherent in the state. According to Gentile, "Liberty is not a right but a duty. Law and the state are the supreme manifestations of liberty."

Rocca observes : "Our concept of liberty is that the individual must be allowed to develop his personality on behalf of the state for the ephemeral and infinitesimal of the complex and permanent life of society determined by their moral growth and development of the state. Freedom is therefore, due to the citizen and to classes on condition that they exercise it as a whole and within the limits set by social exigencies, liberty bings like any other individual right, a concession of the state."

Features of Fascism. Following important features of Fascism may by noted :

1. Fascists assign a very high place to the state. They completely subordinate the individual to the state. They view the state as a spiritual entity and lay stress on the devotion to it.

2. Fascists totally deny the assumptions, institutions, and practice of democracy. They argue that nation must be conceived of qualitatively, not quantitatively as is done in democracy.

3. Fascists believe in leadership, the rare mind and hero-worship.

4. They deny human equality. Women are excluded from leadership, position in government. or party or in armed, forces.

5. They believe in violence. To them international wars are necessary. Mussolini used to say that "There can be no compromise, either we or they."

6. Fascism is opposed to socialism which teaches class conflicts, ignoring the unity of classes under one leader.

7. Fascism believes in expressionism and power and recognises that state dies if its expansion is checked; state is like human will which honours no limits.

8. Rajni Palm Dutta remarks that "Fascism endeavonrs to present itself as a third alternative distinct either from capitalism or socialism to the workers."

9. Fascism accepts the fundamental doctrine of individualism that the possession of private property is essential for economic progress. "It must be preserved if the productive energies of the nation are to be maintained at the highest pitch." But all sorts of property must be subordinated to national interests.

Evaluation of Fascism. Though Fascism brought dictatorship but it also gave strength and efficiency to Italy, Germany and Japan. It made its appearance in Spain, China, Turkey, Argentina, Brazil, etc.

Maxey points out the following achievements of Fascism :

1. It sugar-coated raw power with mystical idealism.
2. It supplied a moral justification for violence.
3. It exploited patriotism to the utmost limit.
4. It subtly rationalized minority rule.
5. It capitalized on the widespread fear of communism.
6. It offered the masses a new religion with a new God to worship.

Fascism has been criticized on the following main grounds :

1. Fascists did not believe in individual liberty and hence checked the individual progress.

2. The general public had no voice of their own. They had to follow the words of the dictator.

3. Fascists totally subordinated the individual to the state. Under such circumstance human welfare is not possible.

4. Doctrine of dictatorship cannot be practicable in the democratic age. Hero worship and blind followership is now out of date.

5. Fascists were opposed to peace and consequently brought wars.

6. It believes in racial discrimination.

7. Lastly in the words of sabine, it is a body of ideas taken from various sources and put together to fit in the exigencies of the situation. It was difficult to combine Hegelian nationalism, Plato's government by aristocracy, Bergeonian anti-intellectualism, etc. and to work them successfully in actual practice.

In short, Fascism became the basis for dictatorship. It is anti-communistic and the last resort of bourgeois against the proletariat. It attempts to exclude hostile elements from any share in the control of the state, its will to co-ordinate all active forms of voluntary associations and communal life under the direction of the state. It may be taken to represent the dialectical antithesis of communism. No association of any kind can exist without the permission of the state. Freedom of association, expression and conscience depends upon the sweet will of the state. In short, it believes, "Everything within the state, nothing against the state, nothing outside the state." This makes the state absolute and omnipotent and in the name of state, the person who exercises the power of the state becomes all powerful or rather to say shadow of God on earth.

Fascism and Communism

It is said about Fascism that it is the last bid of finance capital in its most critical and decadent age. It is true that Fascism has opposed communism and socialism but it is difficult to say that it supported the policy of *Laissez Faire.* Perhaps it would be correct to say that it has opposed the policy of *Laissez Faire* in the interest of the state, thus it cannot be fully justified that it is the last hid of "finance capital". Moreover its aim was not to do good to capitalist class but to gain power, establish authority and to oppose democracy with full force. It opposed Marxism because it pleaded for spiritualism while Marx pleads for materialistic conception. Thus though Fascism allowed private property, the main pillar of capitalism and supported party dictatorship of communism but also opposed both of them. Therefore, it cannot be fully justified that either it resembled fully with capitalism or communism though it took something from both of them.

Fascism and Democracy. Fascism opposes both democracy and liberalism. Fascism had no faith in the parliamentary form of government. They describe it as stupid, corrupt, slow-moving, visionary, impracticable, and inefficient. They called it a decaying corpse. They called parliaments as talking shops which could not accomplish anything substantial. They believed democracy something unnatural and believed that the greatest virtue of man was to obey the state and ultimately merge himself into it. Mussolini did not believe in equality and said,

"Fascism affirms the immutable, the beneficial and fruitful inequality of mankind."

According to Mussolin, "Fascism combats the whole complex system of democratic ideology, and repudiates, it, whether it is theoretical premises or in its practical application." "The democratic regime may be defined, says Mussolini, "as from time to time giving the people the illusion of sovereignty, while the real effective sovereignty lies in the hands of other concealed and irresponsible forces."

Liberty under Fascist State. According to Fascists, "Liberty is not a right but a duty." They believe that the liberty of people depended on the strength of nation. According to Gentile, "Law and state are the supreme manifestation of liberty." There was to be military discipline and believed obedience in every way of life. They believed in "Obedience (To have faith, to obey, to fight)." They believe in authoritarian and totalitarian state in which no aspect of social life escapes the wide discipline of Fascism. "There is no place for toleration of other man's views or dissent in Fascism."

Fascism and Equality. The Fascists do not recognize the principle of equality, which is one of the essentials of democracy. They support hero-worship and put emphasis on the principle of leadership. Their slogan was "Command from the above, obedience from below." They believe in hierarchical organization in opposition to equality.

The Corporate State. They do not believe either in *laissez-faire* or in free economy of capitalists. The corporate state applies the principle of organization and control to Fascist economy which is subdivided in state-controlled association of capital and labour, each association having a monopoly in its trade or occupation. The party government is the ultimate arbiter of conflicts between capital and labour.

In the corporate state, there is no place for a free welfare economy whether the same be capitalist or socialist. The reason is that the objective of the corporate state is the power of the state and not the welfare of the individual. The ultimate objective of the corporate organization of the preparation for a permanent war economy as aggressive imperialism, is the ultimate aim of Fascist foreign policy.

Opposition to Majority Rule. Fascists do not believe in majority rule because they put emphasis on quality in opposition to democracy which believes in the majority rule. Fascists do not tolerate opposite party and believe in one-party rule. "Fascist party", says Gentile, "was the conscience of the state." The party monopolised the state.

Fascistic Conception of General Will. Fascistic conception of general will differs with the democratic conception of knowing the will of the people through adult suffrage and ballot box. They believe, it is the opinion of a few able persons that counts. They argue that public opinion is always fickle and it changes continuously, therefore no reliance can be placed on it.

Democratic Government is Weak. Lastly they say that democratic government is not a strong government because there is separation of powers in the government while strength comes through centralization.

Thus Fascism opposes democracy in all aspects and believes in obedience, authority and totalitarianism in place of democratic concepts of liberty, equality, fraternity majority, rule and representative government. They believe in the leadership of supermen like Mussolini and Hitler instead of having their faith in people. Thus Fascism is anti-democratic. Instead of ballot, they believe in bullet and believe that "International peace is a cowards' dream." Instead of equality they believe in racial superiority.

Fascism and Socialism. The Fascists do not believe in the materialistic conception of history or in the theory of class conflict. They rejected the idea that everything in life is controlled by economic factors; they believed in holiness and heroism. According to Mussolini: "Economic well,being, would reduce man to the level of animals caring for one thing only to be fed and well fed and would thus degrade humanity to a purely physical existence". They rejected the idea of class war and stood for co-operation of all the sections of society for the glory of the state. They believed that harmonious relations could be established between the employees and the employer and class antagonism was not natural or inevitable.

Fascism and Communism. It is difficult to narrate exactly the relation of communism and Fascism as there is difference of opinion among the scholars. Some writers point out that they are really blood brothers and each had more in common with the other than either had with democracy. There are others who maintain that communism and Fascism are completely antagonistic, since they are opposed to each other on all basic issues or both of them have more in common with capitalist democracy than with each other. It is difficult to give exact answer, so we may examine both views.

So far as similarities are concerned, both reject individualism and parliamentary democracy based on individual political rights. They repudiate individualism and put emphasis on collectivism. They assert that parliamentary democracy is not true democracy but only a means for the exploitation of society by the bourgeoisie. They place society above individual. Thus both reject bourgeoisie democracy and liberalism.

Both of them deny the universality of knowledge or morality. Communists believe that the knowledge gained in different periods of history is of very different kinds and serves the interest of different classes. Fascists believe that each race or nation has its peculiar genius and science that it produces is suited to and reflects its peculiar genius and spirit. Any knowledge that claims to be universal is a fraud.

Both reject the conception of universal morality. Communists believe that each epoch in history has developed its own morals and ethical ideas. These moral ideas correspond to the interests of a particular class which is dominant at a given time and justifies its rule or authority over other classes. On the other hand, Fascists believe that whatever strengthens the nation against other nations is good, whatever weakens it is evil.

Communists sanction violence if necessary and Fascists glorify violence and believe in hero-worship of those who use violence on a vast scale successfully.

Both the systems do not respect family or old age. Communists decry religion as opium of the people while Fascism subordinates it to the will of the nation or of the fuehrer.

Both are anti-capitalists as Fascists want industries to be run in the interest of the nation especially for strengthening its military power. Communists oppose capitalism due to exploitation of the workers and its crisis and say that the abolition of capitalism is inevitable in the march of history.

In spite of these similarities there are fundamental differences between capitalism, Fascism and communism. Capitalism believes in money and individual liberty and democracy and religion. Fascists believe in state, order and authority and spiritual natures, and communists in class war, materialistic conception of history and in the utopia of classless and stateless society.

Fascists are anti-intellectual or irrationalists but communists are neither anti-intellectuals nor irrationalists. Fascists believe that intellect weakens the inner spiritual strength of the race, because it creates doubts, uncertainty, division and causes people to question authority of their superiors. Fascists glorify force, instinct and muscles but communists depend on the understanding and insight possessed by the leadership, combined with determined action.

Fascists criticize existing religions but support hero- and nation-worship. Communists do not oppose any religion but religious beliefs which give distorted pictures.

Fascists are nationalist and recialists while communists are internationalists and anti-racial. "Marx gave a call Workers of whole world unite" and Fascists cry for the unity of nation and expansion of national frontier.

Communists are humanists and suggest a creative role for the individual. In their ideal society, the interest of the individual will be identical with the interest of the society, for both will be equally free. But in Fascist society, the individual will lose his individuality in the society.

Communists are believer in human equality, capitalists believe in superficial equality but discard economic equality but Fascists openly preach for inequality and oppose liberty.

Communists believe in class struggle, but Fascists believe in class unity in the interest of the nation.

Fascists believe in power and authority and argue that force and violance are the laws of nature and therefore they can never be dispensed with, but communists believe in classless and stateless society, in which force would be unnecessary.

Fascists glorify state but communists desire to abolish state and think it an instrument of class oppression.

Thus, both oppose capitalism or bourgeoisie society. But Fascism looks backward to feudalism and tribalism while communism looks forward where violence and inequality would be abolished. Therefore the similarities between them are superficial while the differences are profound. Though both oppose bourgeoisie liberalism as their joint enemy but Fascists and communists consider each other as their enemy number one and are daggers drawn with each other. Now Fascism has disappeared though in many countries dictators still rule due to military support. Communism has also lost its former influence and popularity.

Nazism

"All that is not race in the world is trash", said Hitler. In Germany Nazism flourished under the leadership of Hitler. Ideals of Nazism were similar to Fascism but Hitler hated Jews and believed in social superiority. In this way, the doctrine of Nazism differed with Fascism. Nazism rose in Germany after World War I. It is difficult to give exact definition of Nazism as there has been no consistent philosophy of Nazism. The Nazi ideology was a cocktail made up of one jigger of simplified Higel, one jigger of Nietzsche and a desk of misunderstood James mixed by Rosenberg and served by Gobbles."

Origin and Growth of Nazism. The humiliation of Germany at Versailles in 1919 and the numerous problems she had to face in the post-war period enabled the Nazi Party to seize power under the leadership of Hitler. Nazis propagated that the Marxists and Jews have stabbed Germany in the back when it was about to win, so German workers or the National Socialist Party or the Nazi Party gained popularity and succeeded in capturing power under the leadership of Hitler.

Salient Features of Nazism. Following features may be noted :

1. Nazism believed in action first. The whole of Germany was utilized to action by Hitler, who pressed the Germans in the service of nation. The German fatherland was glorified.

2. Hitler advocated theory of Nardic superiority and preached anti-Semitism. Hitler said, "All that is not race in this world is trash". According to Rosenburg, race "is the outer form of the soul". The Germans were duty bound to preserve superiority of their race. Physically weak and diseased persons were not to propagate their species. Only pure Aryan men and women were to be encouraged to procreate.

3. About women. Hitler said, "Motherhood is undesirably aim of feminine education". Von Papen said, "Mothers must exhaust themselves in order to give life to children." Thus, women were to Nazis childbearing machines.

4. Nazism was based on authoritarianism. People lost all their liberty and life was fully regimented.

5. Nazism advocated militant nationalism, war and aggressive imperialism. According to Fichte, "Task of the universities is not to teach objective sciences, but the militant, the warlike, the heroic science and literature."

6. Nazism created the worst type of dictatorship. According to Herr Hans Kerl, "Hitler is the true Holy Ghost". Adolph Hitler was infallible and his words were law. Concentration camps were not considered as disgrace.

7. It was anti-religious and cared the least for moral and spiritual values.

8. According to Goering, "We could either buy butter and surrender our freedom or we could seek to win our freedom and give up our butter. We have decided in favour of force." Thus, Germans preferred guns than butter.

9. Tight economic control was enforced and all rights of workers or employers of lock-outs or strikes were suppressed.

10. Germany discarded international outlook and believed in national aggrandizement.

11. They did not believe in ideology or discussion.

Conclusion. Nazism was full of defects and a curse to humanity, but a few drawbacks may be stated :

1. Preaching of militant nationalism and aggressive imperialism plunged mankind in World War II and brought misery to whole mankind.

2. Advocacy of raeialism and anti-Semitism created an atmosphere of hatred and violence.

3. Upholding of law of jungle that "might is right" cannot be justified.

4. Preaching of war and the commission of aggression were inhuman acts.

5. Jettisoning of religion and spiritual values were undesirable.

6. Degrading of women and brutalising of men were done by Nazis.

7. They initiated World War II which brought untold suffering to humanity and woe to mankind.

8. With the defeat of Germany in Second World War and death of Hitler, Nazism disappeared. However, its ideal of racism survived in South Africa and in some other states. But due to efforts of UNO, racism has mostly become non-existent. Jews have formed their own state of Israel and African countries have become free and are occupying important posts in USA and UNO. As such, now Nazism as well as racism have disappeared.

NOTES

1. J.S. Bouch and others, *Introduction to Political Science* (1954), p. 90.
2. *A Revolution in Thought* (1939).
3. J.S. Pounch and others, *Introduction to Political Science*, p. 696.
4. C.C. Maxey, *Political Philosophies* (1959), p. 638.

6

Pluralism

Pluralism is a complicated political idea and it has been defined differently by different writers. Some may be cited here :

"It is clear enough that the theory of the sovereignty of the state has broken down" (Lindsay).

"It is impossible to make the legal theory of sovereignty valid for political philosophy" (Laski).

"The doctrine of state sovereignty is both useless and dangerous" but critics say that "The pluralist political philosophy transforms society into the anarchy of trade unions". Critics have been replied that "The structure of social organization must be federal if it is to be adequate" (Laski).

"The state even if it includes everybody, is still only an association among others, because it cannot include whole of everybody" (Cole).

Introduction. The monistic theory of sovereignty came in for scathing criticism at the hands of pluralists like Harold Laski, J.M. Figgis, Earnest Barker, G.D.H. Cole, A.D. Lindsey, Miss M.P. Follet an others. Pluralism has been explained through different angles by political philosophers, jurists like Karbbe and Leon Diguit, Guild socialists like G.D.H. Cole and socialists. "Not an unusual feature of pluralistic criticism of sovereignty is that the individual writers wish to lay stress on some particular type of autonomous organization or support some special type of social organization such as socialism."

Opposition to Monism. According to pluralists, the state cannot be regarded as "all inclusive, all-mighty or all-comprehensive as stated by monist thinkers who believe that state indicates supreme, final or ultimate authority in the internal and external spheres". The term sovereignty has been derived from the Latin word Superanus which means paramount or supreme. As such, Bodin defines sovereignty "the supreme power over citizens and subjects unrestrained by law". In the words of Hugo Grotius, "Sovereignty is the supreme political power vested in him whose acts are not subject to any other and whose will cannot be overridden." Austin's definition is, "If a determinate human superior, not in a habit of obedience to a like superior, receives habitual obedience from the bulk of a given society, that determinate superior is sovereign in society and society (including the superior) is a society political and independent". Thus, political philosophers who defined sovereignty made the state absolute and omnipotent and pluralism is an attack over monism.

What is Pluralism. Pluralistic theory of the state sovereignty is a reaction against the absolute theory of sovereignty as given by Hegel. In recent years, a number of political thinkers have cast doubts on the doctrine of unified state sovereignty and have revived the belief that foundation of liberty lies in division of powers. They object to new Leviathan with its extensive authority and are of opinion that it destroys democracy and freedom. They oppose the centralization of authority and argue that it is slow, cumbrous and wasteful. They hold that identification of state and society is not in accordance with actual facts in the intricate political and economic relation of the world. They discredit the state, oppose the theory of a single and unified sovereignty and look to other agencies for a large share of control. "If we look at the facts," A.D. Lindsey has said, "it is clear that theory of sovereign state has broken down." Laski writes, "It is impossible to make the legal theory of sovereignty valid for political philosophy" and that "it would be of lasting benefit to political science if the whole concept was surrendered." According to Barker, "No political phenomena have become more arid and unfruitful than the doctrine of sovereignty." Krabbe goes a step further and says, "The notion of sovereignty must be expunged from political theory."

Sources of Attack. The recent attack on sovereign state came from several sources. It was in the main, a result of certain tendencies in legal theory especially in Germany and England and of somewhat parallel theory, specially in France and England. The German jurist Otto Gierke revived the ideas of Athens and the medieval theory of the real personality of corporate associations within the state.

In England, this line of thought was developed by F.W. Maitland. He insisted upon the real personality, the independent origin, and inherent right of associations within the state. Briefly stated, the doctrine of Gierke and Maitland is that the permanent association which arises naturally within any society posseses personalities which are real, not hypothetical, fictions or created from without. Each association has a collective consciousness and wills of its individual members. The state's role in this legal elaboration is principal but not exclusive. They argued that the state should accept the common point of view that permanent associations have rights and duties as groups whether or not the state is bound morally and practically to accept the sense of community that individuals are subjects of rights and duties within themselves, not derived from the state.

Other political thinkers have given special attention to the position considered historically, legally and politically of professional and economic groupings in society. J. Paul Boncours holds that the history of professional association shows that in all countries and ages, such groups have arisen spontaneously, that in time they reach a position where they are able to devise and enforce the conditions under which the vocation for which the aims are pursued and that relation of such associations, to members as well to outsiders tend to acquire an obligatory character. He maintains that the law of associations gives legal conception to this practical development. The law recognizes a free right to associations by giving to associations privileges which put them in position to interdict work. He argues further that these developments are not accidental or avoidable but inherent in the very nature of economic society and conditions that result in accord with the true principles of government. The basic principle of popular sovereignty is that the protection of liberty is the sole end of social organization; necessary limitation upon liberty can properly be made only through the corporations in the formation of laws, of all those, whose liberties are to be limited by the laws. Only in this way there is guarantee that the restrictions which law imposes are an exact reflection of the majority will which necessitates restriction. The right of majority to act for all within any given association is justifiable only upon the assumption that the majority can and does normally act in the common interest of the members of the association. But the majority of an entire nation is not competent to act for the interest of all citizens in all things because these interests are not common in all respects, and there is always danger that the majority will act on behalf of some particular group. Therefore, besides natural sovereign deciding questions in cases affecting the common interest of the country, there should be a particular sovereign to decide in matters where the special interest of some group is more important than the remoter interest of the nation.

Many other thinkers have argued on behalf of the right of associations generally against the prevailing trends of states. Dr. J.M. Figgs criticized the efforts of the modern political leaders to invade the proper spheres of such essential groups as churches, trade union, local bodies and the families and he advocated the policy which would attribute to all such groups the character of public associations and accord them a large discretion and initiative on controlling their respective interests.

Dr. Barker agrees with the main tenets of Gierke. Maitland said that these groups exist prior to any act of the state, earlier than a juristic person created by a common conviction among its members of its corporate character and function. He writes, "We see the state less as an association of individuals, already united in various groups for a future and more embracing common purpose". A.D. Lindsey says that the corporate personalities in society are infinite in number, and that many of them exist because they are more homogenous and represent a closer community of interests, attract deeper loyalties than the state and, if permitted to act autonomously, move themselves to be more effective agencies of social work or co-ordination.

In order to prove that the doctrine of sovereign state is practically untenable, Laski and his associates oftenrefer to actual instances of state impotence in the face of determined resistance by various group loyalties. The state, he says, has no right to the allegiance of an individual conscience and of various group loyalties. The state, he says, has no right to the allegiance of an individual save in so far as his conscience gives assent. "The claim of authority upon myself is ... legitimate proportionately to the moral urgency of its appeal. The only state to which I owe allegiance is the state in which I discover moral adequacy ... our first duty is to be true to our conscience. The state moreover is only one among many forms of human associations." It does not exhaust the associative impulses of man... society should be regarded as essentially federal in its nature. The group is real in the same sense that state is real. No association can legislate for the whole of myself. The state must compete with churches, trade unions, employers, associations, friendly societies, political parties and professional associations. In any instance of conflicting demands, the state's prominence over other associations depends upon the superiority of its moral appeal in that instance. We give to this particular group of the state no peculiar importance.

In this way, Laski criticizes the absolute sovereignty and considers it a legal fiction and barren concept. He argues that doctrine of sovereignty is no longer true and cannot be applied to the modern state of USA which is based on the theory of separation of powers and no person or organ can be considered sovereign.

Laski goes a step further and says that there are many things which the state does not do and cannot do because of opposition of some of its members. He is of opinion that groups within the state may be important for social purposes as the state itself and such groups have an equal claim to the individual's allegiance. The church and labour union may be in their own fields as sovereign as the state. Sovereignty must be shared by many groups. In his later writings, Laksi has added to his earlier emphasis on the corporate personality and rights of groups, juristic theory of Dugiut, with its emphasis on social solidarity and the limitations imposed upon sovereignty by law. Pragmatic philosophy and positivist sociologists are thus combined to discard the state. Individualism and functionalism are continued to oppose a unified and authoritarian political system.

Guild socialists like Hobson and C.D.H. Cole have tried to lay emphasis on the groups within the state to discard omnipotence of the state. A.F. Bentley in his book *The servile state* pleads for a distribution in which corporate guilds would protect the private property assigned to every individual. Graham Wallas suggests a combination of collectivism and representation modified by recognition of groups.

In USA Miss M.P. Fallett while recognizing the superior authority of the state would encourage the active political functioning of various groups within the state. A.F. Bentley argues that the pressure of interests organized in the form of groups is the essential factor interpretation of history. The Italian sociologist and jurist M.A. Vaccoro believes that the future will witness a process of political decentralization and the development of small units adjusted to natural regional advantages and to administrative conveniences. Rudolf Stiner favours a threefold division of the social commonwealth into an economic system, political system and a spiritual system.

The pluralistic theory has a strong tinge of individualism and insists on democracy. They put emphasis on groups and associations which represent the real interests of men. Pluralism favours autonomy or some powers for the groups and associations which represent various interests of men. It opposes a centralized all-powerful state and urges a division of power along the lines of functional democracy. It rejects the psychology of the general will and the conception of absolute sovereignty based on a formal and metaphysical rationalism that does not correspond with actual and changing political reality. In this respect it allies itself to a certain extent with the anti-intellectualism that characterizes social psychology and the new economic conditions.

In addition to opposition of these thinkers, there have appeared various political movements which are pluralistic in tendency. These movements oppose the centralized geographically-based system of state organization and suggest the creation of more varied basis of representation as in Ireland where professional and functional representation has been adopted. They also aim to diffuse social control among various agencies and to remove from the state the regulation of certain interests over which it has assumed authority.

Pluralist Attack on Historical Grounds. Pluralists say that ancient and monarchical states were not sovereign states. There were churches and self-ruled cities and traditions and customs to check the power of the state. Conception of sovereignty is of recent origin and came in prominence in 17th century, as such historical conception of sovereignty is not old.

Attack on Practical Grounds. Pluralists are of opinion that the mightiest rulers have to bow down to public opinion and tradition. Practically no human being can be omnipotent and all powerful so on practical grounds conception of sovereignty cannot be justified. In this realistic world, power of every state is limited.

Attack on Grounds of Justification. Barker, Lindsay and Laski are of opinion that it is not proper to make state all powerful and omnipotent because state is neither the least association in aim nor in individual respect.

Other Associations have not been created by the State. It is also argued that some associations such as church, etc., are not the creation of the state and as such state possesses no right to curb them.

Conception of sovereignty has also been attacked on following grounds :

1. The theory of sovereignty is wrong on moral grounds because it breeds mental outlook of slavery because man had to obey the state like a slave.

2. Monistic state is not efficient because due to centralization, work cannot be carried out efficiently and promptly. Moreover public grievances cannot be removed quickly.

Attack on Sovereignty on Internationalistic Ground. According to Laski, "The concept of an absolute and independent sovereign state which demands an unqualified allegiance from its members and enforces that allegiance by the power at its command is incompatible with the interests of humanity .... In a creative civilization what is important is not the historical accident of separate states, but the scientific fact of world's interindependence". League of Nations and UNO failed on the rock of national sovereignty, so conception of sovereignty is undesirable in international sphere.

Attack on Theory of Sovereignty on Grounds of Law. Jane Austin said that law is command of sovereign but modern jurists Duguit and Karabbe oppose this point of view. According to Duguit, "Law is product of social psychology" and according to Krabbe,

"State depends on law and not the law on state". As such, these jurists attack sovereignty on legal grounds.

Pluralism and State. Anarchists desire even abolition of state but pluralists like Barker and Laski desire organization of society on federal basis and desire to limit the sphere of the state by giving some autonomy and some power to different associations.

Criticism of Theory. 1. The pluralistic conception has been criticized on various grounds. It has been remarked that logical conclusion of pluralism is Anarchism. If every association is given an equal footing with the state and there is no co-ordinating power, there is bound to arise confusion and chaos in the society. The division of sovereignty into many parts, a bit of it given to every association, will destroy the very idea of sovereignty. It is for this reason that even after dividing sovereignty among the groups, the pluralists advocate that the power of co-ordination should be given to the state. But this function cannot be performed unless the state is given the position of legal supremacy. It can perform its function of adjustment and co-ordination only if its authority is supreme over all other associations. If it is done, it becomes final legal authority. As such, state alone should have the final legal authority and not any other association or associations.

2. It is also pointed out that it is based on wrong assumptions. It is wrong to think that the various associations run along on parallel lines and there is no overlapping of functions. As society is constituted, there is always a clash of interests and a conflict of loyalties and for prevention of clashes, some final authority is necessary and it can be only state.

3. It is pointed out that the concept of sovereignty which is attained by the pluralist is not something which is advocated by the exponents of sovereignty. The advocates of sovereignty did not assign omnipotence to the state. They all admitted that in actual practice, the authority of the state was limited in many ways. Neither Bodin nor Austin ever claimed that to criticise or challenge or to disobey or to resist state authority is necessarily immoral, unethical, anti-social or irrational or even impractical. What they meant is that "state as organization of law is superior to all other social groups within such territory." According to Coker, certain theories of monistic conception of sovereignty are correct. State acts as an organization whose function is to co-ordinate the functions of various associations and to keep harmony among them.

4. It has been pointed out that the view of Lindsey is not logical on the one side. Lindsey admits that state is unique in so far as it

possesses coercive authority and on the other side, he is of opinion, that this unique feature is not enough to constitute a sovereign state. In the opinion of Miss Folleit, the state is a unifying force. She says "The state cannot be composed of groups because no group or any member of groups can obtain the whole of me and the ideal state demands whole of me ... my citizenship is something bigger than any membership in the rational group .... The true state must gather up every interest within itself. It must take up many loyalties and find how it can make them one. The home of my soul is the state."

5. It is difficult to imagine that society can be harmoniously organized in a peaceful manner without the authority of the state. Dr. Garner points out, "State renders important service in helping within proper limits the classes and struggles between competing groups and performing the role of referee or umpire and adjusting or reconciling their conflicting interests.

6. It is pointed out that state is necessary for maintaining peace and order and adjusting and co-ordinating the interests of the various associations in order to avoid anarchy of associations. In order to avoid anarchy of associations and to save society from chaos, the authority of state has to be maintained.

7. Lastly, it is pointed out that the pluralist view is full of dangers. If autonomy or authority is granted to group opinion, any group may misuse the authority and all groups may claim it and it may result in anarchy. If state is given authority to check the power of associations, it becomes a super-association and monistic point of view remains justified and unchallenged. Thus pluralists' doctrine hits back the assumptions of pluralists, and monists get an upper hand.

Conclusion. It is difficult to agree with the pluralistic point of view as it will create a problem, if power is given to various associations and it many even result in greater tyranny of various groups. A.F. Zimmern points out that those who talk of state absolutism are ignoring the simple truth that there is no tyranny like the tyranny of near neighbours. The smaller the group, the tighter the stranglehold over your life and actions. According to Gettle, monism is the point of view of a stable political system in which legal norms have been worked out to adjust conflicting jurisdiction and contradictory objections. He points out that monism is a conservative political theory; pluralism is a critical theory. It is no accident that pluralism is lastly associated with Syndicalism, Guild socialism and internationalism.

In spite of the criticism of pluralistic theory, it cannot be denied that it was a welcome reaction against the glorification of state authority. It was a timely protest against the rigid and dogmatic legalism of the Austinian theory of sovereignty. It points out importance of non-political groups. According to Miss. Follet, pluralists stand for the restoration of local life and point out that interests of the state are not always identical with the interests of the parts. To sum up, we many quote Prof. Sabine, "For my own part, then I must reserve the right to be a monist, when I can and a pluralist when I must."

Pluralism (Legal School of Thought) — Duguit and Krabbe

"Law with Duguit is simply the name for the rule of conduct actually controlling men living in society" is Duguit's conception of law and state.

Introduction. French thinker Leon Duguit was essentially a literary man. He was born in the year 1859. He got degree of Doctor of Laws in 1892. He worked as Professor of Law and wrote "Treatise on Constitutional Law" and a book *Transformation of the theory of the state* which was translated by Laski under the title *Law in the Modern State*. He died at the age of 69 in the year 1928. He belonged to pluralistic school of thought.

Duguit conceives of state not as a sovereign power which issues commands having the force of laws but as a collection of individuals who exercise political power. He believes that state is not a separate entity. According to Duguit, "Government and its officials are no longer the masters of men imposing the sovereign will on their subjects (but they are simply the manager of nation's business)." Governmental activities have expanded enormously but he argues that rulers govern not on the basis of the authority but by force and with the sanction of the objective law of social solidarity. They do not rule by any right but by necessity of maintaining social solidarity and keeping the necessary social services of the state in continuous operation.

The theory of absolute sovereignty is termed imperialistic by Duguit. He criticizes the theory of sovereignty. He states, "If we admit the personality of the state and define law as the command of its sovereign will, it is absolutely impossible to understand how against law can be really law since the state cannot address a command to itself." But in some cases, these laws are formulated in written documents called constitutions but in some countries they exist in shape of convention as in England. Now the objection of Duguit is that if states are sovereign they cannot be subject to constitutional laws but actually states follow constitutional laws consequently states cannot be sovereign as they are limited by constitutional, laws. Thus state cannot be source of laws because the state is itself governed by laws; in this way there is no sovereign state.

He refutes the Austinian conception that law is the command of sovereign. He is of opinion that rule of law is not a command but a way of life derived from the necessities of social existence. In other words, sanction of law arises from the necessity of maintaining social solidarity or, more specially those public services that are necessary for the survival of the society. Thus law is a way of life derived from the necessities of social existence. The basic consideration is maintenance of social solidarity or social discipline. Public services such as education, health, transportation are absolutely essential for the existence of society and these services must be kept running. This is the primary business of the state. As such, law expreses the arrangements, the activities, the obligations, that are necessary for the performance of the public services, and for effective operation of division of labour.

In modern days, many laws are issued by public bodies and administrative officials who cannot be said to be sovereign as such laws are not the expression of sovereignty but arise out of social necessity.

Not only this, functional groups and associations enforce disciplinary rules upon their members which have force of law. Thus state maintains social discipline for whole of society and group discipline is maintained by each of its groups.

Like other pluralists and pragmatists, he says, state cannot always command but must increasingly persuade the citizens to obey laws. The laws nowadays take the form of agreements or contracts, arrived at between the different corporate bodies in society such as trade unions and employers.

Lastly, he says that now social discipline takes the place of law. Social discipline is maintained by the tight organization of guilds or associations and on the natural level by the social reaction to disobedience of laws. Law in so far as it is concerned with the maintenance of public services, is an expression of public policy. It satisfies some widely felt need. The laws organizing special public services are obligatory because they have special purpose. Constitutional laws and administrative laws are obligatory because they organize the state as a whole so as best to assure the establishment of civil services.

Function of the State. The traditional conception of state was the concentration of public power enforcing rights and duties. He discarded the view of sovereign will. The idea that state represented the supposed will of the people was untrue to fact. Formulated law was the creation simply of the individuals who happened to possess legislative power and it had no necessary relation with the will of the majority of people. He objected to the traditional conception of the absolute and unquestionable authority of law.

According to Duguit, state is the only central power for the maintenance of public services. As the services daily grow in number and complicity, they must be carried out by means of decentralization.

Authority of State and Law. According to Duguit, both of them reflect facts and both apply to man living in society and give rise to commands which are habitually obeyed. The basis of authority of state is the physical penalties which can be imposed on those who defy the authority of the state. On the other hand, law is independent and anterior to above and more comprehensive than the state. The state acts in a legitimate manner only if it sustains law or guarantees cooperation towards social solidarity. The function of state is to adopt an already existing rule of law to a given set of facts. The legal validity of any act of the state depends upon the end which it serves.

In the words of a commentator, "... behind Duguit's view of the state as a collector of public services, there lies a far reaching change in the conception of law itself. The end of law can no longer be considered as principally the maintenance of rights. The formulation of this point of view is ... the conception of society as a collection of wills each of which is to be defended in the exercise of the largest possible measure of free decision."

It seems that Duguit was influenced by the philosophy of Comte and Emile Durkheim. The growth of Syndicatist philosophy also influenced the view of Duguit.

Rights. Duguit denies that there are any rights. Right is the power of will to impose itself on another will in regard to a particular object and suggests subjective rights (duties to him) to develop himself to the utmost to be able to contribute his best for social solidarity. Any action that is done by an individual in conformity with the law has the right to protection by the material force of the community in the hands of the government and no other individual may interfere with the same. In his words, "every one has duties towards all."

In short we may say that Duguit's view about state is that it is a collection of public services. Rule of social conduct is the product of social environment.

Criticism. Duguit has failed to discriminate state and government properly. In denying rights Duguit's departure from the traditional theory is apparent than real. But even so, the technique of safeguarding right that Duguit adopts is defective and might easily prove dangerous to what it is intended to protect by calling them duties.

Duguit's fact of solidarity on analysis turns out to be a construction of imagination based on obvious interdependencies that are not merely economic but cultural as well. Duguit's assertion that social solidarity parexcellence is to be found in the nation is comforting particularly in India.

Duguit makes the consciousness of the masses of men in a community as maker of law. But can the society dispense with a definite organ of law-making as it is necessary to a modern community.

However, his true merit lies in putting emphasis on the notions of public service and responsibility. These concepts enshrine a moral lesson for humanity and these have never been placed with greater force than Duguit and herein lies his greatness, though judiciary particularly in India do not accept his ideas.

Krabbe

"The notion of sovereignty must be expunged from political theory", Krabbe stated but his views have not been accepted.

Hugo Krabbe, the Dutch jurist, tried to find out an ethical basis for law. He was educated at Leydon, took his doctorate in the civil service in Netherlands and worked on different posts. In 1908, he was appointed as Professor of Constitutional Law and retired in 1927. His important books are *The theory of sovereignty of law* and *The modern idea of the state.*

Krabbe belongs to sociological school of law. According to him "Law is the expression of one of the many judgements of value which we human beings make by virtue of our disposition and nature". We obey law because it appears just and good from our standard of value and judgement. It is not a matter of external legal authority but an internal human matter. Krabbe narrows down the state to a legal community and makes the judge the centre of power in society. He was an internationalist. According to him, there is one source of law and that is feeling or sense of right.

Krabbe's theory of state asserts that state is based on the rule of law. In fact, it is law and not the state which is sovereign for the state itself is subject to laws as in case of constitutional law. Law rests upon an evaluation of actual interests found in society. Law depends on devices from evaluation of interests both public and private.

All political institutions are legal bodies and they are sustained by the consensus of men as to the value of human interests so that judgment of men and social structure rests on its general harmony with human needs and interests. Conscience of institutions is descriptive as well as informative; it includes values and judgements. In other words, political organization is rooted in laws, in settled ideas of right, good and bad, and these ideas in turn are rooted in consciousness from which the notion of valuation is inseparable. The fundamental concept for the theory of modern state is law.

Moral and social values are connected with and are dependent upon human needs and interests. Thus, values of the institutions must conform with human needs and interests.

Law is only one aspect of society and culture and it is influenced by the other aspects such as religion. The state is "community that possesses common law". The state is an association of men occupying definite territory, in which a common sense of right leads to general agreement of both public and private interests. Such a common agreement expresses itself in organs to maintain a common interest.

According to Krabbe, state is not to be identified with legislature nor with the law enforcement agencies, *i.e.*, courts and administrative organs which enforce law.

He states that law is the basis of public services and not public services that are the basis of law. State may maintain or contain many communities with laws of their own because law fosters private services as well as public services.

Krabbe discards the old concept of sovereignty and he is of opinion that the concept of sovereignty should be expunged from political theory because in Krabbe's political theory law is not the command of sovereign but it is law that is sovereign. Ultimately sanction of law is not the command of sovereign but that of valuation of interests, public and private. The community of man is bound by legal and moral relations and the organs and agencies of government serve these relations. The basic reality is rule of relations and state and various agencies are somehow secondary. Law is the main expression of political activity in the community and everyone is subject to law, *i.e.*, law is above all and nobody is above law. Law is the instrument of its self-government. Authority of state is nothing except authority of law and law depends on the feeling or sense of right. In short, we can say according to Krabbe a law state is based on law and law is supreme and sovereign. Thus law according to Krabbe is independent of the state and he accepts no authority as valid except that of law; the sovereign disappears as source of law from both legal and political theory.

According to Leon Duguit, the basis of political obligation lies in the existence of society, just as cells of an organism act for the benefit of the organism so that the members of society live and act for the survival of society.

He is of opinion that the basic principle that binds members of society together into an inter-related whole is the principle of social solidarity. It is the law of existence for society, because it may continue as an integrated whole only if the principle of social solidarity is operative. As per principle of social solidarity, members of society should do everything which increases the solidarity of society and should avoid every act which affects adversely the solidarity of society. All persons including rulers and leaders are bound by social solidarity. Only that action is proper which promotes social solidarity and that action is improper which harms the social solidarity. According to Duguit, social solidarity means, "The cells composing an organism are submitted to the laws of organism. Everyone recognizes it that the law of that organism is that which governs its formation and development. In the same manner, the individuals composing a social group are submitted to the law of that group, a law which governs its formation and development, *i.e.*, law of co-ordination. We do not call the law of the organism a norm because cells are not conscious but the law of a social group we call a norm because the individuals who are its members act consciously, will a thing that they have in view and in virtue of a motive of which they are conscious. This is the only difference between the law of living organism and the law of a human society; and if one admits that the biological organism is founded on the fact that constitutes this organism, there is no reason, why one should not look on the social norm as based on the fact that is society." This is an important factor for understanding Duguit's, philosophy.

Duguit discards the idea of social contract and builds his theory on scientific facts. To him, the only existence of society is real and society imposes certain obligations which are necessary for social existence. The members of society are bound together in a chain of organic interdependence for their satisfaction of wants. Individuals are governed by the division of labour because the existence of society depends on the various functions to be carried out by different persons. This social character is characterized by division of labour which is necessary for social existence and is independent of the will of individuals.

Individuals work in the society according to their capacity and merit. Individuals who are superior in intelligence, morals or in economic power become rulers, because they are able to exert their will more effectively than others. Thus ruling individuals, writes Duguit, "are stronger than others who will and who can impose their will on the rest. The rulers who possess by definition the greatest force existing in the society are obliged by the rule of law of social solidarity to employ this greatest force at their disposal for the realisation of social solidarity". In this way, rulers find their power defacto but they exercise it de jure, *i.e.*, according to and through the law. Thus, in other words, facts are stronger than laws, for laws follow facts but do not constitute facts. Therefore, rulers also must serve the ends of social solidarity and it is the governing principle of laws, statutes, ordinances and decisions of the courts.

Duguit's theory of social solidarity has been criticized on following grounds :

1. Duguit's analogy of society and organism is false, because individuals are different from the cells of an organism.

2. Duguit himself has admitted that individuals are conscious while the cells are not. But it is a basic difference because on account of their consciousness, men have the power and desire to change the society and to make it serve their ends or at least to change the ends that the society should serve. In this way, individuals can play a creative role which cells cannot do. So far as actual, facts are concerned individuals are able to choose their goals and sometimes to adopt something else than social solidarity as their basic principle.

The principle of political leadership as developed by Duguit who says that the political rulers are superior to other individuals, is fascistic and reactionary as it did not conform to democratic notions and democratic societies that believe in equality and not on the maxim that stronger should rule over the weaker. If superior men rule, it is for them to decide what should be done; and inferior men, *i.e.*, masses have little to say about government but democracy believes in the government of the people, therefore such a notion is unjustifiable in a democratic set-up of the society.

We have already discussed the social solidarity of Duguit which is his main contribution and in this basic difference between Duguit and Krabbe lies; now it will be easier for us to have a comparison between them.

Duguit and Krabbe utilized the growing knowledge of social history, political history, psychology and the impact of other sciences such as the biological theory of evolution. Thus they resemble as both of them consider power as only one aspect of the social and cultural life of the people. The new thinkers do not take it for granted that the state exists at some particular geographical point and that if it is a state at all, it exercises unlimited sovereignty.

Following the development of modern sociological theories especially that developed by Durkheim, Duguit believes that the basic fact of social life is that of social solidarity. Members of society do everything to maintain solidarity and avoid everything that diminishes it. Regarding sanction, according to Duguit, the final sanction is society's reaction to acts that are disruptive of its solidarity. There is nothing like state in Duguit's political theory because men rule on account of their superior power, physical, moral or economic. Thus Duguit denies that there is a single determinate source of political power or sovereignty in the state, social discipline in associations and syndicates. On the national level, discipline is maintained by rulers on one side and the reactions of the society to the action of rulers on the other. The main problem is maintenance of public services, such as education, transportation, sanitation and health, etc. In this way, everything revolves around the maintenance of public services and according to him, any measure which is required to maintain public services is thereby justified.

Krabbe agrees as well as differs with Duguit on certain points. Krabbe supports the contention of Duguit that there is no such thing as sovereignty in modern political community and says that institutions that are generally recognised as sovereign, such as the legislature or judiciary, are themselves subject to laws, hence they cannot be considered sovereign law-givers. According to him, legislatures are not the law-givers but an instrument that discovers law and codifies it. Thus both agree that law emerges from society rather than being legislated by the parliament or commanded by the sovereign. But the basic reality for Krabbe is not social solidarity but sense of right dependent upon human needs and interests. These needs and interests are evaluated by individuals and groups and law fosters these values. Even legislatures do not create laws but find them in the social process where values are generated. In Duguit's philosophy, society is the basic fact, not the individuals. Social needs, especially needs for social solidarity, come before human needs and interests. Duguit's political philosophy is collectivist. Krabbe's is humanitarian and democratic. In Duguit's philosophy, social structure determines human needs but in Karbbe's philosophy the needs determine the social structure, subject to existence of the transitions. In Duguit's philosophy, main purpose of social and political organization and of law is the maintenance of social solidarity and running of public service. In Krabbe's philosophy, values are not predetermined, but members of society are free to develop and support any value with which the members of society agree, *i.e.*, there is basic freedom in Krabbe's philosophy which is lacking in Duguit's philosophy.

Similarly emphasis of running public services is missing in Krabbe's philosophy and in fact in Duguit's philosophy individual is subordinated to social needs and in this way he is totalitarian. But according to Krabbe, law is the basis of public services as much as public services are the source of law. The distinction between public service and private interest is one of proper method of enforcement. Some interests are served by public services, while others are served more efficiently in the form of private interests.

It is difficult to agree with cooker when he maintains that there is "nothing in juristic doctrines of Duguit or Laski that is inconsistent with the theories of the strictly analytical jurists such as Austin or Laband." The concept of law as the expression of social process is fundamentally different from the concept of law as command of sovereign will, whose sanction is the overriding power of the sovereign. Duguit and Krabbe regard law as natural product inherent in the social process, result of social evolution and not the whim or command of sovereign. Law is rooted in the soil where it grows and draws nourishment from the soil of society but it is not the light of the sun of sovereignty as the analytical philosophers make out to be. In England, Analytical school of law is still in existence but in other countries Duguit and Krabbe have changed the outlook.

7

Harold Laski, G.D.H. Cole and Bertrand Russell

Brief Life Sketch of Harold J. Laski and His Main Political Ideas

Laski is considered a great thinker of modern age and his famous quotations are :

"The essential feature of the state is not its search for a common welfare but its power to compel acceptance of certain class relationships which make that common welfare peripheral and not central to its aim."

The State in Theory and Practice in his famous book. He further states.

"The structure of social organization must be federal if it is to be adequate".

"Normally the basis of state sovereignty is the contingent power to use the armed forces of the state to compel obedience to its wills".

As such, study of the main features of Laski's theory of the state is necessary.

Prof. Laski was one of the greatest political scientists of our times. He was born on 30th June, 1893 at Manchester in a respectable Jew family. He was the second son of Nathan and Sahara Laski, who came from Hungary. He was a good student. He was educated at first at Manchester grammar school and later on at New College, Oxford. At the age of 18 he married Fida Laski, an English Christian without the approval of his parents. He studied at New College, Oxford and got first class in History in 1914. His teachers at Oxford were H.A.L. Fisher, F.W. Maitland and Earnest Barker. He taught first as a lecturer in History at Macgill University. In 1920, he came back to England and joined London School of Economics and worked there till his death in 1950. He took an active part in politics. He had been member of the Fabian Society and played a notable part in labour politics from 1930 to 1940. In 1930, he insisted on the abdication of

Edward VIII. In 1934, he visited Russia and also delivered many lectures there. He also visited America very often and was on friendly terms with President Roosevelt.

In fact, Laski was a scholar and political philosopher, politician, author, journalist and above all, a teacher and a friend.

According to Kingsly Martin, English political thought "was more dominated by Laski than any other personality" and it might be called "the age of Laski." According to Kingsly Martin, Laski once said to his father, "I am English, not Polish, an agnostic, not Jew. I cannot reconcile Maimonides with Mill, nor Ann Veronica with Mosaic Law."[1] Later on he became Marxist and wrote, "Out of all, the great lesson I have learnt is the broad truth of the Marxian philosophy ... it (is) impossible for the democratic idea to transcend the barriers of class without the capture of the state power by the working class."

He wrote a lot of books but the most important of them are given below :

1. *A Grammar of Politics* (1925)
2. *Studies in Problem of Sovereignty* (1917)
3. *Authority in Modern State* (1918)
4. *Karl Marx* (1921)
5. *Socialism and Freedom*
6. *Communism* (1927)
7. *Liberty in Modern State* (1930)
8. *The Dangers of Obedience* (1930)
9. *Where Socialism stands Today*? (1933)
10. *Recovery through Revolution* (1933)
11. *Democracy in Crisis* (1933)
12. *Parliamentary Government in England* (1938)
13. *The State in Theory and Practice* (1934)
14. *The Rise of European Liberalism* (1936)
15. *An Introduction to Politics*
16. *Studies in Law and Politics*
17. *The Socialist Tradition in the French Revolution*
18. *Political Thought in England from Lock to Bentham*
19. *The Foundation of Sovereignty*
20. *The American Presidency*
21. *The American Democracy*
22. *What I Believe*? (1940)
23. *The Dilemma of our Times* (1952)

Laski on State and Sovereignty

Laski belongs to pluralistic school of thought and his thinking conflicts with the theory of political monism which believes in all powerful and unified sovereignty.

Background to political pluralism as of Laski is the theory of *Laissez Faire*, which confines the state to a limited supervisory function. The state merely kept law and order and helped the business organizations and associations, mainly in their foreign operations. Herald Laski is of view that the state supplies framework of law and order but the different activities of the society are conducted by various associations. Laski considers state to be a service organization and as a co-ordinating body as the primary services are performed by these associations, so associations have primacy in man's loyalties while the state is secondary. In case of family, church, etc. or worker's union, generally these capture the primary loyalty of an individual. State is an association with the special duty of co-ordinating other groups and associations. There is no sovereign, no human superior. Law is not the command of the state.

Laski repudiates the theory of sovereignty on the following grounds :

1. Authority of state is neither absolute nor unlimited. There are numerous checks over state's sovereign power. Laski observes, no sovereign has anywhere possessed unlimited power; and the attempt to exert it has always resulted in the establishment of safeguards. Even Sultan of Turkey and Czar of Russia in the height of their powers were bound down to a code of traditional observance, obedience of which was practically compulsory upon them. In law, there was no part of the social fact, they could not alter in practice. They survived only by willing submission and not by those changes which might have proved them the sovereigns of Austinian jurisprudenue.

2. Concept of sovereignty cannot be defended according to Laski ethically. He is of opinion that "The Austinian theory of sovereignty, uncongenial enough even in its abstract presentation, would as a fact breed simple servility were it capable of practical application."

3. In some modern states as in U.S.A. which rest on the theory of separation of powers, it is very difficult to locate sovereignty. In USA neither President nor Congress nor judges of Supreme Court are sovereign. Laski writes, "In theoretical sense, the USA has no sovereign organ, for the judges of the Supreme Court, being over-ridden by constitutional amendments are a court of reference."

4. In a centralized monistic state where all powers are centralized at one place, the administration will be inefficient and incomplete.

Laski like Green wanted decentralized state. He desired power of the state split up, divided and thrown widespread among men.

Laski holds that state alone cannot perform all the functions of different associations because every association has got its own importance in its own place, as different parts of the body are important in their respective places. Any attempt on the part of the state for the performance of any action independently would lead to its decay. Each association has its own sphere of activity. Different groups are set up for achieving different aims. No association can interfere in the affairs of other associations. It fact, different groups or associations constituting the parts of the state do not differ with it in any essential manner, so state should not interfere and even power of legislation should be shared by the state with other groups. To sum up Laski holds :

1. That there is no fundamental difference between the nature of the state and nature of any other association.

2. That the state is only one of many forms of associations.

3. That state cannot claim any pre-eminence or superiority over other associations.

4. State can co-ordinate other groups without forcing them for subordination.

5. Power of the legislation should be shared by other groups.

Authority as Federal. According to Laski, all authority is federal. It means that there is no authority which can claim absolute control over individuals. State can only exercise partial control. Man possesses various wants and to fulfil these wants which may be political, economic, social or religious, he joins many associations, each one of which makes contribution for, development of his personality, but all make only partial contribution. A trade union safe-guards or looks after the economic interests of the individual while church takes care of his spiritual uplift and state which satisfied the political needs of people cannot replace these associations properly. As such, contribution made by state to our lives is partial and so we owe only partial obedience to state.

According to Laski, whatever aspect of life we may take, authority is everywhere federal. Even in case of legislation, work cannot be given to any single individual. As a law has to serve the interests of all, all should be consulted in the making of law, so that their points of view may be taken into consideration at the time of enactment of a bill into law. At least those people who are going to be affected by a particular law should be consulted and by this process people will feel moral obligation to obey law.

He believes that no law passed by the rich in the interests of the poor can satisfy unless they are made partner in making law because they understand their own difficulties. Giving example of the Treaty of Varsailles, he says, "Unless a law represents the wishes of the people, the people are not morally bound to obey the state."

He is of opinion that function of the state does not extend to the regulation of whole life of man. Its function is essentially of co-ordination. He is definitely of the view that state should always take into consideration public opinion and as such it cannot be absolute and sovereign and centralized to one place only, but federal.

It is said that days of pluralism are over and now theory of pluralism is declining. Developments have contradicted the theory of political pluralism due to following reasons :

1. Due to disharmony of the associations, state took over and it is taking more and more functions of arbitration and adjudication.

2. With the extension of state's welfare activities, state now possesses more responsibility and authority whether it may be education or sanitation or any other thing.

3. World wars give unlimited powers to the states to mobilize all resources and whole society for defence or attack.

4. With the discovery of new inventions and atomic weapons, now state wields unlimited power and it is futile to think that public upheaval may bring any revolution as was the case in France in 18th and 19th centuries. As such now state is most powerful and wields unlimited power, so pluralism cannot succeed in the present set-up.

LASKI ON RIGHTS

Laski's Theory of Rights

> "Every state is known by the rights that it maintains. They (rights) have a content which changes with time and place."
>
> "Rights in fact are those conditions of social life without which no man can seek, in general, to be himself at his best."
>
> Laski's theory of rights is very popular. He further says that :
>
> "We do not mean by rights the grant of some historical conditions possessed in the childhood of race; but lost in the process of time."
>
> "Rights are not the creation of law but its conditions precedent Laski."

Harold Laski is of opinion that the state is a way of regulating human behaviour. Legally it means that the state is an organization with power to enforce its will upon the individuals who live within its jurisdiction, and for enforcement of which it may use physical force. Thus, in theory, state is sovereign. But he maintains that state is not an end but it may be judged by the service or welfare which it performs.

Rights spring from the urge of every man to be happy according to his will as individual possesses free-will and freedom of decision. The association as well as the state are means to the fulfilment of man's basic demand for happiness. Man cannot be happy without the satisfaction of his materialistic wants and so the right to work, right to proper wages, that is, adequate means of livelihood and proper working conditions is essential. Thus right of adequate wages is most important.

Right to education is also one of the fundamental rights as without it man cannot be at his best and it implies freedom of expression and association also.

Laski considers political democracy as another right and this right means the right to choose the government and to be part of it, if elected.

An individual also possesses the right to apply the lessons of his experience to the decisions of Government. He agrees that the rights are not absolute and nobody has right to misuse the rights.

From, above contentions the Laski comes to conclusion that state is not the source of right for rights are inherent in the individual who strives for happiness by satisfying his desires. Happiness for Laski is the self-realization of the individual. As such, these rights are prior to the state, not in time but in importance. The utility of the state is to be judged by its ability to fulfil these rights as to him individual and individual's happiness is the end and state is the means.

Laski's theory of rights has been criticized as individualistic and ignores that state is not merely a means, it is also the creator of rights and may mould the citizen in a particular manner so that desires may follow a given pattern; as such it ignores constructive contribution of the state.

"The state is a fellowship of man aiming at the enrichment of common life. It is an association like others, churches, trade unions and the rest", states Laski, so study of the leading ideas of Laski and in brief main tenets of his political thereby is necessary.

Laski on Law. Austin's notion that law is the expression of the will of the sovereign authority has not been accepted by Laski. To him, this theory of law is relic of the days when king was absolute. According to him, source of law is to be found in social forces operating independently of the will of the sovereign.

He believes that the end of law is the promotion of social stability and its growth totally depends upon the growth of this sentiment. "To regard law as command of sovereign is a view too dangerous and of the time when the courts held that they were to do no more than apply a given remedy to a given set of facts … with a lofty unconcern for the world at large."

Other Political Ideas of Laski. Liberty is the eager maintenance of that atmosphere in which men have the opportunity to be their best selves and liberty is a product of rights. Without rights there can be no liberty because in that case men are subjects of law unrelated to the needs of personality.

Laski discusses three aspects of liberty: individual liberty, political liberty and economic liberty. Individual liberty means legal protection to all persons without any distinction of caste, creed, race, religion or sex. For political liberty, Laski desires two conditions of education and freedom of press. Basing his conception on sophist outlook, he says "first of all things, I place education." As such, he pleads right of minimum education to everybody. By economic liberty, he means that everybody has got the right to earn his livelihood. He must possess right to work and he must be provided employment by the government.

Laski is a socialist and democrat and opposes capitalism. He states, "The problem of capitalist democracy, save in dubious events of economic recovery can only be solved either by the suppression of capitalism or by the suppression of democracy." He is of view that if democracy is to work without being in constant danger of being destroyed, the only way is that capitalism should be destroyed. He pleads for democracy which he defines as "aristocracy of talents by delegation."

His Contribution. Laski was a great political philosopher. Laski's *Grammar of Politics* is really a grammar of politics for a student of political thought. His other works are also valuable and famous, such as *American presidency*, *Parliamentary Government in England* and *State in Theory and Practice* etc.

Laski's political philosophy is unique contribution of individualism and authoritarian-ism. He discarded the monistic theory of law in most forceful language and supported pluralistic ideas.

1. Laski follows the utilitarians in seeking maximum good of individuals.

2. He is of the view that state is to be obeyed only so far as it serves the good of individuals.

3. Dominant classes also dominate the state and lower classes are neglected and exploited.

4. Law is name of rules which a dominant or ruling class frames to perpetuate its own rule.

5. Individuals can make their voice heard through the associations.

6. He is of the view that in case of conflict, an individual may support his association as is generally done by the trade unions which resort to strike even against the government at the call of their union, thus Laski is pluralist.

7. Modern society is too complex and even state must win public support.

8. He pleads for close co-operation between individuals and the state for mutual benefit.

9. State is a sovereign organization; it should be judged by its beneficial acts.

10. He discards old point of view about democracy and pleads for aristocracy of talents by delegation.

11. He discards the view that rights are the creation of the state.

Thus, Laski's political philosophy is queer mixture of various political ideas. At one place he says that whether one in willing or not, he is automatically born as a citizen of a state. But at another place he says that all men are not actively and continuously political animal. All this leads us to conclude that Laski was neither a champion of extreme individualism, nor of extreme authoritarianism. His contention is influenced by Marxism and he has blended authoritarianism, rank individualism and radical Marxism with a tinge of democracy. He pleaded for rights, equality, liberty and for democracy and pluralism.

Main contributions of Laski may be given as below :

1. His conception of sovereignty.
2. His concept of law.
3. His demand for individual rights.
4. His conception to liberty.
5. His opposition of capitalism.

We may conclude evaluation of Laski with the words of his biographer Martin : "Laski, a political genius is one of the greatest political thinkers of the modern times and he is one that comes nearer to the galaxy of Jewish thinkers, Sigmand Freud, Marx and Albert Einstein."

G.D.H. COLE

Introduction. G.D.H. Cole was the main exponent of Guild socialism. He was born in 1889. After completing his early education, he graduated from Oxford University. He first joined the Fabian Society in 1912, but later on drifted to Guild socialism. He was a scholar and devoted his life in academic pursuits. He died in 1958.

His Works. He wrote a lot of books but most important of them are following :

1. *Social Theory* (1920)
2. *World of Labour* (1913)
3. *Self-Government in Industry* (1917)
4. *Guild Socialism Restated*
5. *Intelligent Men's Guide to Post-War World*
6. *An review of Europe*
7. *Great Britain in Post-War World*
8. *Principles of Economic Planning*
9. *Fabian Socialism*
10. *Essays in Social Theory*

His Political Philosophy. Cole advocated the pluralistic conception of society. He championed for the cause of functional principles of guild society. He desired replacement of territorial representation to functional representation. He discarded the territorial representation on the ground that it is not possible to represent the views of all the persons residing in a particular area. He preferred the functional representation to territorial representation.

Cole demanded that workers should be protected against poverty and slavery. He pleaded for freedom at work. Workers should have the right to work under supervisors and managers of their own choice. He desired that workers should have no fear of unemployment. Cole desired to give complete control of industry to the workers and recommended for industrial democracy.

He considered state most unsuitable for controlling the industry. To him, state exists primarily to deal with things which affect all its members more or less equally and in the same way. The spheres of social action which affect different members of the state in different degrees and in different ways are not included among its primary functions. He emphasised the fact that the state should control the consumption of commodities but it should not control the production and producer. He insisted that "The production of things should be made the concern of the workers concerned; it is only income and prices which seem to fall clearly within the province of the state. The state should manage political activities and not the economic activities." According to Cole, great national industries and services, the mines, the railways, coal, shipping and so forth will be owned by the state.

G.D.H. Cole is a pluralistic thinker and opposes the sovereignty of the state. He says man's social experience is not limited upon state only. About the functions of state, he says, "The state ... ignores the differences between men because it is concerned not with their differences but with their identity, and its function and interests are with men's identity and not with their differences .... The concern of the state, as an association including all sorts and conditions of men, must be with things which concern all sorts and conditions of men, and concern them, broadly speaking, in the same way, that is, in relation to their identity, and not their points of difference."[2] He opposed state socialism because he feared that instead of giving power to labourers to have managers of their own choice, it may impose bureaucratic rule. He was a Guild socialist and remained so up to the last breath of his life.

Cole's Estimate. He has been called "secular saint" by kingsly Martin because he cared little for his self interest. According to Gray, Guild socialism came to be identified with him. He gave a new life to Guild Socialistmoment. His works are landmarks in the history of political philosophy of modern times.

BERTRAND RUSSELL

Life Sketch of Russell and His Main Political Ideas.

Bertrand Russell was a great thinker so his quotations are important. Some are given below :

> "But although Guild socialism represents an attempt at adjustment between two equally legitimate points of view, its impulse and force are derived from what it has taken over from Syndicalism".
>
> "The only philosophy that efforts a theoretical justification of democracy in its temper of mind, is empiricism."
>
> "One ought to be made to feel that self interest itself, when it is fully understood, can be better served by a life which is useful to the community than by one which is harmful. For this purpose it is chiefly necessary to widen his outlook and increase the scope of his desires."

Bertrand Russell was born on 18th May 1872, in one of the most respectable family of England and succeeded to the earldom as third Lord Russell in 1931. His grandfather was Lord John Russell, a Whig Prime Minister of Victorian age.

He had a bitter experience of life as he was left an orphan when he was three years' old and became a ward of court. He received his early education at the University of Cambridge and distinguished himself as a keen lover of philosophy and mathematics. In 1895, he became a Fellow of Trinity.

He opposed war of 1914-18, so he was deprived of his University lectureship, fined and sentenced to six months' imprisonment in 1918. He went to Russia and lectured also at Peking University in China. He won Nobel Prize for literature and the Order of Merit in his own country. He opposed Trueman for atomic bombs hurled in Japan. Russell is the greatest living political philosopher who has been honoured by Mahatma Gandhi as well as by Kruschev.

Russell's Work. His some of the important works are given below :

1. *The Principles of Mathematics* (1903)
2. *On Education* (1926)
3. *Outline of Philosophy* (1928)
4. *Mysticism and Logic* (1929)
5. *The History of Western Philosophy* (1947) won Nobel Prize
6. *Freedom and Organization* (1934)
7. *Analysis of Matter* (1927)
8. *Roads to Freedom* (1918)
9. *Why Men Fight* (1917)

Political Philosophy of Russell

State and Government. According to Russell, the end of political life is the free growth of individuals and to achieve this end, he presents views corresponding to the views of Kroptkin. He regards individual liberty as greatest good and considers state and law as restriction on individual liberty, but he supports the existence of state as it is essential for the enjoyment of individual liberty. He says, "The state in spite of what Anarchists urge, seems a necessary institution for certain purposes. Peace and war, tariffs, regulation of sanitary conditions and of the sale of noxious drugs, the presentation of a just system of distribution there among others are functions which could hardly be performed in a community in which there was no central government." He allows following main functions to Central Government :

1. Internal peace.

2. Regulation of sanitary conditions and protection of health of the members of the state against disease.

3. Preservation of a just system of distribution.

4. Sale of noxious drugs.

He says that "its (state's) powers should be strictly limited to what is absolutely necessary. There is no way of limiting its powers except by means of groups which are jealous of their privileges and determined to preserve their autonomy, even if this should invoke resistance to law declared by state .... The state though at present a source of much evil is also a means to certain good things, and will be needed so long as violent and destructive impulses remain common. But it is merely a means and a means which needs to be very carefully and sparingly used if it is not to do more harm than good".[3]

Russell on Freedom. Russell regarded freedom supreme good, for without it personality is impossible; life and knowledge today are complex and only by debates clear conceptions may be formed. Not only this, freedom of thought may lessen the world conflict because hatred and war come largely of fixed ideas or dogmatic faith.

Russell on Private Property and Imperialism. Russell discards private property of land and he writes, "No good to the humanity of any sort or kind results from the ownership of land".

Russell is opposed to imperialism. When in 1922 Gandhiji was imprisoned, Russell wrote "... the living saint prophet has been gaoled. What consequences it will bring to imperialism." He bitterly attacked imperialistic policy of England and wrote, "Is it not savagery of British imperialism that four hundred million of God fearing human beings have been bound hand and feet behind the fast moving Chariot of British Imperialism ruthlessly dragging them over hard stones and whipping at their naked backs, if they feel too weak to drag."

Russell's opinion that rule of the people means that people should allow themselves to be governed and led by most capable individuals, is true. Perhaps no modern democracy can do without being popular, at the same time capable leaders, "have a tendency to develop into the cult of dictator." But it is at the same time also true that "Sentiment of democracy if it is sufficiently intelligent and alert will at once put a substantially effective check upon it."

Evaluation. L.F. White sees four aspects of the work of Russell which need comment :

1. He is one of the greatest mathematician of our age.

2. His importance as a philosopher.

3. He is a great populariser of scientific and philosophical ideas.

4. He has become the mediator with the limited power of expression in an extremely technical vocabulary and the non-specialist language. He has been able to interpret in the broadest possible way the generalizations and achievements of scientists to the ordinary public. It may bring to him enduring fame.

"Russell" says William Durant, "has poured into his philosophy the mysticism and the sentiment which he had so resolutely repressed in his attitude towards metaphysics and religion. He has not applied to his economic and political theories the same rigid scrutiny of assumptions, the same scepticism of axioms, which gave him such satisfaction in mathematics and logic. His passion for *a priori*, his love of perfection more than life, lead him here to splendid picture that serves rather as poetic relief to the prose of the world than as a practicable approach to the problems of life."

Mahatma Gandhi calls him a Karmyogi. Krushchev on 10th May 1961 called him "a courageous fighter for peace." Pandit Nehru observes, "Russell is indeed, the greatest living philosopher and thinker of our age .... Russell's greatness lies in his wonderful capacity of bringing about a harmonious synthesis between the deep philosophical reflections and the concrete facts of science."

Russell, according to Dr. Radhakrishnan, is "an embodiment of all perfection". But Prof. Suda is of opinion, for philosophy of love and compassion we should look to Gandhi than Laski, Cole or Russell, so we may proceed to Gandhian philosophy. The view of Russell has been to establish peace all over the world, so he had always condemned war and condemned Indo-Pakistan conflict as well as Vietnam war.

After these thinkers, now ideas of Behaviouralism, traditionalists and of Post-Behaviouralism and Neoclassical theory and Integrated approach and about Autonomous Character of Political Science along with Empirical and Normative theories came into existence in Western political thought, so before proceeding to modern Indian political thought, a brief description of new western ideas is given here.

NOTES

1. Quoted by Kingsley Martin in *Harold Laski : A Biographical Memories,* p. 9.
2. *Social Theory,* Chapter V, p. 96, 4th edition.
3. *Roads to Freedom,* pp. 144-45.

8
New Political Traditions in the West

Recently new political thoughts have been propounded by Western thinkers, therefore, brief introduction is given below :

BEHAVIOURALISM — MEANING, ASSUMPTIONS AND CRITICISM

Meaning of Behaviouralism

According to J. David Easton, Behaviouralism is a psychological concept originating with J.B. Watson and aiming at the elimination from scientific research of all references to such subjective data as purposes, intentions, desires or ideas. It puts emphasis on the validity of only that data which is based on observations obtained through the use of sense organs or mechanical equipment to be admitted as data. By the passage of time, even the psychologists began to realise that between the external stimulus and the observable response, there are some subjective experiences. These experience influence the interpretation and effects of the stimulus and thereby the nature of the response — thus replacing S.R. paradigm (stimulus-response) with S.O.R. paradigm (stimulus-organism-response). Evidently the correct adjective for the new development of political science concentrating on the study of political behaviour is behaviouralist, as is borne out in the titles of various institutions. A few examples are : The Centre for Advanced Study in the Behavioural Sciences at Stanford, Behavioural Science Division of the Ford Foundation, Institute of Behavioural Sciences at the University of Colorado, and the journals of *Behavioural Science* and *The American Behavioural Scientist.* David Easton has warned repeatedly against using the term "behaviouristic" for behavioural as it would be entirely confusing and misleading about the scope and direction of interest of the institution or publication involved.

According to Robert Dahl, behaviouralism is "a protest movement within political science ... associated with a number of political scientists, mainly American", who shared (a) "a strong sense of dissatisfaction with the achievements of conventional political science, particularly through historical, philosophical and the descriptive-institutional approaches" and (b) "a belief that additional methods and approaches either existed or could be developed that would help to provide political science with empirical propositions and theories of a systematic sort, tested by closer, more direct and more rigorously controlled observations of political events." Dahl adds that behaviouralism is a movement for "bringing political studies into closer affiliation with theories, methods, findings, and outlooks in modern psychology, sociology, anthropology and economics". It is an attempt to make the empirical component of political science more scientific. It "aims at *stating all the phenomena of government in terms of observed and observable* behaviour of men." It calls for "closer attention to methodological niceties, to problems of observation and verification, to the task of giving operational meaning to political concepts, to quantification and testing, to eliminating unproductive intervening variables, to sources of data hypothesis and theory in the other social sciences" in search of "explanations of some important aspects of politics that are more thoroughly verified, less open to methodological objections richer in implications for further explanation, and more useful in meeting the perennial problems of political life than the explanations they are intended to replace."

Nature of Behaviouralism. There are three main opinions about the nature of Behaviouralism.

1. Behaviouralism not only a Mood. Robert Dahl has raised the fundamental question if the behavioural approach is anything more than a "mood" — of protest, scepticism, reform or optimism about the possibilities of improving the study of politics; if it consists of definite belief assumptions, methods, or topics constituting political behaviour or the behavioural approach. The SSRC Report of 1944-45 and David Easton in his *Political System*, 1953, answer this question in the affirmative. Behaviouralism is more than a mood, as the researcher working with the concept of political behaviour wishes to look at participants in the political system as individuals who have the emotions, prejudices, and predispositions of human beings. "Behavioural research," writes Easton "seeks to elevate the actual human being to the centre of attention. Its premise is that the traditionalists have been ratifying institutions virtually looking at them as entities apart from their component individuals". But others differ.

2. Opposite View. However, according to Alfred de Grazia of Chicago University, a member of SSRC Committee on Political

Behaviour, and editor of *PROD*, Behaviouralism was not and could not be referred to as "a subject matter, an interdisciplinary focus, quantification, any specific efforts at new methods, behaviourist psychology, 'realism' as opposed to 'idealism', empiricism in contrast with deductive systems, or voting behaviour".

3. Third View. According to a third view, behaviouralism is nothing more than "an attempt to make the empirical component of the discipline more scientific". Robert Dahl has explained this view well. According to this view, behaviouralism is an "approach" aimed at improving our understanding of politics "by seeking to explain the empirical aspect of political life by means of methods, theories, and criteria of proof that are acceptable according to the canons, conventions, and assumptions of modern empirical science."

According to Dahl, it is "simply an attempt to make the empirical components of the discipline more scientific, as that term is generally understood in the empirical sciences". This view is also supported by David Truman. In a seminar on political behaviour research held at the University of Chicago in 1951, he defined political behaviour as comprehending "those actions and interactions of men and groups which are involved in the process of governing ...". David Truman opines that all that behavioural political science demands, is that (a) "research must be systematic" and (b) it "must place primary emphasis upon empirical methods". He defines "systematic research" as "a precise statement of hypotheses, and a rigorous ordering of evidence."

The Middle Course. David Truman has avoided the two extremes and adopted a middle course. These extremes were :

1. First Extreme — The Behaviouralists. He did not follow the extreme behaviouralists, who would refuse to make any difference between political science and other social sciences or stop at nothing but quantification and mathematigation of the highest order.

2. Second Extreme — The Traditionalists. Nor did he follow the extreme traditionalists, who would refuse to identify political science with other sciences and reject all attempts at quantification as irrelevant and futile, and regard values to be an indispensable part of the study of politics.

Truman's Course. In this way David Truman avoided to attach too much of importance either to borrowing from other social sciences or to quantification, etc. He admitted that political science should learn from the findings of the other social sciences, yet he did not favour indiscriminate borrowings. He opined that the political scientist should perform his task "in quantitative terms, if he can, and in qualitative terms, if he must". Yet, he realized that the significance of values cannot be completely eliminated from political science studies. He put emphasis on the study of "determinants of man's behaviour"; they had got to be taken into consideration. He gave due regards to the values of the investigator. These values played a role as important in social sciences as in natural sciences in the selection of the objects for study and in determining the lines of enquiry. However, David Truman expected the investigator to keep his own values out of the picture as far as possible. He suggested the behavioural political scientist to take the advantage of the historical knowledge. Historical knowledge was likely to be "an essential supplement to contemporary observation of political behaviour" and as much from it. But while doing so, the investigator should avoid traditions. He argued that "any new departure in an established discipline, must build upon the accomplishments of the past. Although much of the existing literature of politics may be impressionistic, it is extensive and rich in insights. Without a command of the significant portions of that literature, behavioural research ... is likely to be native and unproductive."

Estimate. The above views expressed by David Truman are highly appreciated by the critics. Robert Dahl calls his essay as "wise, judicious, and until very recently neglected essay". He suggests that these characteristics of behavioural political science should be properly understood and accepted by the partisans and critics of the behavioural approach. If they had done so, in his words, "much of the irrelevant, fruitless and ill-informed debates over the behavioural approach over the past decade need never occurred - or at any rate might have been conducted on a rather higher level of intellectual sophistication."

Assumptions and Objectives of Behaviouralism. David Easton has enumerated in his works certain assumptions and objectives of behaviouralism. He regards them as "the intellectual foundation stones" on which this movement has been constructed. These assumptions are : (1) Regularities, (2) Verification, (3) Techniques, (4) Quantification, (5) Values, (6) Systematization, (7) Pure Science and (8) Integration. Here it may be pointed out that these assumptions, besides many other ones of Behaviouralists have been badly criticized by Traditionalists. Their main grounds of criticism are as under :

1. The Behaviouralists have made the discipline more self-conscious and self-critical.

2. They have opened the discipline to vital interdisciplinary influences.

3. The Behaviouralists are aware of the limitations of their theories and conceptual frames of reference and the restrictiveness of

their fields of operationaity, co-exist in a fair state of harmony and understanding.

The main components of Behaviouralism as pointed out by David Easton and other Behaviouralists are given below :

1. Regularities. The Behaviouralists believe that there are certain discernible uniformities in political behaviour. These uniformities can be expressed in generalisations or theories. These theories are capable of explaining and predicting political phenomena. They admit that political behaviour is determined by so many factors, and consequently, it is not always uniform, yet, human beings are observed to behave in certain respects in a more or less similar manner on different occasions. To illustrate, the voters have been known to vote in the same manner, for the same individual or political party, through successive elections. Their voting behaviour can be linked up with their social status, economic position, professional loyalties, regional and caste affiliations, etc. On the basis of this study, a pattern may very well emerge. They hope that on the basis of the observations of the regularities of behaviour, they can explain and predict political phenomena. Political science can, thus, ultimately become a science, capable of explanation and prediction. It is admitted that, due to inherent weaknesses and instability of human nature, political science may not come very close to natural sciences like physics or chemistry, yet it could certainly become comparable to biology or astronomy, *i.e.*, total correctness is not possible but approximate conclusion can be drawn.

Criticism by Traditionalists. The above view is not accepted by Traditionalists. They hold that it is impossible for political science to become a science. They give arguments as under :

(a) Rigorous Study not Possible. First of all, the political phenomena cannot be subjected to any rigorous study. Human behaviour cannot be studied with the objectivity, while objectivity is necessary in the acquisition of scientific knowledge.

(b) Beyond Experimental Inquiry. Political phenomena are not amenable to experimental inquiry. Political phenomena contain too many variables and historical contingencies. Thus, a political scientist can make, at the most, only a very general kind of statement of regularities. But this statement cannot lead to generalisation, or the discovery of laws of human behaviour in all circumstances.

(c) Of no Validity. The Traditionalists argue that in case it is admitted that such laws could be discovered, they would have no validity because human ingenuity was always capable of evading them.

(d) Useless Attempt. The Traditionalists argue that the attempts of the Behaviouralists are of not say much avail. They that a purely descriptive approach was also equally advantageous. They add that an analysis of political phenomena, based on minute description and arrangement of its various aspects in a sequence of development, has proved its worth in the past. It will continue to be an important factor in our understanding of political phenomena through history, but not future.

To sum up, the Traditionalists hold that regularities in political behaviour cannot be discovered as the political reality consists largely of unique elements. In case any regularities are discovered, they would be of a trivial nature. These arguments have not been able to convince the Behaviouralists. They realise that a certain number of political phenomena cannot be subjected to scientific scrutiny and research. Yet, it does not mean that we must give up all such attempts. Instead, it is worthwhile to use still more sophisticated tools of research.

2. Verification. Behaviouralists believe that knowledge, should consist of propositions that have been subjected to empirical tests. They desire that all evidences must be based on observations to them. Political science is concerned primarily with phenomena which can actually be observed — with what is said or done, with the behaviour of individuals and/or political aggregates.

Criticism by Traditionalists. The Traditionalists are not convinced with Behaviouralists as the phenomena which can be actually observed form only a small part of the entire story. Hence an investigator should be prepared to go beyond observable behaviour. Moreover, individuals or groups do not behave in a vacuum. Instead of it, their behaviour is determined, by and large, by the institutional and the social setting in which they work. Knowledge of that setting is, therefore, essential to a meaningful explanation of the behaviour. They argue that we cannot ignore the study of what goes on beneath the surface of human action as motives are difficult to be studied.

Reply of Behaviouralists. The Behaviouralists do not admit that they are ignoring what is beneath the surface. On the contrary to it, they too are interested in subsurface dynamics. However, in their opinion, it is not so unknowable as the Traditionalists seem to think.

3. Techniques. Behaviouralists plead for adopting correct techniques for acquiring and interpreting data, and the use of research tools or methods. They are sure that these generate valid, reliable and comparative data. They also insist on using sophistical tools — like multivariate analysis, sample surveys, mathematical models, simulation, etc., because, this would enable the researcher to discount his own "value" preferences in planning, executing and assessing his research work. According to them, the technique should be refined and validated. As a result, rigorous means could be found for observing, recording and analysing data, etc.

Criticism by Traditionalists. However, the Traditionalists point out that data in social sciences can never be objective because passion follows the reason. As such, it is futile to exalt technique at the cost of content. They fear that too much self-consciousness about methodology may impede the pursuit of knowledge.

4. Quantification. Behaviouralists emphasise that recourse should be taken to *measurement and quantification*. They argue that imprecise qualitative judgements should be replaced by vigorous measurement and data manipulation procedures. Otherwise, it would be impossible to obtain precise and accurate knowledge about the complexities of political life. Their suggestion is : (a) as we find in other sciences, data for research in political science should be quantified and (b) all "findings" should be based upon quantifiable data.

Criticism by Traditionalists. The Traditionalists opine that quantification is an unattainable goal — a vain attempt to "quantify" the unquantifiable and "measure" the unmeasurable. They add that quantification requires extremely precise concepts and matrices, which political science does not possess. Significant questions cannot be quantified. They argue that it is impossible to mathematicige, that which is by its very nature both imprecise and immeasurable and uncertain.

5. Values. Behaviouralists hold that ethical evaluation is different from empirical explanation. Values and facts are two separate things. Hence one should keep them analytically distinct. They may be studied separately, or even in combination, but the one should not be mixed up with the other. To illustrate, democracy, equality or freedom may by excellent values to uphold, but their truth or falsity cannot be proved in a scientific manner. Scientific inquiry to be objective must be value-free. Behaviouralists do not altogether oppose values. Values might be brought in for scientific analysis to the extent they determine political behaviour, as in the case of voting. However, it is desirable that the researcher must keep his own values rigidly aloof from his studies. They hold that political science is a scientific study of politics in its functional aspect, carried through empirical methods. As such, it has nothing to do with moral or ethical questions etc.

Criticism by Traditionalists. The Traditionalists do not accept this plea. They say that significant political issues invariably involve moral and ethical issues, and political science is bound to show concern with questions of right and wrong, even if it might not be possible to resolve them "scientifically". They do not accept the plea of Behaviouralists that values cannot be demonstrated as true or false. They add, the researcher cannot keep his value preferences away from his study. They inevitably creep into his research. Even from the back-door, it will succeed in understanding the political aspect of his social life which he is keen to study.

The Traditionalists admit that in many areas in the study of political phenomena, an interdisciplinary approach is useful, but too much emphasis on interdependence of the political phenomena under study to other aspects of the individual's behaviour may result in losing the sight of what he is primarily interested in, namely the study of the political behaviour. Hence, it is essential to preserve the identity, integrity and autonomy of political science.

6. Systematization. It is claimed by the Behaviouralists that research in political science should be systematic. By the term "systematic" they mean that it must be "theory-oriented and theory-directed". They hold that theory and research should form as "closely inter-related parts of a coherent and orderly body of knowledge". The reason is, that "research, untutored by theory, may prove trivial and theory, unsupported by data, futile." The Behaviouralists claim that in this way, they are putting a greater emphasis on theory than the Traditionalists. However, unlike Traditionalists who talk in terms of value theory, they are evolving a causal theory. Theory should consist of the analysis, explanation, prediction, etc. The hypotheses should advance on the basis of a well-organized, logically inter-related, structure of concepts and propositions. The hypotheses also have to be capable of undergoing rigorous testing, and then alone, should form the basis of new theories. They have discussed various levels of theories. These are :

Low Level. (i) The theory may be low level consisting of singular generalizations. (ii) The theory may be middle level, synthetic or narrow gauge. (iii) The theory may be "general", broad gauge, systematic or overarching.

However, the ultimate objective of Behaviouralists' research is the development of overarching "generalizations". They aim at discovering laws for describing and inter-relating political phenomena with as great an accuracy as laws of mechanics or physics.

The Traditionalists regard it as ridiculous to talk of an "overarching", or "general", theory because in political science there are no accepted low-and middle-level formulations.

7. Pure Science. Behaviouralists insist on the "pure science" approach. The theoretical understanding may lead to an application of this knowledge to problems of life. Both the theory and its application are parts of the scientific enterprise. But the understanding and explanation of political behaviour provide the basis for efforts for the utilization of that knowledge in the solution of urgent practical problems of society. As such, they pay greater importance to pure research. They would not be discontented if it fails to be applied to specific and minimum social problems. They have rejected "majority, programmatic ventures", as these ventures produce little valid scientific knowledge.

Criticism by Traditionalists. The Traditionalists hold that theory has no value unless it is applied to the political problems of society and helps us in finding out solutions to them. The social scientists should aim at understanding social phenomena as to find out how a proper solution of the existing difficulties can be found and the society can be reformed.

8. Integration. As regards the question of integration of political science with other social sciences, the Behaviouralists agree that man is a social animal. A person may distinguish and draw boundary lines between his various activities, *e.g.*, social, political, economic, cultural, etc. yet none of these activities can be understood without placing them in the wider context of his entire life. As such, while studying a political phenomenon, there is need of understanding, how the economic, cultural and other phenomena in society are unfolding themselves. If political man is separated from the economic, social or cultural man, his political behaviour will never be understood. On the contrary to it, a political scientist is aware of this interrelationship between one aspect of the individual's life and another.

BEHAVIOURALISM'S CRITICISM BY TRADITIONALISTS

Criticism of Behaviouralism as offered by Traditionalists and the Main Bases on which Traditionalists have criticized Behaviouralism.`

Though the traditional political scientists have appreciated the Behaviouralist approach on a number of points, yet, there are a few critical areas in which they find it almost impossible to reconcile themselves with the position taken by the Behaviourlists. Although they admit that Behaviouralism in its several forms has an important contribution to make in the study of politics, they find behavioural approach to be adequate in itself for an understanding of politics. They hold that Behavioural tools can help us in the analysis and understanding of the parts or the relationship between parts, as well as in understanding the relationship between the parts and the whole. But these tools are far too inadequate to be able to comprehend the realities of the whole. They opine that the "politicist", *i.e.*, the political scientist cannot remain confined to be a Behaviouralist. Instead he has to be a historian, a lawyer, an ethicist. Mulford Sibley says, "To understand politics implies the kind of insight characteristic of the artist, as well as the precision which we usually associate with science — the comprehension of interrelations of parts to wholes in addition to the analysis of parts themselves."

The Traditionalists state the following drawbacks or shortcomings of the Behaviouralists.

1. Lacking Clear-cut Starting. Traditionalists say that the Behaviouralists proceed to study politics without first defining what politics is and how it is to be distinguished from non-political things. It leads to the conclusion that the Bevavioural political scientists are prepared to adopt more and more the concepts evolved in the fields of sociology, psychology, psychiatry, etc. although they do not know how the political sphere can be demarcated from the sphere of society or human mind. Its evil consequences are before us as we find the political science research of the behavioural era being dominated by the professional scholars of sociology, psychology, psychiatry, etc. who lack expert knowledge of politics.

2. Politics not defined Behaviourally. The Traditionalists contend that politics cannot be defined behaviourally. Instead it can only be grasped by the "eye of the mind". Sibley states, "Whatever the value we attribute to behavioural studies as such — and here we include under the term both the scientific theory and the process of verification — the ideas with which we begin and the conceptions which lead us to scientific investigation must rest ultimately on overall insights, and what Leo Strauss has called pre-scientific knowledge, as well as on something very akin to aesthetic experience."

3. Behaviouralists unable to forecast. It is admitted by the Traditionalists that behavioural methods can accomplish many things in the fields of scientific exploration and scientific prediction. However, they warn that scientific prediction should not be confused with forecasting. The "scientific" predictions of the political scientist remain confined to "if-then" propositions. To illustrate, it can be said that if certain things happen, certain other things might be predicted. However, Behaviouralists cannot say with any definiteness that things are bound to happen in a particular way.

4. Limited Field. The Traditionalists argue that there are many things which the political scientist tries to understand, and about which the Behaviouralist approach fails to give us any proper understanding. For example, the Behavioural research is unable to tell us what goals we are to seek as ends in themselves. Arnold Brech says that (1) "The question whether something is 'valuable' can be answered scientifically only in relation to (a) some goal or purpose for the pursuit of which it is or is not useful (valuable), or to (b) the ideas held by some person or group of persons regarding what is or is not valuable; and that, consequently, (2) it is impossible to establish scientifically what goals or purposes are valuable irrespective of (a) the value they have in the pursuit of other goals or surposes, or (b) of someone's ideas about ulterior or ultimate goals or purposes."

5. Limited Use. Traditionalists admit that the behavioural approach is useful only up to a point. Joseph R. Royce, a psychologist, writes that we may be keen enough to apply the "scientific method" to "any and all problems", but "the final putting together of the segments of life will always be a highly subjective and individual task... which cannot be scientized." Sibely states, "... if-then behavioural science takes us far out of the world of macro-cosmic political 'reality' into the universe of pure scientific speculation, and it is indeed an important universe to which we are invited by behavioural scientist." Sibely adds, "But if the understanding of politics includes comprehension not only of conduct as it could be under specified conditions but also of what it is, has been, will be and ought to be ... we must turn not only to the Behaviouralist but also to the historian of political ideas, the moral philosopher, the cultural historian, the speculative political philosopher of the classical tradition, the descriptive politicist, and the man of direct political experience.' Limited use points out its shortcomings.

6. Inadequacy. The Traditionalists hold that Behavioural approach is inadequate from the point of view of policy-making in all its aspects, the moral, the empirical and also the legislative. The Behaviouralist can not contribute anything to the first aspect, which involves awareness and formulation of the value hierarchies which are to be used. It may be a bit relevant in the second aspect. However, it cannot transcend his understanding of fragments and go to an understanding of the whole, which involves practically no use in the third, the legislative, aspect, built as it is upon the foundations of practical science and philosophy. To the argument that behavioural political science may be able to tackle all these problems when it comes of age and when it develops still more sophisticated tools for the understanding of larger problems. The Traditionalists point out that the limitations of behavioural science cannot be removed. It can never become perfect. The reason is, the limitations are inherent in the if-then nature of hypothetical knowledge itself. They argue that, "It requires more than behaviourally derived statement to 'understand' politics... there are other methods of understanding than those of science." Some other critics also opine that the practice of emphasizing the behavioural approach beyond all other approaches and the exclusive reliance on "scientific methods" has proved harmful. Alfred Cobban states that it has reduced political science, "a device, invented by university teachers for avoiding that dangerous subject politics, without achieving a science."

POST-BEHAVIOURALISM — MAIN ASSUMPTIONS

The Factors that led to the Rise of Post-Behavioural Revolution and the Main Assumptions of Post-Behaviouralism

The Behavioural revolution seemed to be satisfactory for some time. But such a state did not remain for any longer. Although David Easton was one of the leading advocates of the revolution, yet it was he, who towards the end of the 1960s made a powerful attack on the Behaviouralist position and their thinking.

Factors giving Birth to Post-Behaviouralism. The following factors gave birth to the Post-Behavioural revolution :

(i) Discontentment. The Post-behavioural revolution arose out of a deep dissatisfaction with the kind of political research and teaching in the American universities in the 1950s and 1960s. It was felt that this process was trying to convert the study of politics into a more rigorously scientific discipline based on the methodology of the natural sciences.

(ii) Wastage of Time. It was alleged by the Behaviouralists, now turned Post-Behaviouralists, that too much time had been spent by them on trivial, and irrelevant research.

(iii) Unaware of the Need of Time. The Post-Behaviouralists condemn the behavioural thinkers on the ground that at a time, while they were engaged in the building up of various paradigms, conceptual frameworks, models, theories and meta-theories, the world was facing more and more acute social, economic and cultural crises. However, they seemed to be completely unaware of these problems.

(iv) Assiduous Readers in Libraries. The Behaviouralists worked assiduously in their libraries, situated in the ivory towers of exclusive university campuses, worrying over problems of stability, equilibrium, pattern maintenance, etc. without paying attention to practical problems.

(v) Unaware of their Surroundings. The Behaviouralists were unaware of the fear of the nuclear bomb, mounting internal cleavages in the United States, an undeclared war in Vietnam that violated the moral conscience of the world. These were the fearful conditions which no school of political science, whether behavioural or traditional had predicted. Change is inevitable law of life and Behaviouralists cannot predict about changes.

(vi) Useless Research. A question arose from various corners, if there was any use of this kind of research which did not take note of these acute social maladies and problems.

(vii) Doubtful Technical Adequacy. The Post-Behaviouralists felt that there was no use of developing high technical adequacy and sophisticated research tools, if the political scientist was not able to comprehend contemporary social and political problems and make his own contribution towards resolving them.

In the above said situation it had become apparent that some new approach was needed. "Must we be committed eternally," asked David Easton "to an unchanging image of the discipline, behavioural or otherwise? Is it not incumbent on us to take account of changing conditions and to be ready and willing to reconsider old images and modify them to the extent deemed necessary?"

Nature of Post-Behaviouralism. Post-Behaviouralism was a revolt against Behaviouralism. But, it does not mean that it was Traditionalism. Although it was critical of Behaviouralism, its distinction from Traditionalism was quite clear. It can be explained as given below :

(i) Validity of Behavioural Approach. Whereas traditionalism denied the validity of behavioural approach and reiterated its faith in the classical traditions of political science, the Post-Behaviouralist accepts the achievements of the bahavoural era.

(ii) Further Development. Traditionalism is reactionary while Post-Behaviouralism seeks to push political science farther and towards new horizons. Post-Behaviouralism, as Easton pointed out, was future-oriented, seeking to propel political science in new directions. It was a "a genuine revolution, not a reaction; a becoming, not a preservation; a reform not a counter-reformation."

(iii) A Movement. Traditionalists stuck to traditions while Post-Behaviouralism was both a movement and an intellectual tendency.

Post-Behaviouralism all Comprising. One should not identify Post-Behaviouralism with any particular political ideology, since its advocates included political scientists of all hues and colours. They were not only rank conservatists but extreme leftists also. They were of all methodological commitments - rigorous scientists as dedicated classicists, and of all age groups. All this diversity was threaded together by one sentiment alone, a deep discontent with the direction of contemporary political research.

Traits of Post-Behaviouralism. Post-Behaviouralism puts two demands. These are : relevance and action. Easton came out with seven major traits of Post-Behaviouralism and described them as the "Credo of Relevance" or "a distillation of the maximal image". They can be summarised as given below :

1. Substance followed by Technique. In political science research, substance must come before technique. Although sophisticated tools of investigation are needed yet the more important point is the purpose to which these tools were being applied. The scientific research should be relevant and meaningful for contemporary urgent social problems. Otherwise, it would not be worth being undertaken. The slogan raised by the Behaviouralists that it was better to be wrong, than vague, was replaced by the Post-Behaviouralists' counter-slogan that it was better to be vague than non-relevantly precise.

2. Emphasis on Social Change. Contemporary political science should lay emphasis on social change, instead of social preservation, as the Behaviouralists seemed to be doing. The Behaviouralists had confined themselves exclusively to the description and analysis of facts, without understanding these facts in their broad social context. As a result of it, behavioural political science came to be "an ideology of social conservatism tempered by modest incremental change," while change is law of life.

3. To be close to Reality. Political science, during the behavioural period, had severed itself from the brute realities of politics. Since the heart of behavioural inquiry was abstraction and analysis, the political scientists could not keep their eyes open to the realities of the situation. The times were of crisis and anxiety. The political scientist, being affected by Behaviouralism, did not pay any attention to the western world which was moving towards increasing social conflicts and deepening fears and anxieties about the future. Post-Behaviouralists asserted that it was the responsibility of the political scientist to reach out to the real needs of mankind. Otherwise political science was of no use to society.

4. Values not to be neglected. Behaviouralists' role of value had put excessive and even uncalled for emphasis on scientificism and value-free approaches. Consequently, values had been, for all practical purposes, thrown out of consideration. This was a very unhappy situation. They forgot, in their zeal, that it was on value premises that all knowledge stood. In case values were not regarded as the propelling force behind knowledge, there was a danger that knowledge would be used for wrong purposes. Values have an important role to play in politics and research. Values had to be restored to the central position for using knowledge for right goals and results.

5. Responsibility of the Political Scientists. The Post-Behaviouralists conveyed a message to the political scientists that, being intellectuals, they had a role to play — "major tasks to perform" — in society. They ought to do the best to protect the humane values of civilization. If the political scientists, in their zeal or efforts for detachment and objectivity and time-consuming research, overlooked the social problems they would become "mere technicians, mechanics for tinkering with society", their purposes of study would be defeated and its utility will be lost.

6. Demand for Contemplative Science. Post-Behaviouralists opine that it is the duty of the intellectuals to understand the social problems and feel themselves involved in them. In such a position, they would not be able to keep themselves away from action. Knowledge must be put to work. "To know", as Easton describes, "is to bear the responsibility for acting and to act is to engage in reshaping society." Contemplative science might have been the demand of the nineteenth century. Because, at that time, there was a broader moral agreement among nations. But the contemporary society is sharply divided over ideals and ideologies. In such a society, there is need for action science in place of a contemplative science.

7. Politicisation. The Post-Behaviouralists put emphasis on two assumptions : (a) The intellectuals have a positive role to play in society. (b) This role is to try to determine proper goals for society and make society move in the direction of these goals to achieve them.

It can be concluded from the foregoing two assumptions that the politicisation of the professions — of all professional associations as well as universities — becomes not only inescapable but highly desirable.

Post-Behaviouralists' Image of Science. It was argued by the Behaviouralists that science had some ideal commitments, and that Behaviouralism shared these ideal commitments of science. The Post-Behaviouralists contend if science led its votaries to close their eyes in the face of urged social problems, the very image of science should change. Before presenting their outlook, it is worth our while to go into the Behaviouralist image of science. It had so far been associated mainly with the following things :

(a) A technical proficiency in research for reliable knowledge.

(b) The pursuit of basic understanding, with its necessary divorce from practical concerns.

(c) The exclusion of value sophistication as something beyond the competence of science.

The Post-Behaviouralists admitted the importance of technical proficiency. But they did not agree to the following on — (a) The plea that the search for basic understanding and reliable knowledge implied that the scientist should cut himself adrift from the practical concerns of society, (b) That values could be kept out of all scientific pursuits.

Post-behaviouralists held that the following should be the purposes of research and of researchers : (i) Research was to be related to urgent social problems and was to be *purposive*. (ii) A political scientist must find out solutions to contemporary problems. (iii) The objective of a political scientist could not be mere stability or the maintenance of the *status quo*. (iv) Political science in its tools of research should no longer remain subservient to the task of preserving the existing social order. (v) The research should be *relevant* to the understanding of these social problems. (vi) In addition to suggesting solutions, the political scientists must play the leading role in *acting* for the desired social change. (vii) It is the duty of the political scientists to take necessary actions for resolution of the conflicts if the present crisis in society arose out of deep social conflicts. (viii) In case the resolution of the conflicts needed breaking up of the existing political order, the political scientist should boldly ask for that. (ix) A political scientist must not rest content with suggesting reforms but contribute his best to the reshaping of society. He should make his maximum efforts for reshaping the society in the direction in which it could serve the desired goals more effectively and positively.

NEOCLASSICAL THEORY

Main Assumptions of Neoclassical Theory

The neoclassical thinkers are those contemporary political thinkers, who not only continue to defend and uphold the traditional-classical political theory but severely criticise the empirical-analytical approaches. They may not be very large in numbers but they belong to different countries and exercise a great deal of influence over a large number of their students and admirers. Michael Oakeshott, Hannah Arendt, Bertrand, Jouvenel, Leo Strauss and Eric Voegelin, etc., are prominent among these political thinkers.

Michael Oakeshott. Michael Oakeshott took over the chair of

Political Science in the London School of Economics and Political Science from Harold Laski in 1951. The scholars identify him with the resurgence of conservative thinking in England. However, Dr. Vibasi holds that Oakeshott was not merely a conservative. He made successful efforts to recover political theory as a tradition of enquiry and regain for political science the possibility of a critical, theoretical analysis. He enunciated a doctrine which was completely different from Behaviouralists. He did this in his lectures and seminars to his students at the London School of Economics and through his publications. His philosophical analysis was based on experience which seeks to rediscover the multidimensionality that had been denied to experience by the ideological and positivist writers. His main views may be summarised as given below :

1. Distinction between Philosophy and Science. Michael Oakeshott treats philosophy and science as basically two different kinds of activities. He states that any attempt to transfer the methods and concerns of the one to the other is wrong. He writes that, "The notion that philosophy has anything to learn from the methods of scientific thought is altogether false". Philosophy must be pursued for its own sake, and must "maintain its independence from all extraneous interests, and particularly from the practical interest."

2. Limited Activity of Political Philosophy. In his opinion, political philosophy is a limited activity within the context of the larger role of philosophising — in his words, the attempt "to see particular mode of experience — practical experience — from the standpoint of the totality of experience."

3. Levels of Reflection. Michael Oakeshott opines that reflection about political life can be at a variety of levels. It has the tendency to flow from one level to another. On the contrary to it, political philosophy is, in our minds, the world of political activity and also "another world," and our endeavour is to explore "the coherence of the two worlds together."

4. Nature of Political Philosophy. Oakeshott opines that political philosophy is "the consideration of the relation between politics and eternity." "Politics is contributory to the fulfilment of an end which it cannot itself bring about."

5. Criticism of Behaviouralists' views. Oakeshott attacks Behaviouralists' views about political science as political philosophy a "progressive" science which accumulates social results and reaches conclusions leading to further research.

6. Integrated to History. Political science to him is closely integrated to history — "indeed, in a sense it has nothing but a history, which is a history of the problems philosophers have detected and the manner of solution they have proposed, rather than a history of doctrines...." History and Political Science are related.

Hannah Arendt. Hannah Arendt is a more prolific writer. She claims to have published extensively on the major problems of political theory and established her reputation as a thinker of exceptional originality. Her ideas can be summarised as given below :

(i) Uniqueness of Individual. She believes in the uniqueness and responsibility of the individual human being. Individuals possess their own personality.

(ii) Opponent of Totalitarianism. Hannah is opposed to totalitarianism of all kinds.

(iii) Opponent of Behaviouralism. Hannah Arendt is an opponent of the Behaviouralist approach in social sciences. She thinks that this approach prepares the ground for Totalitarianism. She fears that this approach, in its search of uniformity in human behaviour, will itself contribute to the making of a uniform stereotyped "man". In her own words, "The unfortunate truth about Behaviourism and the validity of its 'laws' is that the more people there are, the more likely they are to behave and the less likely to tolerate non-behaviour." Hannah is afraid of the evil consequences that are likely to follow the Behavioural approach. She gives example of Eichmann, who was responsible for sending off train-loads of Jews to the place of their execution in the most punctilious and efficient manner. She brands him to be a typical example of the kind of man that this system thinking of our time is likely to produce. In this way, this system will produce a creature, who knew how to "behave" efficiently, but had suppressed entirely the knowledge of how to "act" responsibly and properly.

Bertrand de Jouvenel. Like Hannah, de Jouvenel also believes that politics has a potentiality for creative activity. It should not be transformed into the dead uniformity of administration. His main ideas may be summarised as given below :

(i) Opposition to Totalitarianism. Like Hannah, de Jouvenel is against Totalitarianism, which threatens to become the predominant phenomenon of the twentieth century. He has tried to examine its intellectual and moral roots with his expert knowledge.

(ii) Opposition to making Political Science Value Free. de Jouvenel, although less passionate and more careful in making evaluations, yet, like Hannah Arendt, strongly believes that political science cannot and should not be value free. It must possess values.

(iii) Emphasis on Evolving Criteria. de Jouvenel believes that instead of spending time over trying to discover uniformities in human behaviour, political scientists must evolve valid criteria for evaluating major developments in the life of the society.

(iv) Defining Politics. He defines politics "as an activity that builds; consolidates and keeps in being aggregates of men."

(v) Conception of Society. His conception of society is that it rests ultimately on authority rather than on force or consent. Consent is not spontaneous but has to be promoted or aroused as such authority is basic.

(vi) Aristotelean Concept of Politics. de Jouvenel's concept of politics is Aristotelean, in the sense that he regards politics as a far more pervasive activity than what the government does. It is an activity which covers the entire social existence of human beings.

Leo Strauss. Leo Strauss is Professor of Political Science at the University of Chicago. He is one of the most outstanding contemporary theorists, a supporter of Neoclassical school and a staunch critic of the Behaviouralist approach. He claims to have exercised great impact on American philosophy and political science. In Chicago, a large number of political scientists regard it as their privilege to be considered his disciples. As a true follower of Neoclassical school, he believes in taking the study of political philosophers in general and of Plato, Aristotle and of Greek political philosophers in particular, very seriously. Main characteristics of his views are given below :

(i) His Hellenism. His interest in Greek political philosophers is not out of mere antiquarianism. Instead, he takes interest in ancient political thought, because he is deeply aware of the crisis of the modern civilisation.

(ii) Understanding in an Untraditional Manner. Leo Strauss hopes that the crisis of our time may enable us to understand ancient political thought in "an untraditional or fresh manner" not in a "traditional or derivative manner." For this new approach is necessary.

(iii) Practical Approach. Strauss regards an adequate understanding of the principles as elaborated by the classics as "the indispensable starting point for an adequate analysis, to be achieved by us, of present-day society in its peculiar character, and for the wise application, to be achieved by us, of these principles to our tasks."

(iv) Recapturing Original Intention. Strauss determines to recapture the original intention and meaning of the great writers of the past to question the predominant assumptions of positivist social science and the fact-value dichotomy.

(v) Refutal of the Charge of Ideology. Strauss criticises the view that all political theories are ideological in character, reflecting a given socio-economic interest. A political thinker who is not a philosopher may be interested in a specific order or policy, but "the political philosopher is primarily interested in, or attached to, the truth."

(vi) A Historian. Strauss calls himself as principally a historian. He aims at presenting the political thought of the great political philosophers as they "intended it to be understood." He gives importance to historical approach.

(vii) Studying and Reinterpreting Political Teachings. The primary work of Strauss in the field of political science lies in the study and reinterpretation of the political teachings of masters of political thought such as Plato, Aristotle, Thucydydes, Machiavelli, Hobbes, Locke, etc. He thinks that this was a necessary preliminary effort before the actual rebirth of political theory.

(viii) Classical Political Theory to be Model. According to Leo Strauss, the classical political theory can place a model of what a political theory ought to be before the political theorists of today.

(ix) Flaws of Behaviouralism. According to him, Behaviouralism "views human beings as an engineer would view material for building bridges." This is a wrong approach as human beings possess own thinking power.

(x) Human Activities in Terms of Political Activities. Strauss puts emphasis on understanding human activities in terms of political activities. He states, it is the highest, most distinctively human type of activity. He feels sad to find that Behaviouralism deals with the political as a function of the sub-political. He feels that it has failed to bring to light anything of political importance which intelligent political practitioners with a deep knowledge of history, nay, intelligent and educated journalists, to say nothing of the old political science at its best, did not know at least as well beforehand.

(xi) Wrong Claim to be Value-Neutral. Strauss states that the behavioural political science claims to be value-neutral. Yet it is committed to an implicit value judgement in favour of a society grounded on "permissive egalitarianism" and promotes a creed which can be called "democratism". He puts a premium on observations which can be made with the utmost frequency and, therefore, by people of the meanest capacity. Thus, it frequently culminates in observations made by people who are not intelligent.

(xii) New Political Science not Diabolic. Strauss writes that it is false to "call the new political science diabolic : it has no attributes peculiar to fallen angels....Nor it is Neronian. Nevertheless, one may say of it that it fiddles while Rome burns. It is excused by two facts: it does not know that it fiddles and it does not know that Rome burns."

Eric Vogelin. Eric Vogelin is a prolific writer, though his style is somewhat complicated. His views may be summarised as given below :

(i) No Distinction. According to him, there is no distinction between political theory and political science.

(ii) Meaning of Political Theory. To him, political theory would mean a critical reflection on politics, in the absence whereof there can be no political science.

(iii) Hellenic Impact. Like the ancient Greeks, Vogelin regards political science the *episteme politike,* rooted in *theoria,* or contemplation. He thinks that man never had the materials available and the intellectual climate suitable for great advances in the theoretical analysis as now.

(iv) Opposition of System Building. Vogelin opposes system building in modern philosophy because, in his opinion, the system-constructors are ignorant of the basic experience of existence.

(v) Belief in Metaphysics. Like Bergson, he also believes in a metaphysics which passes "from reality to concepts and no longer from concepts to reality."

(vi) Views on Reality. He opines that "reality" possesses a structure, or constitution, independent of human thinking and willing.

(vii) Aspiration. In his views, it must be the aspiration of the philosopher to attune his thinking to that reality rather than attempt to force that reality to conform to his concepts or ideas, etc.

(viii) Duty of Political Theorist. Vogelin opines that it is the duty of the political theorist to empirically examine, and critically evaluate man's experiences through history. He must seek the light which they shed upon his own search for the truth about order in human society, a task which was superbly done by the Greek philosophers and the Christian theologians.

(ix) Flaws of Modern Political Theorists. Vogelin points out a great flaw in modern political theorists, who would treat political Theory as essentially methodology and its task as merely acting "as the hand-maiden of research into behavioural regularities on the phenomenological level."

(x) True Nature of Political Theory. According to Vogelin, political theory is "an experimental science of right order, based on the total experience of the existing human person."

(xi) The Task of Political Theory. Vogelin thinks that political Theory should elaborate "empirically and critically, the problems of order which derive from philosophical anthropology as part of a general ontology."

INTEGRATED APPROACH

Integrated Approach as Presented by Carl J. Friedrich

It was often argued by the political theorists that political science should not be lost in scientism or moralism. Some other political thinkers have put emphasis on the fact that both the scientific and philosophic aspects of political theory should be properly understood and emphasised.

Meaning of Science. Science has been variously described as under : (i) "A branch of knowledge or study dealing with a body of facts or truths systematically arranged and showing the operation of general laws," (ii) "knowledge, as of facts or principles, gained by systematic study" and (iii) "a branch or body of organised knowledge."

Scientific Approach. It becomes evident from the aforesaid that a scientific approach to the study of problem, involves two things :

(a) the agreement on methods and

(b) the training of human beings in scientific work.

Carl J. Friedrich takes these two aspects into consideration and defines science as "a body of ordered knowledge, known to progressively enlarged by the specialists in that field of knowledge through the use of methods which they as a group accept as workable ways for arriving at that particular kind of knowledge." Science is, thus, "organized" knowledge. Friedrich makes it clear that, "Neither the degree of generalization, nor the degree of quantification, are in themselves 'absolute' criteria of scientific progress, but must be evaluated in relation to the material in hand and to be assessed," and he quotes Aristotle with approval, when he describes it as "the mark of an educated man" "to look for precision in each class of things just so far as the nature of the subject admits."

Need of Several Methods. Friedrich thinks that political science is a comprehensive discipline. As such, it may need not one but several methods. He distinguishes it from sociology or psychology, where the study of the group or the individual is involved, a study which can be carried on through methods involving precision, accuracy, etc. In political science, we deal with the territorial state, state as the largest organised form of society, which changes its character, form and goals from time to time, and from country to country. In every change, there may be need of a different approach or method, or sometimes a combination of different approaches and methods. It may be explained with the help of an illustration. A particular kind of method may be needed by the emergence of a constitutional form of government and its justification. Likewise, the emergence of a totalitarian dictatorship needs quite another kind. In the history of politics, help will be needed of prehistory, history, ethnology, anthropology, psychology and also of several other approaches. It may not be done by the help of any single approach. Instead it may sometimes require documentary method of history, and on another occasion the analytical and case study method of legal studies. Again, on some other occasions, it may need the statistical and interview methods. Hence, it is essential for political theory to continue to possess a scientific character. It leads to the conclusion that science does not necessarily mean the use of the same methodology in social sciences as in natural sciences, like physics and chemistry.

Scientific Character and Philosophical Character. The scientific character of political science does not deprive it of, in any way, having its philosophical character. In order to be a good political theory, it ought to be both philosophical and scientific.

Philosophy. Here it is felt necessary to interpret and define philosophy. Philosophy has been variously defined as under : (i) "the study or science of the truths or principles underlying all knowledge and being (or reality)", (ii) "the study of science of the principles of a particular branch or subject of knowledge" and (iii) "love of wisdom or knowledge, specially that which deals with ultimate reality or with the most general causes and principles of being."

In view of the above diversity in definitions, philosophy can be broadly treated as knowledge of a very general kind.

Bertrand Russell opines that philosophy consists of two parts : (a) it is "a theory as to the nature of the world" and (b) it is "an ethical or political doctrine as to the best way of living." Friedrich also says that philosophy generally deals with problems which can be comprehended within the framework of existing knowledge. However, it does not remain confined to it. Instead, it attempts to go beyond it. It may put up "metaphysical" questions and also try to give answers to them either on rational or on mythical irrational grounds.

Philosophy and Science. As such, philosophy is clearly distinct from science. Here one may see interdependence of science and philosophy as under : (a) Political science brings to philosophy both facts and generalisations. (b) In turn, it receives from philosophy the capacity to deal with these problems, in a comprehensive manner. A political philosopher can in no way develop his framework of political knowledge without his having a general philosophy of life. It is evident from the thoughts of Aristotle, Laski and other modern political thinkers.

Detachment of Political Science from Philosophy. It is believed that the political philosophers cannot detach themselves from their philosophical moorings. In such a position, some contemporary political scientists argue that whatever might have been true of the earlier ages, the time has come now for a change. Now, come in political science as it has come in physics. We may detach ourselves from such teleological views and concentrate more on the non-normative and non-philosophical aspects of political science, and build up a "positive" science of politics. Friedrich opines that such attempts are not possible. He argues that political scientists are bound to have a discussion of concepts like "power" or "justice" or "value", or "group" or "notion" or "society." These concepts cannot be used without some reference to the general philosophy for the writer. Friedrich faces the challenge given by the political scientists and holds that they in order to emphasise their "scientificness", may try to break away from philosophy. Even then the philosophers will not stop discussing these concepts. In support of his statement, Friedrich gives the examples of philosophers like Leo Strauss, and of the existentialists, more especially of Paul Tillich and Maurice Cranston. These philosophers have written at length on the role of power, law, freedom, authority in politics. They have largely influenced, and will continue to influence the thinking of political scientists for a long time to come. A political scientist may not agree with the views of Strauss, Tillich, Cranston and the host of philosophers dealing with concepts which lie at the core of political science. Yet he has only two alternatives before him : (a) he has to discuss them and (b) he has either to appreciate or contradict them.

To conclude, Friedrich says "Political science and political philosophy are intimately tied, that the one cannot be usefully pursued without the other, and that political science in this respect is not at all different from other sciences which likewise are linked with philosophy."

NORMAN JACOBSONV's VIEWS ON AUTONOMOUS CHARACTER OF POLITICAL SCIENCE

Views of Norman Jacobson on Autonomous Character of Political Science

In the recent times, attempts have been made from various corners for the close identification of political science with either science or philosophy. Such attempts have led to another kind of danger. According to Norman Jacobson, it is the danger of political theory ending up in some kind of "scientism" or "moralism".

Nature of Political Science. While expressing his views on the nature of political science, Jacobson has tried to make it clear that political science is neither sceintism nor moralism. To him, it is neither completely identified with science nor with morality. Instead of any such identification, it is separate from them both. Not only this, but it maintains an identity of its own also. The political scientists attempting to mould political science in the perfect image of science and trying to apply methods and procedures of science to it have failed to understand the real nature of science. It cannot be denied that it is advantageous to utilize the knowledge of one field for the better understanding of another, but the distinction between the two fields cannot be overlooked. Jacobson is of the view that contemporary political scientists are trying to make of political science anything but political science. "It would seem", he writes, "that politics is psychology, or it is sociology" that it is moral philosophy or theology — that it is "almost anything but politics." He considers politics to be a special kind of intellectual activity. Jacobson does not object to drawing upon the best that the fields of enquiry in other disciplines have to offer. But this should be done only with a view to help us in the better understanding of politics.

Need of Science and Philosophy. Jacobson lays emphasis on both, *i.e.,* science as well as philosophy. In his opinion, if "science" is taken out of political theory, it might become a worthless "ethical" residue. Likewise, if "philosophy" is taken out of political theory, it might be reduced to mere methodology. Some thinkers have tried to emphasise either the scientific or the philosophical character of political science. They have done it to the extent of identifying political science with one or the other such persons, may be good advocates of "scientism" or "moralism". But, according to Jacobson such persons are devoid of the sense of commitment to political science itself.

To appreciate the unity of political theory, politics should be recognised as a special kind of activity. Besides there shoud be a commitment to the study of politics as a special kind of undertaking. However, the "scientists" and the "moralists" both are too much obsessed with their own commitments to "science" or to "ethics". Consequently, they cannot think of politics as an activity worthy of study in its own right. Jacobson criticises both and accuses them of suffering from a terrible sense of impatience — the one for precision, the other for virtue. He writes that "Scientism would take the politics out of politics. Moralism would destroy it if necessary as the enemy of virtue." He adds that for both, politics is literally a means. He explains them as given below :

(i) For the Scientists. For the scientist, politics is a means "for the attainment of specific ends regardless of their morality".

(ii) For the Moralists. For the moralist, politics is a means "for the realization of morality and rationally sound goals, regardless of their practicability." Jacobson admits that politics is a means but not in the foregoing sense. Politics has got to be studied in its own right. It is essential to distinguish political theory from political processes, attitudes, etc.

Mode of Borrowing. Jacobson is willing to borrow concepts and tools from other sciences. Yet, he does not believe in an indiscriminate borrowing. This applies particularly in the case of vocabularly. Jacobson does not like that the vocabulary of political science should be made extremely precise and scientific. Sterilisation of language can easily lead to sterilisation of thought. We should not attempt at borrowing language indiscriminately from other disciplines, particularly the natural sciences, because, in that case, there is a danger of our thinking being deeply influenced by them.

The Question of Objectivity. As regard the question of objectivity, a political scientist cannot be as objective as a physical scientist. Nor is it desirable. Jacobson writes, "... the physical scientist is not in the least dependent for his knowledge upon the skill with which he is able to imagine the motivation of a falling body or the sentiments of justice obstinately held by a gaseous element. On the other hand, the political theorist is enormously dependent for his knowledge upon self-awareness and introspection. We cannot hope to understand our fellows without seeking to understand ourselves." Nor is it desirable. "To perform relentless surgery on ourselves, to cut out the morally exciting and cramp the flow of the intellectually dramatic", is to reduce the possibility that we will ever understand politics really well. Jacobson remarks that we become like Montaigue's pedant. He would not venture to say that he had an itchy backside before consulting his dictionary to discover the meaning of "itchy" and of "backside."

Jacobson is of the opinion that complete objectivity is never entirely possible in social science. "Detachment", to quote Michael Polyani, "in the rigorous sense of the word, can only be achieved in a state of complete imbecility well below the normal animal's level."

Political Theory not to be confused with Science as well as with Scientism. It is evident from the aforesaid that political theory is not to be confused with scientism. Likewise, it cannot to be confused with moralism. Its relationship to moral philosophy is at least as tenuous as the relationship of scientism to science. The moralist is fond of endless preaching. He seems to ignore the realities of the political life. He attempts at reducing political theory to ethical theory. A search for political theory and a search for ethical theories, are not the same as both Hobbes and Rousseau seemed to have believed. As per Jacobson, political theory "is neither scientism nor moralism, whether viewed separately or taken together." They do not share its central concern. The central concern of political theory is with the search for political wisdom.

Criticque of the Idea of System. Norman Jacobson has criticised the idea of a system, with the consequent stress on methodology. It was evolved by the contemporary political scientists as the central point in their political studies, as an extremely naive approach to the understanding of politics. The system theory is based on the assumption that there already exists such a thing as a political system. Its recent additions are social scientific techniques and knowledge and in symbolic logic and mathematics. The idea of a system can be called to be the product of the ingenuity and training of a particular group of thinkers. These thinkers have devoted a long time to the study and perfection of methodology rather than in the search of political wisdom. Something more than ingenuity and training is needed by the study of political science. It demands a discriminating intellect. It demands knowledge in comparison to the techniques and wisdom in comparison to the blue-prints. On the contrary to it, in case knowledge is subordinated to techniques and wisdom to blue-prints in political theory, there would be a general levelling down of the standards of creativeness in the field. It is required by the knowledge of politics, on the part of the scholar, imagination, experience, judgement, and besides a commitment to the subject. In Jacobson's words, "It is one thing to organize mediocrity for its most efficient performance. It is quite another to regard organized mediocrity as providing the standards by which to judge creativeness and originality in political theory." It would be a pity, if, owing to an emphasis upon system and methodology, the test of worth in political theory were gradually reduced to the test of technical brilliance. Views of Jacobson made great impact on modern political thinking.

EMPIRICAL AND NORMATIVE THEORIES

A comparative study of Empirical and Normative Theories

A Comparative Study. The several approaches to political science may be broadly categorized into two heads :

(a) The legal history and the normative approaches.

(b) The empirical, analytical or the scientific-behavioural approach. Each of these two approaches has been mainly demarcated from the other by the emphasis it lays on values as against facts or on facts as against values. Robert Dahl names them as Empirical Theorists and Trans-empirical Theorists. A brief description thereof is given here :

(i) The Empirical Theorists. The Empirical Theorists opine that an empirical science of politics based on facts alone is possible.

(ii) The Trans-empirical Theorists. Trans-empirical Theorists think that the study of politics neither can nor should be purely scientific. The controversy revolves round two major issues :

(I) Can political analysis be neutral?

(II) Should political analysis be neutral?

1. Can Political Analysis be Neutral? (a) The Empirical Theorists believe that it is possible to isolate and to test the empirical aspect of our beliefs about politics. They do not think that there is any necessity of going into the value-laden question of whether the empirical propositions are true or false. There is always a difference between the "correct" decision on what is empirically true and the "correct" decision on what ought to be. The values are purely subjective in nature. The existentialists believe that facts are there for all to see and can be subjected to empirical tests. On the contrary to it, values cannot be tested in that way.

(b) The Trans-empiricists also believed that irrespective of the situation in the natural sciences, facts and values are closely intertwined with each other. Consequently, in the study of politics, they cannot be separated except in the most trivial instances. Trans-empiricists hold that whatever one might pretend, one is making value judgements all the time. Any comprehensive theory about politics must inevitably contain evaluations of the empirical validity of the factual statements in the theory as well as the moral quality of the political events, processes or systems described in the theory. Hence, to imagine a completely objective theory of politics is merely a utopia *i.e.* unrealisable idea.

Agreement between Empiricists and Trans-Empiricists. Robert Dahl has pointed out a wide area of agreement between the two. Some points of agreement are as under :

Neither of them would deny that values can be completely kept out of empirical studies. The Empiricists would agree with the Trans-empiricists as given here :

1. Values, interests and curiosity of the investigator exercise their influence on his selection of topics - in social sciences as much as in natural sciences.

2. It is not possible to establish criteria of importance and relevance entirely on the basis of empirical knowledge alone. A value of some kind is required to decide which areas of research he regards as more important than others.

3. The value of truth has to be necessarily accepted before undertaking any objective analysis of politics.

4. Certain assumptions regarding the existence of things, the "pre-scientific knowledge" not requiring any proofs, have to be accepted before undertaking any empirical research.

5. It is not so easy to keep the biases of the investigator out of social science research as in natural sciences. The reason is unlike social sciences. In natural sciences, there is a built-in corrective for bias and distortion in the form of comparatively easy verifiability of the results of the research. The Empirical Theorists and the Trans-empirical Theorists do not much differ from each other on the logical question whether the knowledge of what is can be distinguished from the knowledge of what ought to be. Both of them agree what there is and ought to be logically distinguishable — as over its psychological aspect — whether facts and values can be separated psychologically in political matters.

Controversy over Neutrality. A controversy between Empiricists and Trans-empiricists has turned largely on the issue whether political science should be neutral. Trans-empiricists emphasise that the study of politics should have a purpose behind it. The purpose may be as under : (i) it should enable us to act rightly, (ii) it should enable us to choose the best and (iii) it should enable us to make decisions about how best to live with our fellowmen.

All of the above involve appraisal and evaluation. Political appraisal is a constant interweaving of fact-finding and evaluation. Hence, Dahl opines that it is of no help to us "to set our factual knowledge off to one side, neatly sealed up in an aseptic container, and values off to the other side whether they have no bearing on reality."

Charges of Trans-Empiricists against the Empiricists. Robert Dahl has summarised the charges brought by the Trans-empiricists against the Empiricists as under : (i) the Empiricists have no criteria of relevance, (ii) the Empiricists have, in striving for neutrality and objectivity, gone in for a new, complicated and ridiculous jargon, (iii) the Empiricists have in the attempt to eschew values rejected all grounds for evaluation and treat all values as equal and (iv) the empiricists, at the time of professing neutrality, are for the most part partisans of liberal democracy. They are possessing no criteria of relevance because such criteria cannot be drawn simply from empirical knowledge, beyond which the Empiricists would not like to move. Again, having no criteria of relevance, they necessarily indulge in trivial investigations, irrelevant to human purposes. Some other charges by Trans-empiricists against Empiricists are given below :

1. The Empiricists, use of jargon, which makes their concepts difficult to understand is based on profuse extracts from their writings.

2. The Empiricists treat all values as equal or are ideologically committed to liberal democracy. But, Dr. Vibasi holds that these arguments are based on a wrong understanding, or a misrepresentation.

3. The Trans-empiricists allege that in their attempt to eschew values, the Empiricists reject all grounds for evaluation and treat all values as equal. Leo Strauss writes that "By teaching in effect the equality of literally all desires, it teaches in effect that there is nothing that a man ought to be ashamed of; by destroying the possibility of self-contempt, it destroys, with the best of intentions, the possibility of self-respect. By teaching the equality of values, by denying that there are things which are intrinsically high and others which are intrinsically low as well as by denying that there is an essential difference between men and brutes, it unwittingly contributes to the victory of the gutter." Strauss and Vogelin criticise Max Weber. In the views of Strauss, Weber "assumed as a matter of course that there is no hierarchy of values : all values are of the same rank". Vogelin also alleges that Weber "treated all values as equal". They say that Weber believed that science could contribute nothing to the value problem and that he treated values as "beyond science". However, a careful study of Weber's works would have removed these misunderstandings regarding his views. The position of Weber may be given as under :

(a) Weber never treated values as equal but merely their validity as equally undemonstrable. Moreover, this also he wrote with reference to "ultimate" values, and not all values.

(b) Weber did not believe that science could contribute nothing to the value problem. On the other hand, he denied that "value judgments are to be withdrawn from scientific discussion in general".

He said that, "Criticism is not to be suspended in the presence of value judgments."

(c) The Trans-empiricists hold that the scientific method can deal satisfactorily with both facts and values, and that, so far as the use of the scientific method was concerned, it was not necessary to make a distinction between the two. John Dewey and Flex Kaufmann have taken this position.

(d) Another argument brought forwards by some of the Trans-empiricists is that "science" need not be considered in the narrow manner, in which the Empirical Theorists look at it. They plead that the concept of science should be broadened to include value judgments — a line of argument generally adopted by Jacques Maritain, the French philosopher, as well as Erick Voegelin, etc. They argue that if St. Thomas could include within his definition of science supra-empirical and supra-rational kinds of wisdom, the modern scientists could also do it. Science should not be reduced, to the type of empirical-logical science, that is, the physico-mathematical sciences and the sciences of phenomena. There "must" be a non-empirical science, and metaphysics should be included in science in this ampler sense.

(e) The Trans-empiricists allege that under the garb of a value-free analysis of political phenomena, the Empirical theorists smuggle into their theories their own values. They have a commitment to a particular version of liberal democracy — a characteristic for which Strauss has used the term "democratism".

(f) The Trans-empiricists allege that the Empirical theorists are prone to indulge in trivial investigations, irrelevant to human purposes.

(g) The Trans-empiricists allege that in striving for neutrality and objectivity, Empirical theorists find it necessary to invent a new, complicated and even a ridiculous jargon and complicated political ideas.

Refutal by Empiricists. The Empiricists have refuted the allegations made by the Trans-empiricists against them as under :

1. Empiricists contend that they do have criteria of relevance and are mostly concerned with the same questions which have been the focus of inquiry by traditional political theorists. A few examples are the kinds of political systems, problems of stability, change and revolution, of equality and inequality, of freedom and slavery.

2. In reply to the charge that they use a complicated jargon, they hold that this is due partly to their deepening of the understanding of

political behaviour and processes, for which new concepts have to be developed and partly to the need of drawing terms from other social sciences. However, they contend, a number of modern political theorists, Lasswell in particular, have tried to develop as precise a vocabulary as possible. The charge also seems to be based on the confusion which a number of Trans-empiricists have made between Empirical theory and the position taken by some of the early Logical Positivists that all value statements are "meaningless".

The new political ideas are very controversial and complex and require very careful study.

9

Gandhi, Sarvodya and Nehru

GANDHISM

According to some writers, Gandhiji was the greatest personality next to Buddha, therefore, it is necessary to study the political philosophy of Mahatma Gandhi.

Gandhiji pleaded for passive resistance as well as for satyagraha but according to him, "Satyagraha is dynamic, passive resistance is static".

In his non-violence, he is follower of Jainism and Buddha — indebtedness of Mahatma Gandhi to earlier thinkers and his views on non-violence are similiar to Jain Tirthankars and of Buddha.

Gandhiji's views on the relationship between ethics and politics were that not only aim but means should also be moral.

Some writers regard Mahatma Gandhi as a political philosopher because the value of his contribution to the political thinking of our time is very great.

He said, "The rule of majority does not mean it should suppress the opinion of an individual if it is sound. An individual's opinion should have greater weight than the opinion of many, if that opinion is sound. That is my view of real democracy."

Gandhiji's theory of state was, "We have learnt to strike the golden mean between individual and social restraint. Willing submission to social restraint for the sake of the well-being of whole society enriches both the individual and the society of which one is a member".

Gandhi's Theory of the State

About rights and duties, he said, "The true source of right is duty...if we all discharge our duties, rights will not be far to seek."

Different writers have formed different opinions about him. Some call him a philosophical anarchist. Others say, "Gandhism is the very anti-thesis of socialism". J.C. Kumarappa and others were of the opinion that Gandhism and communism, as regards their ends and methods differ but some say Gandhism is communism minus violence. As such, Gandhiji's views should be studied objectively.

Brief Life Sketch. Mahatma Gandhi whose full name was Mohandas Karamchand Gandhi was born on October 2, 1869 at Porbander in Kathiawar. His father was diwan (Prime Minister) at Porbander and Rajkot and his mother was a religious lady. He was married at the age of 12. In 1888, he passed his matriculation examination and was sent to London to qualify for the bar. Before leaving India at the age of 19, he made a promise to his mother that he would avoid meat, wine and women.

After qualifying himself for the bar, he began to practise at Rajkot and from there he shifted to Bombay. During his stay in England, he became interested in "Bhagwat Gita" and was also influenced by Matthew Arnold's "The light of Asia", *i.e.,* poem about Buddha. During his stay at Bombay, he came in contact with Raj Chandra Raujibhai and learnt his first lessons of non-violence and truth.

In 1893, he had to leave for South Africa to conduct the case of a Gujarati Muslim merchant. He was deeply moved by the hard conditions under which his countrymen had to live and was unable to tolerate injustice which they were getting. Gandhiji's opportunity came in 1906 when the Asiatic Registration Act was passed. He protested against it and put into practice his weapon of Satyagraha and developed a self-confidence to lead a struggle which later on became a cause of the downfall of British empire. He along with his other countrymen had to suffer hardships and imprisonment but he got success in his aim there.

Having won his laurals in South Africa, he came to India in 1914. Up-till now he did not oppose British rule in India and in 1915, he said, "I have found that it is possible for me to be governed least under the British empire. Hence my loyalty to British empire...". But passing of Rowlatt Bills in teeth of opposition by the people forced him to change his views and he came to the conclusion that the British rule in India was "satanic." In India, he chose Gopal Krishna Gokhale as his political guru but perhaps he was also influenced by Tilak. Thus he learnt something of Indian diplomacy and was acquainted also with the British diplomacy.

The period of 1914 to 1947 is the most glorious phase of Gandhiji's activities. In 1918, he wrote to the Viceroy, "I would make India offer all her able-bodied persons as a sacrifice to the Empire at this critical moment; and I know that India by this very act, would become the most favoured partner and racial distinction would become a thing of the past". But his hopes were shattered on the sharp rocks of reality; and in August 1920 he wrote, "Events that have happened during the past months have confirmed me in the opinion that the Imperial Government have acted in the Khilafat matter in an unscruplous, immoral and unjust manner...(and estranged me completely from the present Govt. and have disabled me from rendering as I have hitherto wholeheartedly rendered my total co-operation)" He further added, "In European countries condonation of such grievous wrongs as the Khilafat and the Punjab would have resulted in a bloody revolution by the people. They would have resisted at all costs the national emsculation. Half of India is too weak to offer violent resistance and the other half is unwilling to do so. I have therefore decided to suggest the remedy of non-co-operation...."

Gandhiji started his non-violent non-co-operation movement with great hopes but his dream of Swarajya did not materialize. From 1920, when he got his resolution passed at Calcutta, Gandhi era begins as now Mahatma Gandhi became the unquestioned leader of India who lead her to freedom. In 1922, there took place serious rioting at Chaurichaura near Gorakhpur in U.P. and he stopped further activities of the movement.

There was a split within the Congress on the question of Council entry, and Swarajya Party lead by Moti Lal Nehru and C.R. Das favoured Congress entry in the legislatures and fighting the government from within also. But the scheme of Swarajists failed because in the words of Zakaria, "they desired to eat the cake as well as to it."

From then onwards Mahatma Gandhi became the unchallenged leader and dominated the entire politics of the country. In 1931, he went to attend Round Table Conference, but came empty handed. In 1931, he started Civil Disobedience Movement. It was greater success than the movement of 1921. It ended with Gandhi-Irwin Pact which was a victory for Indian National Congress. In 1942, India witnessed Quit India movement under the leadership of Mahatma Gandhi. India won her independence on 15 August, 1947 under the leadership of Mahatma Gandhi. Although he was neither the Prime Minister of India nor the President of Congress, his was the last word on every point. He worked wholeheartedly for Harijan uplift and for the cause of down-trodden peasants and workers and for woman uplift. He also championed the cause of handwoven khadi to provide employment to weavers.

But the greatest hero of the freedom movement and liberator of the country could not breathe in the atmosphere of independence for long. On January 30, 1948 he was shot dead and thus lover of non-violence sacrificed his life on the altar of violence. That was a great blow, not only to India but to the whole world. Dr. Stanley Jones in his book, *Mahatma Gandhi The meaning of his death* writes "If Mahatma Gandhi had been privileged to choose the issue on which he could have died, he could not have chosen a better issue. It exactly sums up his life.... No human being ever summed up more perfectly in his death the things for which he lived in his life."[1]

The French socialist expressed his feelings in the following words.

"I never saw Gandhi. I do not know his language. I never set foot in his country and yet I feel the same sorrow as if I had lost some one near and dear. The whole world has been plunged into mourning by the death of this extraordinary man." He now belongs to ages. He was the greatest man since Buddha that India has ever produced. According to Sheriden, "Gandhi and Lenin gave immortal ideas to the world." According to Dr. Homes, "World has to decide whether it desires atom bomb or non-violence of Mahatma Gandhi and it is the decision of life and death." Gandhiji proved that the spiritual power is more powerful than the physical force.

His Political Philosophy

Introductory. Gandhiji was not a philosopher but a Karmayogi and it is often remarked that there is no "ism" like Gandhism by quoting his words which he observed in 1936, in his book *My experiments with truth*. "There is no such thing as Gandhism and I do not want to leave any sect after me. I do not claim to have originated any new principle and doctrine. I have simply tried in my own way to apply the central truths to our daily life and problems.... You will not call it Gandhism; there is no ism about it."

It is true that the political philosophy of Gandhi was "not a set of doctrines or dogmas, rules or regulations, injunctions or inhibitions but it is a way of life. It indicates a new attitude or restates an old one towards life's issues and offers ancient solution for modern problems." His whole life was an unending experiment. But as a way of life, remarks Prof. Suda, "Gandhism possesses all qualities which are necessary for an 'ism' or ideology and it has a definite philosophy." There are some basic principles on which a special technique has been built to solve national and international problems. The various movements and organisations which were founded by Gandhiji possess basic principles and dogmas. He always followed non-violence and these principles and ideology based on this outlook can be expressed in a systematic way. Gandhism not only exists but has a bright future which can serve and save the humanity from destruction and can also serve as a beacon light to humanity.

Various Influences on Gandhiji. Man is the creature of circumstances as well as the moulder of the circumstances. His thoughts are moulded by the environment and various influences. As such, we may trace out the sources which moulded the political thought of Gandhiji. As narrated before, the Gita influenced him most. Gandhiji himself wrote, "Where doubts surround me, when disappointments stare me in the face, and I see not one ray of light on the horizon, I turn to the Bhagwat Gita and find a verse to comfort me, and I immediately begin to smile in the midst of overwhelming sorrow. My life has been full of external tragedies and if they have not left any visible effect on me, I owe to the teachings of Bhagwat Gita." Perhaps in making Gandhi a Karmyogi, Gita influenced him most.

Jain monk Bechorji Swami and Buddhism also had their influence on Gandhiji. John Rushin's book *Unto the last* and its teaching "the life of labour was the life worth living", profoundly influenced him. Thoreau's "Easay on Civil Disobedience" which he read in prison in 1908 in South Africa also influenced him but it is wrong that he got the idea of Satyagraha from him as he himself refuted it in 1935. Tolestoy also influenced Mahatma Gandhi and particularly his book, *The Kingdom of God is within you* had a profound influence on him. Gandhiji is stated to have remarked that, "Tolstoy is one of the three moderners who have exerted the greatest spiritual influence on my life."

Both Gandhiji and Tolstoy condemn modern civilization based on force and exploitation. Both favoured non-violence and preached the gospel of love but Gandhiji followed the ideal of Gita which stands for action without attachment. Rajchandra, a distinguished social reformer of Bombay, also exercised a lot of influence on him. But in-spite of these influences, he was a Karmayogi, a practical idealist and his philosophy grew out of his own experiences and experiments with truth and non-violence.

Religion and Politics. Gandhiji was not willing to separate religion from politics. He stated, "Those who say that religion has nothing to do with politics, do not know what religion means." Again he does not know what patriotism or feeling for one's country is who does not know true duty or religion. He adds, "If I take part in politics, it is only because politics today encircles us like the coils of the snake from which one cannot get out, no matter how much one tries. I wish to wrestle with the snake. I am trying to introduce religion into politics. There are no politics devoid of religion." He further stated, "I do not know any religion apart from human activity. It provides a moral basis to all other activities which if they would, otherwise done, reduce life to a thing of sound and fury signifying nothing." Religion was the very breath of his life based on love, truth and Ahinsa. His contention was that there could not be two consciences of man, one individual and social and other political.

Means and Ends. Gandhiji discarded the Machiavellian idea that the end justifies the means. He considered means and ends were correlated terms. The two were inseparable and must be pure. He believed, "As the means, so the end." He insisted that our means must be pure as our end.

Non-Violence. He believed that non-violence or Ahinsa was the heart of all religions. He believed truth and Ahinsa as the sides of a smooth unstamped metallic disc and so intertwined that it is difficult to disentangle and separate them.

He referred to three kinds of non-violence :

1. The highest form was the non-violence of the bravely inner connection based on moral considerations. This non-violence was not only political but pervaded every sphere of life.

2. The second kind of non-violence was adopted as a measure of expediency and sound policy in some spheres of life. That was the non-violence of weak or passive non-violence of the helpless.

3. The third kind of non-violence is the passive violence of the coward and the effeminate. To him, vengeance was superior to passive and helpless submission. "It is better to be violent if there is violence in our breasts than to put on the cloak of non-violence to cover impotence". There is nothing like failure in non-violence as there is nothing like success in violence.

Satyagraha

Gandhiji evolved a way of resisting evil through the instrumentality of Satyagraha. The Satyagraha is not new to India. But Gandhiji was the first to make its use for political purpose. "Satyagraha is made of two words, Satya meaning truth, agraha, *i.e.,* insistence. It literally means insistence on truth." Satyagraha to him means holding on to truth or insistence to truth. It is the vindication of the truth not by the infliction of suffering on the opponent but on one's own self. Satyagraha can only be cultivated by strong and the strength lies in absence of fear, not in quantity of flesh and muscle we may have on our bodies. Non-violence and Satyagraha should go together. The courage involved in Satyagraha is the courage of dying without killing and is far superior to that involved in violence. But if one has not that courage, Gandhiji would advise killing and being killed rather than shamefully fleeing away from danger in the name of non-violence. Thus, when Gandhiji chooses non-violence, it is superior to violence because forgiveness is more manly than punishment.

A Satyagrahi aims to winning the opponent from error by bone and patient suffering. In Satyagrahi, there is no room for hatred or ill-will. According to Mahadev Desai, "Satyagraha is dynamic, passive resistance is static. Passive resistance acts negatively and suffers reluctantly. Satyagrahi acts positively and suffers with cheerfulness and makes the suffering fruitful...." Satyagraha can offer more effective and determined opposition to injustice and tyranny than passive resistance.

The technique of Satyagraha may take the form of non-co-operation, civil disobedience, hijrat, *i.e.,* to leave the place, fasting and strike. Gandhiji pointed out that oppression, exploitation and tyranmy were possible on account of the co-operation of the people. If the people refused to co-operate with the government, the latter could not function. To quote him, "Even the most despotic government cannot stand except with the consent of the governed which consent is often forcibly procured by the despot. Immediately the subject ceases to fear, power is gone."

Civil disobedience means not to obey the command or law in a non-violent manner but it must be sincere, respectful, restrained, never defiant and must be based on well understood principles. Hijrat means voluntary exile and it was advised by Gandhiji to the Harijans of Kaitha in 1935.

Fasting means not to eat. It is a non-violent pressure exerted through self suffering by fasting. According to him, strike was a voluntary proof purification, suffering undertaken to convert the erring opponent.

Gandhiji recommended Satyagraha even in case of foreign invasion by non-co-operating with the aggressor and preferring death to submission. It goes to the credit of Gandhiji that he put the doctrine of Satyagraha into practice against the then mightest government on the earth and got success. Satyagraha means an assertion of the power of the human soul against political and economic dominance. Thus "true pressure or Satyagraha" means the exercise of the first soul force against all injustice, oppression and exploitation.

According to Gandhiji, to make Satyagraha effective, certain psychological and sociological condition are required. They may be stated as given below :

1. The Satyagrahi is not to barbour any hatred within his heart against the opponent.

2. The issue for which Satyagraha is launched should be true and substantial.

3. The Satyagrahi should make himself ready to undergo all kinds of sufferings and humiliations. He must be even ready to give up life if occasion so demands.

He also laid some rules for a Satyagrahi :

1. He should be devoid of anger.

2. He will tolerate the anger of the opponent.

3. In doing so, he will never retaliate but he will not submit out of fear or punishment.

4. He should voluntarily court arrest if order is given by proper authority.

5. He will refuse to surrender his property even on the pain of death.

6. A civil resister will never insult his opponent.

7. Non-retaliation excludes swearing and cursing.

8. Compromise is an essential part of Satyagraha.

Gandhiji on State. Gandhiji's grouse against the state is based on the conviction that it is rooted in violence and hence inimical to the development of human personality. To quote, him "The state represents violence in a concentrated and organised form. The individual has a soul but the state is a soulless machine. It can never be weaned from violence to which it owes its very existence." As such, an association based on violence should be banished. If total revolution is not possible, its field of activity should be curtailed to narrowest limit. He followed the maxim "That government is the best that governs the least". He adds, "I look upon an increase in the power of the state with the greatest fear, because although while apparently doing good by minimising exploitation, it does the greatest harm to mankind by destroying individuality, which lies at the root of all progress. We know of so many cases where men have adopted trusteeship, but no state where the state has lived for the poor."

Gandhiji was a philosophical anarchist. He repudiated state on ethical, historical, and economic grounds. The ideal of Mahatma Gandhi was stateless democracy where social life was self-regulated. According to his conception, "In such a state everyone is his own ruler. He rules himself in such a manner that he is never a hindrance to his neighbour. In the ideal state there is no political power because there is no state."

Society based on non-violence can only be of a group settled in villages in which voluntary co-operation is the condition of dignified and peaceful existence. The federation and groups were to be organized on voluntary basis. Society was to be decentralized and equality was to prevail in every sphere of life, In social life, it was to be expressed through the law of Dharma combined with the ideals of non-possession and bread labour. Every individual was to be given fullest freedom to devote himself to social service according to his capacity.

The ideal of non-possession and bread labour implied rural civilization based on cottage industry and handicrafts. There was to be no room in such a society for exploitation. Everybody was to be his master and no one a hired labourer.

Gandhiji was opposed to heavy transport, courts, lawyers and modern system of medicine and big cities. He was confident that the people will not be worse off if all the doctors and lawyers disappeared. He was opposed to the theory of sovereignty. He said, "red Swarajya will come not by the acquisition of authority by a few but by acquisition of the capacity by all to resist authority when abused." He said, "A government cannot succeed in becoming entirely non-violent because it represents all the people. I do not today conceive of such a golden age, but I do believe in the possibility of a predominantly non-violent society and I am working for it."

Representation. Gandhiji was not opposed to the institution of representation and elections. To quote him, "By Swarajya I mean the government of India by the consent of the people ascertained by the largest number of adult population, male or female, native born or domiciled, who have contributed manual labour to the service of the state and who have taken the trouble of having their names registered as voters."

In 1931 and 1942, Gandhiji advocated the system of direct election to the village panchayats. All these villages were to elect their representatives for district administration and district administrations were to elect the representatives for provincial administration. The provincial administrations were to elect the President. In this way, power was to be decentralized among all the villages. Candidates were to be selfless, able and incorruptible based on manual work.

Rule by Majority. He believed that democracy is not a state in which people act like sheep. According to him, "The rule of majority did not mean that it should suppress the opinion of even an individual if it is sound. An individual's opinion should have a greater weight than the opinion of many if that opinion is sound. That is my view of real democracy." It was both the right and duty of the minority to correct the majority to its own point of view. Likewise, the majority was also not to ignore completely the views of the minority.

Sphere of State. Gandhiji was not in favour of multiplying the functions of the state. He believed, self-government means continuous effort to be independent of government control, whether it is foreign or whether it is national. A government that runs its affairs smoothly without much state interference is truly democratic.

Regarding criminals he favoured reformatory theory and said that they should be treated as defective. About police he said that they will be reformer and servants, not masters, of the people.

Regarding taxes he said that these should be realised in the form of labour because payment in labour invigorates the nation.

According to Gandhiji, the administration of justice is to be made cheaper for the man in the street. Parties in civil suits were to be encouraged to refer their matter to arbitration. The decision of Panchayat was to be final except in a case of corruption or misapplication of law. Multiplicity of intermediate courts was to be avoided. Case law was to be abolished and the general procedure was to be simplified. Lawyers may remain but their fees were to be regulated. They were to keep before themselves the ideal of service and not of their enrichment.

Thus, Gandhiji's ideal of Ramrajya is based on mutual goodwill and tolerance. In Ramrajya he pleads for the sovereignty of moral authority. To Gandhiji, the state is not an end in itself but means of enabling people to better their conditions in every department of life.

Private Property and Trusteeship. Gandhiji evolved the formula of trusteeship which means that persons possessing property should utilise their property for the benefit of the community. To quote Gandhiji, "My ideal is equal distribution, but so long as I can see it is not to be realised. I therefore work for equitable distribution."

He was an egalitarian. He said economic equality means that everyone will have a proper means to live in, sufficient and balanced food to eat, and sufficient khadi with which to cover himself. It also means that the cruel inequality that is prevailing today will be removed by purely non-violent means. To achieve this ideal, Gandhiji did not suggest any wholesale confiscation of property of the landlords and capitalists. He was in favour of trying to change their mentality by peaceful means.

The concept of trusteeship was explained by Gandhiji in the following manner :

1. Trusteeship provides a means of transferring the present capitalist order of society into an egalitarian one; it gives no quarter to capitalism but gives owning classes a chance for reforming themselves.

2. It permits ownership of the property only for the welfare of the society.

3. It does not exclude legislative regulation of the ownership.

4. It requires that living minimum wage and maximum limit of property should be fixed.

5. Under the Gandhian economic order, the character of free production will be determined by social necessity and not by personal greed or whim.

Gandhiji's view was that the industries which failed to act as trusts were to be taken over by the Government. As far as possible there was to be decentralization as centralization and large scale production were considered to be the enemies of democracy. He states, "If the state suppresses capitalism by violence, it would be caught in the coils of violence itself...and will fail to develop non-violence at any time. The state represents violence in a concentrated and organized form. The individual has a soul but the state is soulless machine...hence I prefer the doctrine of trusteeship."

Patriotism and Internationalism

Gandhiji put emphasis on duty towards one's own country but he favoured interest of humanity at large. He said, "I want India to rise so that the whole world may benefit. I do not want India to rise on the ruin of other nations." He remarked, "We want freedom of our country but not at the expense of exploitation of others. A country has to be free in order that it may die, if necessary for the benefit of the world." Thus, Gandhiji desired the welfare of whole humankind and believed in the maxim of Vasudhav kutambhmakhm and Vishwa ka Kalyan ho, *i.e.,* all men of the world are of one family and welfare of the whole world may happen. वसुधैवकुटुम्बकम विश्व का कल्याण हो.

On Human Nature. Gandhiji was not a visionary but a practical idealist. He believed that man was a mixture of good and evil. There is no one without shortcomings but he believed that even the most wicked persons can be transformed. He believed, "The soul is one in all. Its possibilities are therefore the same for every one." Thus, he believed in the inherent goodness of human nature.

Rights and Duties. Gandhiji advocated for both rights and duties. He places more emphasis on duties than rights. According to him, the right to perform one's duties was the only right that was worth living for and dying for. To quote Gandhiji, "The true source of right is duty."

Gandhi and Marx. It is generally said that Gandhiji was a communist minus violence. Both had one and same object. But their ways were different. This is the basis of all other differences between these two philosophers.

Both wanted to establish a classless and stateless society, so as to make possible for everyone to get an equal share in the gifts of nature. To achieve this aim, if Gandhiji adopts the way of truth, non-violence and Satyagraha, Marx recommends the way of class struggle, abolition of capitalists, and nationalization of industries. Gandhiji believes in Varnashram Dharma, in Satyagrah, in decentralization, in co-operation, in freedom of the individuals and pure social life and in the principle of democracy. Gandhi attaches more importance to spiritalism whereas communism is purely materialistic. Unlike Marx, Gandhiji prescribes reduction of our wants. He says, mind is a restless bird, the more it gets, the more it wants and remains unsatisfied. For Gandhi, communism is the necessary result of modern materialistic civilization. Gandhiji is totally against violence and atheism, but Marx favours both violence and atheism. Marx states religion as opium of the people but Gandhiji attaches great importance to religion. Gandhism is based on religion while Marxists disfavour it.

Gandhiji attaches equal importance to means and ends but Marxists believe that end justifies the means. But to Gandhiji, as Dhawan says, "As the means, so the end."

Gandhiji discarded violence and said if violence is the law of human existence then men cannot be protected, but communists desire to destroy the capitalists even by violence as a last resort.

Gandhism is a philosophy of love whereas communism is rooted in hatred. Bible says, "Love thy neighbour as thyself" but Gandhiji goes a step further and says that every living being is your neighbour. Two quotations to illustrate the difference of Gandhism and Stalin may be given here :

> "I would not dispossess moneyed men by force, but would invite their co-operation in the process of conversion to state ownership" (Gandhi).
>
> "You cannot conquer the enemy without learning to hate him with all the power of your soul" (Stalin).

Gandhism and communism also differ on the point of leadership. Gandhism believes in democracy while communism believes in dictatorship of proletariat. Gandhiji was really a democrat and believed only democracy can achieve welfare of the individuals.

Gandhiji regarded decentralization essential for democracy and stated that real democracy depends upon people's franchise. Communists believe in the dictatorship of proletariat and they have great faith in centralization.

J.C. Kumarappa stated that "Gandhism is violence minus communism", as their ends and goal are not much different and added that they only disagree about means. It is true that Gandhiji's goal was a classless society, a society in which all are equal. Though this idea of classless society is Marxist's but unlike Marx he did not wish to abolish private enterprize but believes in trusteeship and in a method of love and Sarvodya, *i.e.,* good of all and not the dictatorship of proletarians. In short, following points may be given to prove that Gandhiji is not a Marxist :

1. Gandhiji attaches more importance to truthfulness and purity of means whereas according to Marxists end justifies the means.

2. Gandhiji believes in non-violence while Marxists desire peaceful methods and also violence, if necessary.

3. Gandhiji is spiritualistic while Marxism is purely a materialistic ideology. Gandhiji supports religion while Marx discards it as opium of people.

4. Gandhiji believes in philosophy of love while Marxism is rooted in hatred of the exploiters.

5. Gandhiji believed that change in society can come by changing the outlook of the individual, but Marxists believed in class consciousness.

Thus, Gandhiji believed in a classless and stateless society, yet he is not at all a Marxist and there are basic difference between them. Gandhiji is sometimes described as a philosophical anarchist because he rejects the state totally in any of its form. Perhaps this view Gandhiji had to form because he saw exploitation and ruthless suppression of poor persons by the British imperialism in South Africa and in India. As such, he came to the conclusion that every state exploits the poor and exploitation cannot cease if the state exists in any form. In this connection Dr. Dhawan says, "Gandhiji as is well known, is a philosophical anarchist, who ideally speaking repudiates the state as such, whatever its form. The repudiation has an ethical, historical as well as economic basis. The compulsive nature of the state authority damages the moral value of the individual's action, for any action is moral only when it is voluntary.... Besides, state, even through its machinery may be most democratic, is rooted in violence Violence, implies exploitation and every state exploits the poor."[2] He desired to establish a non-violent society by non-violent means as he succeeded against the British imperialism by non-violent means.

Gandhiji's Contribution. Gandhi was a genius, a great personality of creative and constructive power. He was a teacher and taught the world the lessons of non-violence, Satyagraha and truth. To quote President Dr. Radhakrishanan, "As a great teacher appears once in a while, several centuries may pass without the advent of such a soul. He first lives on it, then tells how others may live. Such a teacher was Gandhi."

Gandhiji's thought influenced not only India but the whole world. Pt. Nehru says, "Gandhiji influenced millions of people of India in varying degree; some changed the whole texture of their lives, others were only partially affected".

Gandhiji has made the following contributions to the history of political philosophy :

1. The philosophy of non-violence.
2. Unification of religion and politics.
3. The philosophy of Satyagraha and its practical application in political field.
4. The conception of freedom of individuals.
5. Equal rights to women. He says, "If by strength is meant moral power, then woman is immeasurably man's superior."
6. Harijan uplift.
7. Khadi uplift to improve the conditions of weavers and poor persons.
8. His humanitarian outlook.

According to Lord Boyd Orr, the fundamental features of Gandhism are : "Truth and truth alone is attained by contemplation, justice for all men; freedom for all nations to develop their own resources according to their own genius, freedom for individuals within nations, *i.e.,* complete freedom...freedom from disease, hunger and poverty, in a word complete freedom for all so that each individual could attain his highest innate capacity for physical, psychological and cultural well being. The most striking feature of Gandhiji's principles is that these great ideals could only be attained by non-violent means. That I think was the most important part of Gandhian teaching in deliberations."

Rabindra Nath Tagore says, "Great as he is as a politician, as an organizer, as a leader of man, as a moral reformer, he is greater than all these as a man, because none of these activities limits his humanity. They are rather inspired and sustained by it." President Dr. Radhakrishnan states, "Gandhiji will ever be remembered as the great prophet of a moral and spiritual revolution without which this distracted world will not find peace."

Pt. Nehru says, "Future will hardly believe that there lived such a man."

Really Mahatma Gandhi will be remembered as one of the greatest men which the world has ever produced. We believe in what Dr. John Hauges said, "Gandhi was the greatest man in the world after Jesus Christ", or as Sir. Tej Bahadur Sapru says, "He was the greatest man after Buddha." In short, place of Gandhiji lies with Jesus Christ, Mohammed, Buddha and Confucius who brought revolution in human thought and left their impact on mankind.

On India, his impact can be stated as follows. India is free. There is equality and individual freedom in the society. Untouchability is no more. Women are enjoying equal rights. But India of Gandhi's dream is a far off goal. He stated, "I will work for an India in which the poorest shall feel that it is their country, in whose making they have an effective voice, an India in which all communities shall live in perfect harmony. There can be no room in such an India for the curse of untouchability or the curse of intoxicating drinks or drugs. Women will enjoy the same rights as men. This is India of my dreams."

Only future will tell how far the dream of Gandhiji materialises in the present set-up of the society.

SARVODYA OR TRUE SOCIALISM

Sarvodya and Bhoodan movements were propounded by Acharya Vinoba Bhave. It is said that the Bhoodan movement of Acharya Vinoba Bhave was an ideological revolution and according to Jayaprakash Narain, "Sarvodya represents distinct advance over the existing social systems and philosophies". As such, there can be comparison between sarvodya and socialism, therefore, their careful study is necessary.

Meaning and Growth of Sarvodya. Sarvodya means the welfare of all and not only the welfare of only one class or section of society. There is vast difference between communism and Sarvodya. Communism stands for the good of proletariat and hates capitalists and bourgeoisie but Sarvodya stands for wefare of all, the rich, the middle class and the poor. Sarvodya goes further than utilitarianism in promoting the happiness of the people while utilitarianism wants the greatest happiness of the greatest number. Sarvodya desires to promote the happiness of all.

When Mahatma Gandhi gave the Gujarati version of Ruskin's *Unto the Last*, he used the title Sarvodya for the work. The gist of *unto the Last* may be summarised as : (1) that good of individual is contained in good of all and (2) all have the right of work to earn their livelihood and discrimination is useless.

According to Bharat Ratan Kumarappa, "Sarvodya as the welfare of all represents the ideal social order according to Gandhiji. Its basis is all embracing love. So it has room in it for all without exception, prince and peasant, Hindu and Muslim, touchable and untouchable, white and black, saint and sinner. No individual or group is to be suppressed, exploited or liquidated. All are to be equally members of this social order, sharing the produce of their labour, the strong protecting the weak and functioning as trustees for the weak, and each promoting the welfare of all." The disciples of Mahatma Gandhi are making efforts to keep alive Gandhiji's spirit and it can be regarded as the projection of Gandhiji's movement carried on by Vinoba Bhave, Jayaprakash Narain, Kaka Kalelkar, etc.

Sarvodya Society. Mahatma Gandhi was aware of the fact that most of his political followers were not deeply interested in Sarvodya, so he put his faith in his more intimate followers to bring about a social revolution. A conference was planned at Wardha around February 1948, but due to Gandhiji's assassination on January 30 1948, it could not be held on scheduled time. On December 22 and 23, 1949, a Sarvodya Economic Conference under the Presidentship of Kaka Kalelkar drew up a plan to put into practice Gandhi's ideas. According to the plan, Sarvodya Society was established. But the chances of disseminating Sarvodya ideas and doing actual work seemed bleak when followers of Gandhiji who held the rein of government adopted economic planning based on Russian and Western models. In spite of all this, Vinoba Bhave carried its message everywhere.

The Ideals of Sarvodya. Acharya Vinoba Bhave speaks in terms of establishing a society in which people are free from exploitation and oppression. Sarvodya is against the state in its present form even if it tries to promote social welfare as it is based on methods of coercion. Jayaprakash Narain and other advocates of Sarvodya criticize the concept of the welfare states as it increases powers and functions of the government as in India. Sarvodya desires no difference between ruler and the ruled for both are "merged in the individual." The ideal of Sarvodya is a stateless society, free from every type of authority.

They oppose the present form of representative government on that following grounds :

1. Decisions are not taken on merits of the case but on party considerations.

2. People are encouraged to form groups against one another.

3. There is lust and scramble for power which spell the ruin of people as a whole.

4. There is bound to be bribery and corruption on a vast scale and money will enable people to realise their selfish ends through the majority party.

5. People who are in minority and poor suffer.

6. Power gets highly centralized and all the evils of bureaucracy manifest themselves.

7. Administration becomes a very costly affair.

Sarvodya Ideals. In the Sarvodya Society, there will be loose federation of autonomous villages, in each of which there is almost self-sufficiency. In a nutshell, features of the Sarvodya Society may be given as below :

1. There is no centralized authority and there is political and economic autonomy in villages.

2. Politics will not be instrument of power, but an agency of service and rajniti will yield place to lokniti.

3. All people will be the imbued with the spirit of love, fraternity, truth, non-violence and self-sacrifice. Society will be functioning on the basis of non-violence.

4. There will be no party system and majority rule, and society will be free from the tyranny of the majority.

5. The Sarvodya Society is socialist in true sense of the term. All callings will have the same moral, social and economic values. The individual's personality has fullest chance for development.

6. The Sarvodya Society is based on equality and liberty. There is no room in it for unhealthy competition, exploitation and class hatred. All will work, and follow the goal of "From each according to his work to each according to his needs. Land and other types of property will exist for the benefit of all. Ideal will be that all fields and birds belong to God and every one should satisfy himself according to his needs."

राम ही की चिड़िया, राम ही के खेत, खाओ चिड़ियों भर भर पेट

The Bhoodan Movement

Vinoba Bhave is quite serious about establishing a Sarvodya society and to realise his object, he launched his Bhoodan movement.

He made the beginning of a great revolution. Vinobaji says, "People should accept the principle that all land belongs to God. If all land is socially owned, the present day discontent would disappear and an era of co-operation and love will take place. What I want people to do is first to give away some of their land, secondly they should engage themselves in service of others."

In April 1951, Sarvodya Sammelan was held at Shinrampalli in Andhra Pradesh and Harijans related their sufferings due to landlessness. Vinobaji made a beginning of Bhoodan or land gift and Shri Ram Chandra Reddy of Panchampalli donated one hundred acres, thus seed of bhoodan was sown on April 18, 1951. In Telegana alone, the Vinobaji was able to collect 1,220 acres of land in course of 51 days.

Basic Ideas of Bhoodan. In a nutshell, the ideas can be given as below :

1. The Bhooden movement upholds the principle of trusteeship. All land belongs to God and human beings are to hold it in trust.

2. Bhoodan or land gift is to be given as justice demands. It is a moral and just act.

3. Land cannot be private property for exploiting others; it is to be held in trust for good of all. Bhoodan will free a man from the sense of attachment, possession and pride and will bring about a change of heart, as man has the moral right only to retain that mach property he really needs. He has to return property to the community which he does not need.

Methods. Vinobaji wants a revolution to take place but not through coercion but through a change of heart.

1. The Acharya collects land from all, whether rich or poor, as he wants to get rid of from the sense of possession and attachment which is to be found even among the poor as among the rich so he accepted gifts even from poor persons.

2. He realised that money is necessary for purchase of seeds, manure and cattle, so he gave rise to the concept of Sampatidan or gift of wealth. He stated, "Along with Bhoodan work, I have recently launched another programme, the Sampatidan Yojna." It is necessary for the fulfilment of the Bhoodan Yojna.[3]

Gramdan and Gramraj. Vinobaji wants to have Bhoodan first and at the next stage Gramdan, which means gift of an entire village. In the beginning, people will donate a part of their land, but ultimately they will give away their entire land. This will make Gramdan a reality and it will provide the basis for Gramraj. When Gramdan is made, no individual will have the ownership of land. Ownership will be vested in the community. It gained considerable support in Orissa. Vinobaji's Gramraj is like Gandhiji's Panchayat Raj.

Briefly main points may be given as below :

1. Just as the people in family work for the good of whole family, people in Gramraj will work for the benefit of whole community. "Each will offer all to their community and the community will take care of him."

2. In Gramraj there will be no violence and coercion. Villages will be republic in miniature with a general Village Council in which every family will send one representative. The Society with its executive committee of fifteen members will conduct all the affairs of the village.

3. In Gramdan, place of rajniti will be taken by lokniti, *i.e.*, service to the people in place of lust for power.

4. People will have freedom, fellowship and equality as they will be free from the tyranny of parties, capitalists and landlords.

5. People will have religious freedom without any caste or class prejudices.

Evaluation of Sarvodya. Much can be said in favour of Sarvodya :

1. Sarvodya sets its face squarely against the politics of power and exploitation. The state is to be an agency of service and not of power based on violence.

2. Sarvodya stands for good of all and discards class conflicts.

3. Sarvodya puts greater emphasis on moral and spiritual values.

4. Sarvodya seeks to establish new social and economic values. The concept of possession yields place to concept of trusteeship and lust of power to sacrifice and service to others.

5. Bhoodan at early stage and Gramdan and Sampatidan later on will bring about a change of heart. All will give up their idea of attachment to property and will work for the good of all.

6. There will be the fullest scope for freedom, fellowship and equality.

The ideals of Sarvodya are very great, noble and lofty. But human nature as we see at present is unable to give up selfishness and attachment to possession, so in practice these are difficult to be realised. Mankind has not yet reached the stage in which all selfishness will disappear and everything can be done through non-violence. In spite of all this, in this vast ocean of corruption in which at present India is mired, Sarvodaya is the only ray of light which can show the true path.

JAWAHAR LAL NEHRU

The contribution of Jawahar Lal Nehru towards the political thinking of our times

Pandit Jawahar Lal Nehru was a freedom fighter, historian, political thinkers and above all a successful ruler who continued as Prime Minister till his death. After him, his daughter, Indira Gandhi and her son Rajiv Gandhi became Prime Ministers.

Pandit Jawahar Lal Nehru was born in 1889 at Allahabad with a silver spoon in his mouth. He was the only son of Pandit Moti Lal Nehru and Swarup Rani Nehru. He was educated at home and later on at Harrow, Cambridge and London. He was called to Bar in 1912 and after taking his degree, he came back to India.

He first practised as an advocate of Allahabad High Court but soon gave up his practice and began to take part in politics. In 1916, he took part in active politics and became Secretary of Annie Besant's Home Rule League branch of Allahabad. In 1926, his name was proposed by Gandhiji for the presidentship of All India Congress Committee and he was duly elected and since then both shaped the destiny of India.

In 1946, he was made Prime Minister of India by English Viceroy Lord Wavel and since then he held that august office till his death in May 1964. If Indian period of 1920 to 1947 can be called Gandhian age, so the period between 1947 to May 1964 may be termed as Nehru age. It is very difficult to give a detached judgement about him because he was one of the most controversial figures not only of India but of whole world. Moreover, historical judgement can be given after a few years of his death as impact and result of his policies are not quite clear even up to now.

Sources of Influence

Pandit Jawahar Lal Nehru was a queer mixture of East and West. He got his education in England, so influence of English culture on him was profound. In political thinking, he was influenced by the thinkers of Fabian Society of which he remained a member for a long time. Particularly George Bernard Shaw influenced him most. He also went to Russia and was profoundly influenced by its progress even in his young age and began to appreciate socialism.

In India he was profoundly influenced by Mahatma Gandhi and in his speeches, there is queer mixture of Gandhism and socialism.

His Political Thoughts

Nehru was not a political philosopher but a Karmayogi or a man of action. Perhaps there can be no Nehruism as there is Gandhism. In spite of all this, Nehru sponsored the idea of Democratic Socialism, Panchsheel, policy of non-alignment, concept of welfare state and economic planning in India.

Great difficulty in assessing Nehru's political thoughts remains that he always praised socialism but also supported capitalism. He talked of following leftist policy but generally favoured rightest policy. He talked almost democratic rights but always gave encouragement and support to bureaucracy. As such, it is difficult to pass any judgement about him.

Democratic Socialism. Under Jawahar Lal Nehru's lead, India chose the road of democratic socialism. Nehru knew fully well that the road to Democratic Socialism will only lead to the goal of social welfare. Nehru declared even in 1929 at Lahore, "I must frankly confess that I am a socialist and republican.... India will have to go that way, too, if she seeks to end her poverty and inequality though she may evolve her own methods and may adopt the ideal to the genius of her race." It was due to his influence that in the Awadi Session of Indian National Congress in 1955, Congress accepted the goal of the socialistic pattern of society. The 68th Session of the Indian National Congress, which met in January 1964, at Bhubneswar also decided to follow the path of democratic socialism for bringing about a social welfare state. K. Kamaraj defined it as socialism without loss of freedom.

Nehru believed that the best way to fight communism is to inject democratic socialist ideas into the country. He favoured mixed economy and economic planners of India inspired by Nehru's socialist spirit are prepared to allow the co-existence of the private sector and the public sector. The significance of India's socialism lies in the fact that it wants gladly to settle down with democracy. To conduct the socialist programme in a democratic set-up is one of the greatest achievements of Nehru.

Welfare State. According to G.D.H. Cole, welfare state is a society in which assured minimum standard of living and opportunity become the possession of every individual. According to Toynbee, it is the first era in history in which people dared to think it practicable to make the benefit of civilisation available for the whole human race.

The preamble of the Constitution itself states in its aim, "To secure to all citizens : Justice, social, economic and political, liberty of thought, expression, belief, faith and worship; equality of status and of opportunity, and to promote fraternity assuming the dignity of the individual and the unity of the nation." As such, under Nehru, India choose the goal of welfare state.

In welfare state, the state itself takes initiative in protecting the health of the people and in promoting their economic security and welfare. The state understakes to abolish illiteracy, poverty and unemployment. It establishes schools, hospitals, and other institutions to meet the needs of the people. Under Nehru's leadership, Indian government launched various social welfare programmes and achieved a notable success. Turning India into a welfare state is the greatest achievement of Nehru.

Planning. Planning sometimes denotes any programme of action but state planning means national centralized control of economy. Planning in practice means the drawing up of preferences and priorities by experts and their imposition on the people who do not actively participate in plan activities at any stage. Planning can be classified into four categories : (1) Central planning under socialism as in Russia and China. (2) Guided capitalism and dynamic competition (post war America and Germany). (3) Planned capitalism (France and Britain). (4) Mixed economy or synthetic approach as adopted by India under the leadership of Nehru.

It goes to the credit of Nehru that he adopted most suitable mixed planning for India, and on account of three five year plans India has made a considerable all-round progress. According to Prof. Hayek, planning and democracy cannot live together but India launched three Five Year plans under the leadership of Pandit Nehru within the democratic framework and it is an astonishing achievement of Nehru.

Panchsheel

Pt. Jawahar Lal Nehru gave the concept of Panchsheel to the world. He was the main figure in sponsoring the idea of Panchsheel. China and India accepted the idea of Panchsheel and it was adopted by many countries. It means five things : (1) Respect of territorial integrity and sovereignty. (2) Mutual non-aggression. (3) Non-interference in internal affairs. (4) Equality and mutual benefit. (5) Peaceful co-existence. However, this concept was shattered on the sharp rocks of reality when China invaded India but it cannot be denied that Nehru gave a unique thing to the humanity.

Policy of Non-alignment. After the Second World War, two giants Russia and America emerged all powerful. Most of the countries aligned themselves either with America or Russia through the pacts like N.A.T.O., S.E.A.T.O. Warshaw Pact, etc. But Nehru followed the neutral policy of non-alignment without offending any country. In the beginning it brought good dividend and in the war between China and U.S.A. in Korea, India was the main country to settle the dispute. Similarly, in all other disputes, India gained an upper hand and played leading role as a mediator as in case of Indonesia or Suez crisis, etc. According to Nehru, "The part our foreign policy and India have played in international affairs...counted far more than its either military or financial strength was entitled to."[4] How far the policy of non-alignment proved successful is a debatable question and only future will tell its fate but it cannot be denied that it is one of the achievements of Nehru to bring such a concept on forefront and other countries followed him. Similarly he favoured the membership of Commonwealth of Nations without giving up republicanism of India. These are the most notable achievements of Nehru. He said about his non-alignment policy : "What was positive in India's non-alignment will be preserved, what was negative — that dream world will be abandoned." Wherever freedom and democracy are in jeopardy, the world will not find India neutral.[5]

Democratic Socialism *Vs.* Gandhism Sarvodya. Gandhiji's greatest political dream was that India's Swaraj should be "Rama-raj." He desired that every man and woman in the country should have fullest opportunity for developing his or her personality; everybody's basic needs should be fulfilled, and everybody should live for himself and others at the same time honestly and conscientiously.

Gandhiji's teachings were not acceptable to Nehru in toto. Nehru borrowed the concept of democratic socialism from the British Labour Party to achieve the political teachings of Gandhiji as well as of western democracy and Russian communism as he was influenced by these two outlooks also in addition to his Gandhian outlook. He felt these concept more practical and easier to implement than the visionary idea of Gandhiji.

In essence, democratic socialism means socialization of means of production for the people. This concept applies to materialistic welfare only while Gandhiji defended spiritualism also.

Socialism involves taking over all the means of production by the state running them efficiently and economically and distributing them equally among all. So far equality or equal distribution is concerned, Gandhiji favoured it but he disfavoured the powers of state and gave the idea of trusteeship which is lacking in it.

In democratic socialism, consent means under the pain of legal penality, *i.e.,* coercion which Gandhiji discarded. However, each and everything cannot be achieved by the state on the basis of Ahinsa as such. Aim of Nehru is based on the basis of power of the state while

Gandhiji believed in gradual change of heart for which his followers such as Vinoba Bhave, Jayaprakash Narain and Kaka Kalelkar are working. Thus Nehru and Gandhi both desired welfare of all and, as such, the goal of both Sarvodya and democratic socialism is to some extent similar but there is a differentce of method and outlook as one is based on change of heart and Gramraj, and other through the power of state by democratic means.

Criticism. Nehru has been praised all over the world but Mao-tse-Tung called him "running dog of British imperialism." Rajni Palm Dutt, an Indian Communist leader called him "New Chiang Kai Shek of Asia or India". In a recent book whose review appeared in the *Journal of Indian History* by historian Dr. R.C. Majumdar, in April, 1965, this has been vehemently criticized. Some quotations may be given here. In his paper "Jawahar Lal : An Engima or a Tragedy," M.N. Roy says, "To purchase popularity, Nehru had to suppress his own personality....Gandhi proved much too strong for Nehru's superficial modernism."

In his article "Roy and Nehru", Spratt says, "Nehru was guided by unconscious thinking which told him...that there was no future for anyone who broke out with Mahatma." S.P. Aiyar in his article "Nehru and Charismatic leadership" called him "The charismatic leader who builds his authority on the irrational elements of mass psychology" and quotes S.K. Dey saying, "We are a nation of hero" worshippers. V.V. Karnik in his article "Jawaharlal Nehru's Foreign policy" states, "Nehru's policy of non-alignment at the beginning was quite justified but Nehru failed to realize that in view of peculiar problems of India-Pakistan, Kashmir, Goa and China. As soon as USA and Russia began to move closer to each other, the policy of non-alignment had lost its value. China's invasion showed the futility and danger of the policy of non-alignment but Nehru clunged to it...it is a painful fact to realize that Nehru's foreign policy left practically all problems of India unsolved.... India was left alone and friendness...as she found to her cost on the occasion of Chinese invasion...hardly any of smaller countries of Afro-Asian landmass came out unequivocally in support of India against Chinese aggression. Shaw points out how Nehru an uncompromising spokesman for freedom and democracy was temperamentally a dictator like the grand Moghul and would never identify himself with the common man."[6] Dr. Lohia said of him that he contributed nothing after Independence. It means that there was no major achievement by Nehru because if he contributed anything before 1947, credit goes to Gandhiji and not to Nehru because not Nehru but Gandhiji shaped India's destiny before 1947.

I have given the above criticism to quote R.C. Majumdar, "to emphasize the view of those whose voice is generally drowned by the servile accultrations of Nehru."

Conclusion. In spite of above-mentioned harsh criticism, we must not forget that Nehru is one of the architects of modern India, "who stood like a colossus on the stage of free India for a period of seventeen years, and made or marred its future for many years to come." Nehru "was an aesthetic, a writer, a champion of modern values with a deep sympathy for the oppressed and the disinherited, and, in spite of un-limited power, detached and lonely in a certain sense...even the best Indian intellectuals considered it a privilege to work as an instrument of his will."[7] He was also an administrator, statesman, political thinker and a man of peace. His influence was so great that after him, his daughter, Indira Gandhi and her son Rajiv Gandhi became Prime Ministers. Nehru's family successors still are playing very important role in Indian politics. As such, Nehru's impact on Indian politics is very great and it has survived throughout 20th century and is continuing even in 21st century.

Impact of his acceptance of Pakistan and policy about Kashmir and foreign policy cannot be judged at present. But it cannot be denied that by giving a set-up of democratic socialism, welfare state, economic planning, Panchsheel, policy of non-alignment and of a secular state, he contributed a lot in the world of political thought as well as in political sphere by applying them. So far as his literary merit is concerned, his speeches and books like *Autobiography*, *Glimpses of World History* and *Discovery of India* have become the classics for the modern world.

NOTES

1. Dr. Stanley Jones, *Mahatma Gandhi : An Interpretation,* pp. 52-54.
2. Dhawan, *The Political Philosophy of Mahatma Gandhi,* p. 312.
3. Vinoba Bhave, *Bhoodan Yojna,* 1957, p. 100.
4. Nehru in Lok Sabha on 19.9.1963.
5. Nehru before American Congress in 1949.
6. R.C. Rajindar, *Journal of Indian History,* April 1965, pp. 332-37.
7. *Jawahar Lal Nehru : A Critical Tribute*, edited by A.B. Shalo and published by the Indian Committee for Cultural Freedom, P.C. Manabutala Iron Private Ltd., Mumbai.

10

Democracy

Essentials of Democracy

About democracy it has been said, "Democracy...is a search for a way of life in which the voluntary free intelligence and activity of man can be harmonized and co-ordinated with the least possible coercion, and it is the belief that way of life is the best way for all mankind, the way most in keeping with the nature of man and the nature of the universe." As such, "Enlightened public opinion is the only guarantee of the successful working of our democratic institutions".

Democracy has been praised as well as criticised from the very beginning. Plato criticised it and criticism is continuous even now and even Coker says, "Democracy is, of all forms of state, the most unfriendly to liberty and individuality."

The explanation and appraisal of democracy have been a favourite theme of discussion since the earliest times. We derive the word from the ancient Greeks and there has been little change in formal meaning. Herodotus in 5th century B.C. understood democracy to mean the "multitude's rule" or a society in which there is equality of rights and the holders of political office are accountable for what they do therein.

Much has been written on democracy. Perhaps few subjects in political science commanded such an attention of a very large number of thinkers as democracy. But "Democracy has come to mean so many different things, some very hostile to each other, that it needs careful analysis".[1] "Few words have been more loosely and variously defined than democracy. It has almost literally meant all things to all men." The confusion is increased because not only western democracies speak of democracy, but communist countries like USSR and China also say that they have people's democracy. Communists say that perfect democracy is to be found in their countries while western countries have democracy in which there is exploitation by capitalists and imperialists. It is interesting to note that Ayub Khan has introduced "basic or controlled democracy" in Pakistan while Sukarno has given "Guided" democracy to Indonesia.

The term democracy is drawn from the Greek word demos (people) and kratas (government) means power or government of the people. The most popular definition is of Abraham Lincoln. He defined, "Democracy is a government of the people, by the people and for the people". According to Seeley, "Democracy is a government in which everyone has a share."

Prof. A.V. Dicey defines "democracy" as that form of government in which the governing body is a comparatively large section of the entire nation.

Lord Bryce defined democracy, "That form of Government in which the ruling power of a state is legally vested not in a particular class or classes but in the members of the community as a whole."

According to J.S. Mill, democracy is that form of government in which "The whole people or some numerous portion of them, exercise the governing power through deputies periodically elected by them."

MacIver observes, "Democracy is not a way of governing whether by majority or otherwise but primarily a way of determining who shall govern and broadly to what ends."

C.C. Maxey's definition on democracy is of great significance at present. "Democracy as reinterpreted in nineteenth century thus seems to be more than a political formula, more than a system of government, more than a social order. It is a search for a way of life in which the voluntary free intelligence and society of men can be harmonised and co-ordinated with the least possible correction, and it is a belief that such a way of life is the best way for all mankind, the way most in keeping with the nature of man and the nature of universe."[2]

Different Senses of Democracy. Democracy has been used in three different senses. It means a form of government, a form of state and a way of life. As a form of government, it means that legal power in the community is vested in the people as a whole and rulers belong to the majority in the electorate in the communities which actually are voting. Thus democracy is regarded as government by consent or public discussion. Modern democracy stands or falls with the right of discussion and with the existence of a recognised opposition.

As a social philosophy, Declaration of America in 1776 and Declaration of the Rights of Man and Citizens based on popular sovereignty and indefensible natural right of man to liberty, property, security and resistance to oppression have been its core. In the possession of these rights, men have been considered as equal.

Democracy as a Way of Life. Democracy, it is said, is not only a form of government but a way of life. Under a democratic government, the dignity of individual personality is recognised. Every individual is free to live in his own way, entertain opinion as he likes, express his opinion freely, move about freely, enjoy the company of people he likes and become a member of associations and parties. In a democratic country, individual enjoys equality and liberty.

Forms of Democracy. Direct democracy according to Garner means "as a form in which the will of the state directly or indirectly is expressed through the people directly." It was practised in Greek city states and now it is practised in Switzerland that is, to a certain extent it can be put into practice easily only in small states. Indirect or representative democracy means that the government is carried on through the periodically elected representatives. It is of three kinds: Presidential, parliamentary and collegiate as practised in Switzerland. Now Concepts of people's (communist) democracy and basic or guided democracy have been added to it though it is difficult to consider them really a democracy.

Conditions Favourable for Democracy

With all its drawbacks, democracy is regarded as the best form of government. At the same time, it should be noted that it is the most difficult form and certain minimum conditions are necessary for its successful working. According to E.E. Sehnla, following are the requirements of a democratic type of government : (a) Popular control of key officials, etc. (b) Liberal suffrage. (c) Willingness to adhere to the rules of democratic process. (d) Freedom of speech, of assembly of association and safeguards against arbitrary imprisonment. (e) Adequate sources of information.[3]

According to Prof. Hearnshaw, democracy demands that there should be :

1. A high standard of honesty and honour among the people. There should be equality of opportunity and equality in law.

2. The people should have a high level of intelligence and a sound system of education.

3. It is necessary that the people should be conscious of the community as a whole. They should always remember that as "the strength of a wolf is the pack, the strength of the pack is wolf.

4. There should be a strong and vigorous public opinion.

5. There should be democracy not only in political field but also in the social and economic fields.

According to Prof. Garner, the essential conditions for democracy are a high moral level among the people, their training in the habits of self-government, education among the people and "a relatively high degree of political intelligence and abiding interest in public affairs, a keen sense of public responsibility, and a readiness to abide and accept decisions of majority" and respect for the rights of minorities.

E.F. Durbin puts emphasis on the ability of people to choose a government and freedom to oppose the government of the day and tolerance of opposition. According to Dr. Hocking, democracy demands education and training of the people. According to Dr. Lindsey, the essence of democracy is contained in the insistence of a tolerated official opposition. According to him, in democracy, in final decision, every one should have somehow made his contribution in that decision. Sir Henry Maine desires a "wise constitution" and Lackey wants a written constitution for the successful working of democracy. Ebenston pleads for political climate in which political liberty can thrive.

According to Prof. Coker, the success of democracy is dependent upon the existence of a civic sense among the people generally; a rational likemindedness and an imaginative sympathy that in some degree transcend economic and cultural differences, and a general disposition among the people to put into high government office the sort of persons who act largely under the influence of such attitudes. It presupposses also that citizens have intellectual and moral vigour to withstand persistent deception by demagogues and to apply some discriminating judgements to the policies of their chosen leaders.

In short, the essential conditions of democracy are desire for democracy and "a tradition of ethical liberalism, a strong middle class, widespread education, safeguards for civil liberties and regard for political dissent."[4] Eternal vigilance is the price of liberty so people should be vigilant for safeguarding democracy. People should possess peace, sympathy, understanding and tolerance. They should know that they have to solve their problems through arguments and discussions and not through violence, education, public spirit, good leadership, a free press and minimum economic satisfaction among all.

Principles of Democracy. In democracy, utmost importance is placed on public. State is regarded merely as a means.

Public Representation. Democracy puts its faith in election by public and not on heredity or wealth or any other consideration. Elections are necessary for democracy.

3. Constitutional Change. In democracy, public possesses the right to change the government or the Constitution.

4. Freedom of Thinking and Expression. Democracy believes in freedom of expression because without it there can be no discussion and democracy is government by discussion.

5. Equality before law is also one of the important principles of democracy.

Merits of Democracy. Among the various forms of government, with all defects, democracy has been regarded as the best.

Democracy upholds certain values. Some of them may be mentioned below :

1. Peaceful voluntary adjustment of disputes.
2. Ensuring peaceful change in a changing society.
3. Orderly succession of rulers.
4. The minimum of coercion.
5. Diversity.
6. Attainment of justice.
7. Promotion of science.
8. Freedom etc.[5]

A classical case has been prepared on certain grounds.

1. Precautionary. Democracy takes into consideration the wishes and sufferings of the people.

2. Psychological. Democracy seeks the co-operation of all in solving the problems of all. It lays greater emphasis on co-operation than efficiency.

3. Educational. Democracy provides training to the people in citizenship and government.

4. Moral. Democracy possess moral value as it develops the spirit of partiotism and eliminates the risk of revolution.

5. Practical. Democracy is of practical use as it develops the spirit of participation in state affairs and eliminates the risk of revolution.

6. Democracy protects the interest of all as it is based on consent and criticism. A monarchy or aristocracy may not know where the shoe pinches, but democracy is bound to know where exactly the people suffer.

7. Democracy respects the dignity of the human personality as in democracy each individual is regarded as an end in himself.

8. Democracy upholds liberty and equality. A.D. Condsey says,[6] democracy is a revolutionary form of government, for its aim is to find a place for continual change within government, its law exists to foster freedom, its force exists to protect law. It is an organisation to preserve, and leave room for all these precious things of the spirit, which in their nature cannot be organized.

9. A democratic government is responsible to the people and if rulers want to continue in power, they must serve the public interest.

10. In democracy people have scope to learn how to run their own institutions. According to Garner, "...the greatest glory of democracy in the opinion of votaries does not flow so much from its own inherent excellence as a form of government as from its influence in elavating the masses of the people, developing their faculties, stimulating interest among them in public affairs and strengthening their patriotism by allowing them a share in government."

11. Democracies in the modern times are guided by the principle of the welfare state. Only democracy can serve the people's welfare without destroying the dignity of human personality.

12. Democracy puts faith in human capacity to attend to political and other affairs. It is the only system of government that permits the people to bring about a change in a peaceful and orderly manner as soon as, or at least shortly after, dissatisfactory policies are put into effect.

13. A great merit of democracy is the spirit of compromise and agreement. According to Basset, "The democratic method involves the determination of political principles on the basis of discussion which generally ends in compromise."

14. Democracy ennobles the people. According to Mill, "It promotes a better and higher form of national character than any other polity whatever". According to President Lowell, "The best government in the long run is one that nurtures a people strong in moral fibre in integrity, industry, self- reliance and courage." Democracy comes out successful in that taste. According to Lord Bryce, right of vote gives dignity to individual.

15. It is the glory of democracy that it elavates the masses, the people feel that the government is their own creation and government service is really the service of the people.

16. Democracy is government by representation and by its tactics of persuasion, it reduces the danger of revolution.

17. Democracy results in greater efficiency than any other form of government. A popular election, popular control and popular

responsibility are more likely to ensure a great degree of efficiency than any other system of the government.

18. According to Coker, rank and file in democracy are generally able to make a relatively intelligent discrimination between a group that intends to further the public interest and some other group animated by narrower motives. Their participation in political power is indispensable for developing in them the interest in government, respect for law, and co-operative feeling which are in a measure essential to stable government in any community.

19. Democracies have proved more stronger governments in First and Second Worlds wars as they defeated dictators like Hitler and Mussolini.

20. Democracy is the from of government which pays attention to every citizen as it believes in equality. According to Lowell, in true democracy, nobody can complain that his voice has not been heard.

21. Democracy is a self-government and self-government is the best government.

22. From Utilitarian point of view, it is the best form government.

23. It helps in development of art and literature.

Evils of Democracy

Much was expected of democracy in the first two decades of twentieth century but after the First World War all hopes have been shattered on the rocks of reality and it has been very harshly criticized. Juraz defined it as the government of the cattle by the cattle and for the cattle. Tellyrand defined democracy as "an aristocracy of black guards", Carlyle sneeringly referred to the people as a certain number of millions mostly fools, H.G. Wells asserts there is no case for the elective democratic government in modern states that cannot be knocked to pieces in five minutes.

1. Criticism of democracy began with Plato. He said, administration is a very difficult job and everybody is not fit for it, so only expert and able persons should be entrusted with the administration and not the masses.

2. Democracy believes in equality but critics say that men are not equal. They differ in physical force, intelligence, character and capacity so democracy is basically found as wrong principle.

3. Some modern writers on the basis of psychological research say that hereditary characteristics are so important that they cannot be changed and so it is futile to hope that they will become intelligent in a democratic set-up as democracy believes.

4. One school of thought do not believe that man is rational being. They say that man acts due to instincts and emotions and some-times acts in a foolish manner, therefore, in democracy only those people get success who are expert in mass psychology and in taking advantage of unitelligent feelings of the masses.

5. On biological grounds, some thinkers say that state is like an organ or body and as the work and function of everyone is divided so work and function of every man should vary in the state.

6. It is pointed out that the working of democracy brings out all the evils of petty politics. Everything is decided on the basis of party. According to A.R. Lord, "To the critics of representation, the party system seems to be toomechanical, a method of dividing opinions to represent the popular will without any approach to exactness."

7. Democracy has been described as "exaggerated committee". It is a very expensive form of government because a lot of money is spent on organisation of public opinion, propaganda, frequent elections and on committees, commissions, etc.

8. In democracy, there is no love for the truth and justice. The foremost thought is to capture votes.

9. Bribery and corruption are the common diseases of democracy. Not only voters but members of legislatures submit to this. Money plays a very important part in politics and so it lowers the standard of the people.

10. In a democracy, there is a craze for legislation to impress the people and consequently increasing mass of hasty and ill-digested legislation comes into existence.

11. Critics point out that local interests tend "to obscure and to defeat the interests of the state at large" as representative of every place tries to compete one another to gain advantage for his constituency to please the voters.

12. According to President Lowell, democracy in the U.S.A. has resulted in mis-government of the large cities. The national interests have been subordinated to private or party interests.

13. According to Faguat, "Democracy is a cult of incompetence. It is a government by amateur or those who are hopelessly immature. It rests upon multitude which consists of incompetent, ungrateful, emotional and passionate persons." Robert Browning in his poem "Patriot" shows how people applauded a leader one time and sent him to gallows at another time, same as happened during French revolution.

14. People are short-sighted and do not see far enough in future. According to Prof. Hernshaw, leaders are like schoolmasters

elected by their public and are liable to be punished and dismissed by them.

15. In allegorical paintings, aristocracy was shown in the guise of solemn senate, monarchy as a brooding despot receiving homage and democracy as a drunken clown surrounded by a yelling mob, *i.e.,* worst.

16. Democracy puts emphasis on quantity and not on quality but generally intelligent persons are always in minority and numerically less than common persons.

17. According to Faguet, "Government is an art and it presupposes knowledge but the people are governed by men who have neither knowledge nor art and were chosen because they have them not." He attributed all incompetence in France to democracy. Bathemy pointed out that in democracy leaders govern without any technical skill to govern due to belief that everybody was fit to rule.

18. According to A.G. Sidgewick, democracy lacks adequate means for securing an enforcible responsibility.

19. Sir Henry Maine criticised democracy in his book called *Popular Government*. He pointed out democracy as of ephemeral duration and fragile government.

20. Maine's view was that there is no connection between liberty and democracy. There has hardly been a community, says Maine, in which weak have been pushed to the wall, in which those who have succeeded uniformly have been the strong, and in which in so short a time, there has arisen so great inequality of private fortune and domestic luxury.

21. Lecky says in *Democracy and liberty* that it is government by the "poorest, the most ignorant, the most incapable, who are necessarily the most numerous."

22. Critics point out that democracy is opposed to liberty and individuality as persons become victim of tyranny of the masses and those who hold view in advance of their time, such as Socrates or Bertrand Russell are persecuted.

23. According to Henry Maine, democracy is unfriendly to the growth of knowledge as public do not tolerate anything progressive but generally people are conservative and do not tolerate new things.

24. Critics also maintain that democracy is an unscientific idea. They support their view by referring to psychology of mobs or crowds, the law of heredity and measurement of human intelligence. Labon points out, democracies work under influence of crowds and consequently cannot be efficient.

25. One of the main defects of democracy is that it gives rise to professional politicians who do nothing to earn their livelihood and are good for nothing, who promise as pointed out by Plato all qualities and all things to public to befool it. Today he may preach gospel of peace and after a short time of war, to maintain himself in power. Dr. Johnson says, "Politics is the last refuge of a scoundrel."

26. Politicians get an upper hand in politics and interfere in all affairs and are called everywhere for honourable inaugration, etc. and consequently in social service noble-hearted do not enter at all as honour goes to a politician, not to a social worker.

27. In democracy, each and everything is decided by the whim of the politicians and only flatterers, group sponsors and opportunists flourish and honest or meritorious persons have to go to wall. As such, really efficient and capable cannot come on top; those who succeed are generally inefficient.

28. Democracy is also slow as it is government by consultation and criticism which make it necessary to take much time in coming to a decision.

29. It is wrong to say that power resides in the hands of the people. Generally the poor are controlled and blindly led by a few people, who rise to the top by fair or foul means. In various ways, people are deceived and made to feel that power is located in their hands. Unorganized masses are controlled by some alert, resolute, organized minority, military despots, big businessmen, party managers or social reformers who are skilful in adjusting popular ideas and emotions to the limited interests or beliefs of some small groups *i.e.,* top bureaucrats or capitalists who may be in actual power in that set-up.

30. In democracy, there is a wide gap in profession and practice. Democracy "rests upon certain pretences, not to say frauds...political parties are supposed to be free associations. But, in fact, members of a party belong to it because of their parents or due to some locality or due to economic interest or due to religion." There is wide gap between principles and practice because true democracy cannot be realised. Democracy ensures neither better government nor greater liberty as said by Garner and Coker. Indeed, some of the strongest tendencies are adverse to liberty. History justifies that democracy often proves opposite to liberty.

31. Fascists call democracy false ideal and say it leads to the rule of demogogues who are expert in the art of manipulating elections.

32. Communists say bourgeoisie democracy is false as no poor person can be elected as he lacks power to spend money in elections

without which election cannot be won. Political equality under capitalist democracy is merely a protective shell of capitalism.

Even freedom in Greek democracy meant freedom to slave-owners and now to capitalists to exploit wage slaves. Poor persons can never move the Apex Court for protection of their rights. As such, democracy in captalist countries is a mirage and false notion.

33. Socialists also oppose democracy and say, without economic security, it is false to think that there can be political rights of a person who may find sword of unemployment of hunger hanging over his head.

Far off fields look green, so there were great hopes with the advent of democracy but all hopes have proved false. Some of the defects have been accepted by democratic thinkers such as Lord Bryce. He mentions certain defects :

1. The power of money to pervert administration.
2. The tendency to make politics a gainful profession.
3. The abuse of doctrine of equality and failure to appreciate the value of administrative skill.
4. The tendency of legislatures and political officials to play for votes in the passing of laws and in tolerating breaches of order.
5. The undue power of party organization.
6. The extravagance in administration.

Suggestions for Improvement of Democracy. Various suggestions have been given for the improvement of democracy. These suggestions do not count much. If persons are educated, honest and capable, all governments can succeed, not only democracy. But certain suggestions may be mentioned. Lord Lothian desires guarantee of freedom of speech and criticism and economic initiative for the individual. Andre Maurois recommended "an individual leadership for a fixed period." Lord Percy favours general power to Prime Minister and policy making power to parliament. Sir Stafford Cripps favours functional and administrative committees to supervise the work.

Conclusion. In spite of all these defects, it may be said that democracy has provided the best form of government. According to Lord Bryce, democracy has maintained public order and secured the liberty of individuals. It has given an efficient civil administration. Legislature in democracy has been directed for the welfare of poor whose condition is better than ever before. It has encouraged patriotism and enthusiasm of the masses. Thus it has proved better than the rule of one or the rule of many. Whatever defects have been pointed out are not of real democracy but of democracy which is controlled by a particular class, whether it may be bureaucratic class, capitalist class, particular class in Finer's words is oligarchy of judges or military class, or a particular class of politicians who may exploit the name and slogan for their own benefit. As such cure of democracy lies in more democracy so that no class may dominate all the population. However, we may quote Ednard Carpenter, "O disrespectable democracy I love you". The reason is obvious. There is no better alternative to democracy.

Democracy in the Present World. The word democracy has gained such a reputation that now majority or rather to say all nations use the word democracy for their own set-up. Communists condemn England and America as capitalist democracy while call their own government as people's democracy. Similarly, American and English writers condemn communist countries as based on party dictatorship but their own governments as ideal democracies. Raimsay Muer, Lord Hewart and Allen have pointed out power of bureaucracy in England and Finer calls American democracy as judicial oligarchy. In such controversies, a student of politics finds that though the word democracy has gained supremacy and popularity but actually democracy has disappeared even in Switzerland as women possess no right of vote and it is difficult to agree with that. However, every rose has a thorn and perfection is not to be found in this imperfect world dominated by men of flesh and blood but the most wonderful thing is that people have become dumb-driven cattle. Whoever captures the powers of the state, gains support of public as in case of Iraq, public supported Col. Kaseem and later on Gen. Arief and similarly Pakistan supported Mohd. Ayub khan as soon as he captured the power of the state. In this bewilderment, new concepts of democracy have come into existence.

Of "Democratic socialism of India, De Gaulle's democracy of France and basic or controlled democracy in Pakistan under Mohd. Ayub khan and guided democracy in Indonesia", a brief description may be given here. Democratic socialism of India can be termed democracy as has been shown before. France was the home of democracy and there is still democracy but with the advent of De Gaulle substance has gone.

So far as Pakistan's guided democracy or Sukarno's guided democracy are concerned, strictly speaking these are no democracies at all. In Pakistan, the President enjoys overwhelming powers, sovereignty is vested not in people but in military dictatorship and people neither possess justiciable fundamental rights nor free press, nor freedom of religion.

Same is the case of guided democracy of Indonesia. In guided democracy or democracy of leadership, President is supreme and possesses all real power, parliament has become powerless with the formation of National Council or Supreme Advisory Council and everything is done by decrees. Parties have lost their freedom, people lost civil liberties and press its freedom of expression.

Such democracies are a cloak to cover dictatorship. The lust for power, very backward conditions and political instability give rise to these peculiar forms of democracy.

The problem of future of democracy is agitating the minds of thinkers. The spread of communism and of military and hidden dictators and other dangers hold up the work of democracy. Whether the democracy will have a good or bleak future depends upon the attitude of people in a country. People used to liberal traditions cherish democratic ideals and will protect democratic institutions as best as they can. The future of democracy will depend upon the way in which democracies are able to handle people's programme.

The problem of democracy in underdeveloped countries is indeed very great. Ignorance, illiteracy, poverty and apathy to democracy are the worst enemies of democracy. The setback democracy got in Pakistan, Indonesia and in other countries makes people seriously think of future. India is a democratic island in the occean of non-democratic countries and let us hope that it will serve as beacon light to humanity and government. of the people, by the people and for the people will not perish from the earth. Let us be optimistic and hope for the best to democracy and to future of humanity. What is hidden in the wombs of future nobody can foretell but humanity is on march and is progressing in every walk of life so it is possible that real democracy may emerge out of chaos and an utopian regime may emerge in which peace, prosperity and plenty may prevail for the welfare of all.

Now all over the world, democracy has triumphed. Fascism has disappeared, communism has lost its former influence and socialism has lost its former popularity and it has survived now as Democratic Socialism. Thus democracy has gained an upperhand all over the world except in few countries. Racialism has disappeared and sex discrimination has become a thing of past. Women rulers are playing most important role.

So far as India is concerned, democracy has survived fully upto the end of 20th century and the future is bright at the dawn of 21st century all over the world.

NOTES

1. H. Finer, *The Theory and Practice of Modern Governments*, 1960, p. 67.
2. C.C. Maxey, *Political Philosophies*, 1960, p. 69.
3. *Ibid.*
4. *Essential of Government*, p. 218.
5. H.B. Ray, *An Intrcduction to Democratic Theory*, 1960.
6. A.D. Condsey, *The Modern Democtatic State,* p. 266.